HURDLES

The Admissions Dilemma in American Higher Education

HURDLES

The Admissions Dilemma in
American Higher Education

HERBERT S. SACKS, M.D.

and Associates

ATHENEUM

New York

1978

Library of Congress Cataloging in Publication Data

Hurdles.
  Bibliography: p.
  Includes index.
  1. Universities and colleges—United States—
Admission. I. Sacks, Herbert S.
LB2351.H87 1978   378.1′05′60973   77–15350
ISBN 0–689–10857–5

For Helen

THE ASSOCIATES

Henry-Louis Gates, Jr.

Eric K. Goodman

Harold L. Hodgkinson

Joseph Katz

Morton Levitt

Howard B. London

Angela S. Moger

Etta S. Onat

Philip R. Rever

Herbert S. Sacks

James A. Thomas

David C. Tilley

Peter H. Wells

Preface

THE CENTRAL THEME of this collection emphasizes the normal developmental crises students endure in clearing the admissions hurdles in the American university at every level: high school to college, community college to senior level college, college to graduate or professional school. The essays spell out the effects of these crises on students' personality development and on national and university policy-making. This volume claims that the present system of admissions tends to disregard educational principles and is often insensitive to what we know of adolescent and young adult development. The stiff entry fees students pay to the admissions track meet frequently warp the purposes of education and promote the tendency for premature closure in career choice. Some of the excessive costs for high school seniors include motivational distortions in the pursuit of grades and the mastery of the material, in the character and volume of their extracurricular activities and in the emergence of insincere relationships with teachers. Premedical students, beleaguered by the necessity of satisfying real and imagined requirements for medical school admission, often abandon the prospect of more profound studies in the humanities. Among preprofessional students and graduate school aspirants, there is a reluctance to venture into academic courses that lie outside their field of concentration simply because final grades may prove to be damaging to their records.

Too often, anxious candidates for admission to selective higher educational programs are caught between a rock and a hard place.

> To stand up straight and tread the turning mill,
> To lie flat and know nothing and be still,
>   Are the two trades of man; and which is worse
> I know not, but I know both are ill.[1]

Too many students share the bleakness of Housman's alternatives. Obviously, admissions candidates to ranking university programs were able to perform well in their preparatory work, but those for whom normal conflicts and expectable adolescent turmoil invited a slackening of attention to scholarship, however ephemeral, won't be readily forgiven, if forgiven at all by the selection apparatus.

The notion of admissions hurdles is a broad concept and is inclusive of phenomena beyond the immediate admissions procedure, phenomena triggered by the central event.

Hurdling takes into account the journey from high school to college, whether in public- or private-sector institutions, with the complex psychosocial changes elicited in students by the hurdle labeled emancipation, and the effects of the movement of this student population upon institutional and public policy.

Hurdling takes into account the plight of the working class community college student, for whom the initial barrier is non-existent, but for whom the move to senior level college (junior and senior years) is burdened by personal conflict and social dissonance.

Hurdling takes into account the lower hurdles set for talented black students who find it relatively easy to gain admission to first-rank colleges, but for whom the subsequent experiences of culture shock and the emergence from that state carry with them specific emotional conflicts superimposed upon the psychological problems usually seen in admissible whites for whom the obstacles are initially set higher.

Hurdling takes into account the fierce fight to gain entry into law and medical schools modulated by compassionate guardians at the entry portals, who are all but swept away by the tide of battle as they try to make sense out of an educational predicament not properly addressed by public policy studies.

Hurdling takes into account products of the higher educational system whose giftedness and personality structure permit them to take the hurdles deftly, but whose development has been skewed through meeting rigorous institutional demands.

Hurdling takes into account qualified women who gain entry into graduate schools only to find themselves subjected to continuing discrimination based upon gender, economic considerations, and probable fear of displacement by those in positions of power and influence.

Important as admissions policies are in shaping the character of the student body and in determining institutional direction, a review of the literature reveals very few studies. The dimensions of the problem are vast; this small contribution is a pioneering venture onto a relatively untouched terrain. There are over 3,000 institutions of higher education in the nation, and the admissions dilemma is perceived and managed quite differently in the various groupings of schools. The desire for admission to a relatively small number of highly selective institutions is cause for intense competition among well-qualified applicants who endure an anxiety-evoking test. This book stresses the effects of the admissions hurdles upon the student applicants and upon this selective group of universities and colleges. Since many graduates of these schools develop into leaders in the political, intellectual, and financial affairs of the nation, scrutiny of the relationship between admissions policy and behavioral changes induced in the applicants is merited. The public sector's recent history, its institutional dynamics and moves toward democratic access are explored with the recognition that every applicant will be admitted somewhere. Nearly half the freshmen across the nation applied only to the school they attend and about half of the entering students do not graduate but drop out or transfer. Their hurdling exercises and concomitant growth-related crisis experiences often commence after admission. We have not attempted to address specifically each of the diverse institutional models and groupings in our country.

Each chapter underscores recurrent critical themes which are often identifiable to the concerned observer. In no way are the essays intended to provide, for instance, comprehensive overviews, touching upon every feature of the experience of the black student, the woman in graduate school, the undecided applicant to professional school, or the internal social conflicts in community colleges throughout the country.

The reader will note that although half of the contributors have Yale associations, their observations and commentary have national scope and are not narrow reflections of the first-rank schools of the private sector. Historically, alterations in national educational policy have often been derived from experimentation in the private sector, so no apologies are in order when examples of attempts at problem-solving within the private sector are cited.

This book grew out of the senior author's clinical observations over a period of time which called attention to the crisis of the high school senior making application to selective colleges. The subject was then expanded to include transitions between different levels within the higher educational system. The contributors, distinguished men and women from a variety of disciplines and professions who are veteran players in the admissions tournament, were charged to write trenchantly and without apology, following after Marianne Moore, who blessed the man

> who does not sit in the seat of the scoffer—
> the man who does not denigrate, depreciate, denunciate;
>   who is not "characteristically intemperate,"
> who does not "excuse, retreat, equivocate and will be heard."[2]

Each essayist worked closely with the senior author and each contribution was reworked in several drafts. There is a clear synthesis in the development of the material and the organization of the chapters—a synthesis which nevertheless respects the character and style of the individual author. Where possible, the student view is brought forward, and, indeed, two of the authors at the time of the writing were themselves students.

The volume is directed to a broad readership. Educators, administrators, and policy-makers on a secondary school, college, professional school, and graduate educational level may be interested in our positions and conclusions. Parents accustomed to reading thoughtful journals may be attracted to essays which broaden their grasp of a national dilemma and expand their insight into their children's situations. Finally, young people in transition may be drawn to the book, to argue the views presented, and, we hope, to enlarge and enrich the debate so urgently needed.

H.S.S.

REFERENCES

1. A. E. Housman, "To Stand Up Straight," 1936, *The Collected Poems of A. E. Housman* (New York: Holt, Rinehart and Winston, 1965), p. 186.

2. Marianne Moore, "Blessed Is the Man," 1956, *A Marianne Moore Reader* (New York: Viking Press, 1961), p. 61.

Acknowledgments

First, I wish to record my gratitude to the twelve colleagues who entered into this collaboration eagerly, supporting the central theme of this volume—that normal developmental crises in students and their individual and institutional aftereffects are triggered by the admissions hurdles set by the American university at every transitional point in the system.

To Albert Solnit I owe a special debt of appreciation for encouraging me to see the application of developmental psychological theory and clinical practice to matters of social policy. David Riesman confirmed the validity of my excursions into the world of admissions issues. Ernst Prelinger and Kenneth Keniston were partners in making new findings about young adults derived from our consultative experience with the Yale College Five Year B.A. Program. Jay Katz's suggestions about both the project and my own contribution to this book have added clarity and richness. I am grateful for Joseph Katz's untiring interest in this enterprise and his wisdom in interpreting changes appearing on the canvas of American education. Lisa Adams, a recent Dartmouth graduate, was a persevering assistant who responded generously to countless demands. I thank Judith Kern of Atheneum Publishers for her fine editorial work.

My wife, Helen, has supported these time-consuming efforts with much understanding and little complaint. Finally, I want to acknowledge the influence of my children, who frequently refresh my own youthful memories. Their individually distinct hurdling styles and barked shins sometimes give their parents pause.

H.S.S.

CONTENTS

XV

xvi

HURDLES

The Admissions Dilemma in
American Higher Education

HAROLD L. HODGKINSON

Foreword

WHAT YOU ARE about to read is a fascinating book addressing for the first time a comprehensive set of problems which could be called "getting into the adult world." These rites of passage deal with both the quantitative and qualitative aspects of going to college. During the 1950s there was an enormous rush in the United States to attend the most selective colleges because it was believed that graduation from a high status college or university would virtually guarantee one's success in life. Deans and presidents of distinguished institutions when reporting on the success of their institutions would speak not of the number of students who benefited from their education, but of the number of students who sought admission and were *rejected*. (In general this is a rather meaningless measure of a college's or a university's performance, except insofar as it affects those who have been rejected.)

During the late 1950s and early 1960s our national aspirations for education were most pervasive and all but unquestioned. We believed that in the early grades, through the interventions of such programs as Head Start, Follow Through, and Right to Read, we could use the schools to overthrow inequities of race and class, and, at the same time, that the veteran returning from the Korean War could assure his future with a degree from the rapidly burgeoning state college or university. Since the fifties there has been a vast increase in the numbers of people going on to higher education. Access to institutions of postsecondary education has grown significantly as a result of the community college movement and the expansion in the length of the working day during which colleges and universities are available for study. An increased variety in the student population—whether measured by race, social class, previous success in school, or other factors—has drastically changed the nature of the student culture in American higher education over the last fifteen years. We then have moved out of a *meritocratic* phase and have approached an *egalitarian* era in which almost everyone can gain access to some form of postsecondary education.

As this book points out, however, many of the highly selective institutions are retaining their selectivity even though the alternative of attending a local community college is now available to children from upwardly mobile families and families with a tradition of attending institutions associated with excellence. These children are compelled by family ambiance—almost from birth—to consider nothing but Harvard, Yale, or Stanford. Children from such families opt for the community college only at a price.

I recall vividly about eighteen years ago sitting in a high school gymnasium with 300 very frightened high school students who were about to take the Scholastic Aptitude examinations. When the guidance counselor entered, a dramatic and unexpected hush came over the room. She strode dramatically to the lectern and announced loudly (and one could tell this was her finest hour) "What you all do in the next five hours will determine the rest of your life!" During the examination two students became sick to their stomachs and one young man fainted. That experience was memorable not only for the high school students, but for me, too, because it made me realize just how much stress we place upon young people by proclaiming that there is only one road to heaven and that only very few can pass through its tollgate. Although there are many institutions willing to take almost anyone, the ad-

4

missions problem with its tensions and potential for trauma still prevails for the qualified youth who wishes to attend the highly selective institution.

A new problem to arise in this egalitarian era is that some students in community colleges may feel they are receiving only a second-rate education, partly because their teachers would prefer to teach in more prestigious institutions and partly because the students themselves do not feel that they have really been extended or pushed to maximize their education. As one black student in a community college told me recently, "If I don't try very hard I can't fail very much." To say this, however, is to overlook the fact that most community colleges have performed a great national service by opening up access to further education to literally millions of energetic and able Americans. Further, in many of the community colleges with which I am familiar the quality of teaching is often inspired. Relatively speaking, these students often move further in educational competence than their counterparts in many first-rank institutions who begin undergraduate education with a higher level of preparation and better proofs of academic achievement and who are bound to succeed anyway. The accounts of community college students in this book tell an engrossing but not necessarily a complete story.

Admission to professional schools may be for today's youth what admission to undergraduate schools was fifteen years ago. Because there are more candidates than the market can possibly bear, professional and graduate schools often use distorted criteria for making selections among legions of applicants who seem to be equally qualified by all the conventional measures of academic aptitude and previous performance. The adaptations required in order for one to become and to be a graduate student are particularly difficult, and those required of the female graduate student are even more difficult. One unexplained phenomenon is the very high dropout rate among black women graduate students. We speak often of the role problems of individuals in terms of sex and of race but we do not put those phenomena together often enough. Black women still have a long way to go before achieving equity in access to higher education as well as to many other areas of American life. And there is yet to be a black female director of admissions to any Ivy professional school who might give us some insight into the problems of trying to manage the admissions process from her unique perspective.

Hurdles, then, are devices produced by society to mark the occasion of the movement of an individual to a new status in life as well as to provide for some sort of selection based on skill. For example, the circumcision rituals practiced by many tribes serve as both a rite of passage from puberty into adulthood and a test of physical tolerance. In this case, however, everyone "passes," because social sanctions are so strong that it would be truly impossible for any young man to flee or escape such a test. But to become a hunter in any tribe is not without challenge, because it requires the passing of a "competency-based curriculum" to guarantee to society the competency of the hunters upon whom other people's lives will depend. Thus, rituals may serve two purposes: (1) providing focal events for the celebration of transition to new life stages and (2) demonstrating and certifying the competency of those who move into leadership roles.

Hurdles in American higher education attain the same ends, although the processes have been heavily bureaucratized. Hurdling, through the rites of getting into higher education and getting out of it, provides both a developmental social event and to some extent a generalized statement of competence. In the language of the general psychologists, "getting into the adult world" through participation in the higher educational rites is a task specific to youth moving forward on the developmental spectrum toward adulthood. Institutions such as the military and the residential college provide transitional settings with some degree of monitoring where adult roles can be tried out. Even the summer camp experience is an example of a supervised environment in which adolescents can experiment with various adult roles while minimizing risk.

After reading this book, one should recognize two important changes in the rites of passage mentioned above. First, for many the college graduation no longer clearly marks off the point of entry into adulthood. In the graduation line today one sees not only the expected callow youths, now ready, with degrees in hand, to try the wings of adulthood for the first time, but also grandmothers, forty-year-old veterans, and career women who have returned for an advanced degree.

The second change concerns the granting of a college degree as a demonstration of competence. We have known for years that the possession of the B.A. degree does not guarantee any level of minimal knowledge of skills for its holders. Indeed, entering freshmen at some institutions know more at admission than graduating seniors from other institutions with sheepskins in their hands. Studies of the relationship of grades in college to success in later life, no matter how success is determined, have shown little or no positive correlation. Thus, the filtering and selecting process of higher education in terms of who is granted the degree does not seem to be functionally related to what works in American life.

It is for this reason that American industry is putting over $2 billion into education programs of its own, with the prospect that the amount will grow substantially by 1980. One recent study indicates that of a large sample of college graduates ten years out of college, over half of the males and two-thirds of the females are now working in an area unrelated to what they studied in college. For most, a primary career choice was made after graduation. And, indeed, many had moved to second or third careers in the postgraduate decade.

Given this lack of relationship between the things learned at college and the chances for success, one could argue that the name of the college one attended might yet become even more important than in the past. The networks of influential people in Washington are constituted primarily of graduates from the most prestigious colleges and professional schools in the country. (I must confess that one reason I attended Harvard for doctoral study was my conviction that whatever happened, a degree from Harvard probably wouldn't hurt.)

In the future we can expect more attention to be given to:

• *The nature of the hurdles themselves.* For instance, *Griggs versus Duke Power** will make us a trifle more modest in broadcasting the virtues of all holders of our degrees.

• *Those who go over the hurdles.* How many who don't clear them make it anyway in life? How many get over the obstacles but prove themselves incompetent? What impact do instructional methods and curricula have on the professional and personal development of those who succeed and those who fail?

• *Those who govern the hurdling system for both individuals and institutions.* What will the consequences be of lawsuits directed at admissions officers and institutions based upon certain objections to affirmative action and special programs? Can we anticipate the effects of increasing pressure brought by accrediting organizations, such as the ABA and AMA on law and medical school

---

* Subsequent to the 1964 Desegregation Act, the Duke Power Company altered a job requirement to include a high school diploma and adequate scores on one of two tests—the Wunderlic Personnel Test, which purports to measure general intelligence, and the Bennett Mechanical Comprehension Test, an aptitude test. In *Griggs versus Duke Power* in 1971, the Supreme Court ruled against Duke Power, striking down the new discriminatory job requirement, indicating that the use of such considerations for employment purposes must be specifically related to the needs of the job. Thus, with educational credentials related to the job description for employability at the high school graduate level, might this ruling be extended to include holders of university degrees? Recent lower court decisions have begun to move in this direction, raising perplexing questions about the translation of higher level education into careers for those without back-up course work from college days. If employability must relate to college training, then institutions will have to reexamine the nature of the hurdles they set before student applicants and the character of their curricula.

admissions policies? Certainly, institutions must first leap hurdles in order to run *people* through hurdles. And faculty and trustees ought to examine more closely just how admissions decisions shape institutional policy.

Hurdles will demand more evidence of performance rather than aptitude, and measures will need to be better suited to a wider range of applicant ages, ethnicities, and social backgrounds. Work is becoming a scarce resource, as there is not enough to go around, particularly for the well-educated. This will make hurdling more pragmatic, more vocationally oriented, and perhaps more important as a key to entering the estates which dominate the country (communications, technology, politics, research and development, etc.).

In some respects this book may seem to be looking backward in its concern with students entering the most selective institutions, both undergraduate and graduate, as well as with the fate of those who know they are in second-rate institutions and thus will be second-rate people. However, the future may well see the development of new kinds of elite institutions to which this book should be very relevant. We need different kinds of excellence, each admired and respected for its own sake. This book may help to show us how to make the necessary but difficult journey.

HERBERT S. SACKS

"Bloody Monday"
The Crisis of the High School Seniors

Herbert Sacks focuses upon a high school population eager to gain admission to highly-selective colleges. Building upon ideas he first offered in an Op-Ed piece published in the New York Times* *where he discussed some of the psychodynamic features of the student and family response to the admissions crisis, Sacks weaves observations of student behavior with those of institutional conflict and compromise. He sees present-day problems mirrored in the motion picture* American Graffiti *and then takes us to parallels with Dickens's* Dombey and Son. *He offers several corrective models for consideration but also suggests that "this developmental hurdle seems to be so necessary in our society today that if the institution of college did not exist it would have to be invented."*

His clinical analysis of the cost of the academic lock-step, the intellectual drivenness of achieving students in the most selective undergraduate schools is confirmed by the recent early results of longitudinal research work employing different assessment measures. A study of graduates of a selective male undergraduate college suggests that the price of scholarly accomplishment for many was a postponement of the resolution of important developmental tasks of young

* *The New York Times*, April 12, 1975, p. 27.

10

*adulthood giving rise to marital and work problems and depression.**

Prologue

The material that follows is based upon a study of fifty-two high school seniors, forty of whom I have treated over the past five years. Twelve more high school seniors, not in psychotherapy, were also observed. The fifty-two students were in the mainstream of late adolescent behavior. In the treatment group, a preponderant number were suffering from normal developmental difficulties sometimes called adolescent turmoil, and only a few had neurotic complaints, largely of an hysterical nature. No psychotically disturbed adolescents were in the treatment group. The students in treatment were distinguished by their psychological awareness and their readiness to look at themselves. Observation of the total group exposed the anatomy of a clear-cut universally experienced developmental syndrome manifesting common themes. While clinical anecdotes and vignettes express the acutely felt experiences of individual students, every senior does not consciously recognize each of the components of the syndrome. But concerned students, parents, teachers, and clinicians can often identify some topographical features of this developmental map although the details are usually hidden from view.

The group was largely upper middle class, half coming from the public schools and half from independent day and boarding schools. They were evenly divided in gender. Half were Protestant, one-third were Jewish and the remainder were Roman Catholic. Formal religious commitments were minimal but all had

* Douglas Heath, "Academic Predictors of Adult Maturity and Competence," *Journal of Higher Education*, Vol. 48, No. 6, November–December, 1977, pp. 613–632.

significant moral positions and important ethnic, national, and racial identifications. The students ranged from children of immigrants to the offspring of old Yankee families. All but ten parents had earned baccalaureates, and more than thirty held advanced degrees.

The Framework of Crisis

On Monday, April 18, 1977, hundreds of thousands of American high school seniors streamed to their mailboxes and to post offices to intercept the morning mail and to learn which colleges and universities would admit them to the class of 1981. "Bloody Monday," as it was known to young students, kaleidoscopically revealed the fears, struggles, and aspirations of late adolescents. What are the issues involved in this awesome moment, a moment which occurs each April—a time to be savored by some, for others a moment of humiliation and embarrassment?

The present system of college admissions tends to disregard educational principles and is often insensitive to what we know of adolescent development. The admissions community has failed to identify its work with the mission of education: to master knowledge so as to enrich one's existence, to elaborate the spirit of inquiry for critical exploration of intellectual and political life, and to illumine the personal inner world. Those who do seek to uphold these lofty principles are also hampered by the secondary school students' absorption with rank, grade, and score distinctions. But the students have not arrived at this position simply by chance; they were guided there by signposts installed by the current admissions system. Normal adolescent development is tumultuous, never straight-line, with dramatic regressions and progressions. Admissions judgments are intolerant of these peaks and nadirs in the students' mental lives which encumber academic performance. The system rewards those fortunate young people whose learning experiences occur in a relatively conflict-free sphere of ego functioning, away from the ongoing *Sturm und Drang,* or those whose excessive defenses against their adolescent drives permit them to repress conflict successfully.

Although they recognize the hard decisions and inexact judgments which must be made of a sea of applicants, many of whom seem to be similarly qualified on paper, college admissions personnel worry primarily about how to select the best candidates for their institutions while avoiding reflection upon the underlying meaning to youth of this farrago of life crises which, though artificially induced, are expectable for this stage of development.

The normal late adolescent is naturally preoccupied with thoughts of emancipation from parents and home, with the strengthening of autonomous strivings, the achievement of mastery over impulses and capacities, with a firming of sexual identity, the evolution of love relationships, and the early moves toward a vocational choice. The knowledge of impending departure from home is a pressure cooker which, over a period of months, leads toward a coalescence of emerging identity fragments, the residues and precipitates from other life crises experienced since infancy.[1] The admissions process becomes a lightning rod for more intrinsic normative issues in human development and the distortions which result often lead us to ignore the harsh realities of the process itself.

Eager American parents with regard for intelligence and respect for scholarship, and spurred by economic and social considerations, have set the stage for the college matriculation process. Even at the junior high school level, educators assist in laying down the foundations of the admissions crisis by subtle coercion and threats about the necessity of making a good record for the future.

> History to the defeated
> may say alas but cannot help or pardon.[2]

Surely, the wicked doctrine of these lines published more than thirty years ago by W. H. Auden is part and parcel of the tenets offered students by teachers and parents. When narrowly applied to education, his words indicate a lack of appreciation for the vicissitudes of development which frequently occur during the school years and which contain within them the possibility of re-working unstable solutions resulting from crises of earlier times. The personal accounts of academically successful adults are re-splendent with tales of difficulties in school—both academic and behavioral—from which they emerged, strengthened by the influ-ences of accidental events, encounters with new models and re-worked solutions to older developmental problems.

Those who work with the young will readily testify to the effectiveness of "treatment" in helping to achieve a healthy resolu-tion when crises damage the progress of growth, and sometimes invade the realm of learning. "Treatment" is not generic to psy-chotherapy alone, but to many forms of help available in our soci-ety to almost all social classes. For the "defeated" who are young there are multiple ways of securing "help or pardon" within the formal educational system. There are high school equivalency tests, community colleges, ABC programs for high-schoolers, af-firmative-action programs for the neglected, and in some colleges there are admission opportunities for the carefully screened high-risk, high-gain candidates. For example, Williams College in the past five years has taken as much as 10 percent of its enter-ing class from this latter grouping.

A chorus of concern about college admissions begins to be heard by the tenth grade, when many schools, especially the private ones, urge their students to take the Preliminary Scholastic Aptitude Tests (PSAT's) in a trial run before October of their junior year when the test really counts. These test results will be used to derive National Merit Scholarship Qualifying Scores which publicly identify high performers. Students are well apprised of the necessity of performing well in the junior year and in the first half of the senior year. With the SAT's and achievement tests taken more than once, the preliminaries are over and the crunch is on.

In the fall of the senior year, applications and catalogs must be secured, visits and interviews arranged, and an estimate made of how many and what quality colleges the students ought to consider. Parental clamor urging their children forward as if they were race horses is often greeted with agreement but with no follow-through action by late adolescents. The stubbornness of youth is a good match for the chivvying behavior of parents. The conscious awareness of seniors that they have not sent for applications is counterpoint to their rich fantasies of crisp autumn days in sought-after colleges.

After irritable confrontations with parents, marked by children's claims of usurpation of their independence, and painful sessions with low-keyed but insistent school guidance personnel, the applications begin to appear in the mail. Their deadlines are noted by the students and then brochures and application forms are swiftly put away in desk drawers.

After a period of quiescence, the skirmishes are renewed with provocative contributions offered by uncomfortable parents, dismayed by their own periodic loss of control. In the seesawing arguments, the reluctance of the seniors to fill out the applications, combined with parental intensity and irrationality, stir up a recapitulation of earlier childhood struggles. Questions of trust, responsibility, duty, ability to govern themselves, flood the dialogue between old and young. It often seems that the joint regression of parents and children is necessary in order for the participants to begin to appreciate the roots of the brouhaha, and to discover a little more about each other before they can disengage and move forward, together and separately.

These issues are always worse in families where the impending loss of an important child threatens the integrity of the family structure. In such families a child often recognizes the signals indicating that a parent wants him or her to remain at home. These elements contribute to guilt and ambivalence about departing and cause the emergence of symptomatic behavior which suggests that it may be dangerous to consider leaving home. Psychiatrists who work with this age group see unwanted pregnancies in the senior year, car accidents, and reawakened psychosomatic symptoms of moderate severity which require continuing care.

For a smaller group of high school seniors, there is little parental involvement in the admissions process. These parents frequently have little information about the procedure and do not try to become acquainted with its features. Some of the reasons for parental distance include residual divorce issues which often lead parents to impute to their children a measure of responsibility for the rupture of the marriage, rejection growing out of long-standing conflicts or illness, or grave disturbance in other family members. This second group of late adolescents have a few of the earmarks of children, described by Anna Freud, who had temporarily or prematurely lost their mothers. These children substituted themselves for their mothers by perpetuating the bodily care once received from them. In mothering themselves the children would not shed their sweaters in hot weather, would not dare to eat green apples, and asked for galoshes in threatening weather so as not to get their feet wet.[3] So it is that high school seniors with uninvolved parents manage their own applications and interviews quietly, pursue advice and recommendations independently and invite scholarship aid with minimal parental acknowledgment. When admitted to first-rank colleges of their choice they are sometimes subjected to muted parental criticism. Their acceptances augur an increase in parental obligations and in some cases confirm the children's desire to achieve goals incompatible with parental value systems and attainments. Freshman college counselors refer to these pseudoautonomous students as "eighteen years old going on forty."

The Application Form

Finally, the applications are carefully read by the senior. Most of them are composed of straightforward biographical questions followed by an exploratory essay focused upon an autobiographical theme designed to gain a simple grasp of the applicant's beliefs and life experience. The autobiographical statement unsettles many students who are concerned with how much to tell, how to decide which vignettes show growth rather than vulnerability, and how to sort out passing moral positions and social postures without appearing to be on an "ego trip."

Another often-troublesome section of the application is a career-choice question which permits some colleges in the private sector to admit applicants with identifiable interests without excessively burdening the teaching loads of particular departments weakened by budgetary strains. For most late adolescents, probing questions about career choice present unreasonable demands for a decision which they obviously are not ready to make. Career-choice questions are seen by some as accusations of how incompetent they are to handle the personal and academic requirements of college, because the colleges explicitly want to know in which majors and departments the matriculants will spend most of their time.

In 1977, eighty-three private colleges from Columbia to Colorado recognized a new common application form in order to simplify the admissions process.[4] Some colleges will require both the new form and their own application form in the beginning years, with the expectation that the latter will ultimately be dropped. Advocates emphasize that the six-page common application form, photocopied for the participating colleges on the student's list, will reduce the paperwork of students and secondary school guidance departments and improve the quality of the application. The effort to promote the ease of application to multiple institutions derives from the increasing economic and recruitment problems of private colleges. But with the adoption of the common form, and the possibility of the ultimate abandonment of individual college forms, the admissions community will be without an instrument that reflects change within a specific institution and the ongoing findings of individual admissions office research.

The clearing-house psychology implied by the new system

may deprive many colleges of particular information they require to serve their entrants better, to change recruitment policies and to rough out a profile of expectable departmental needs. The common form not so subtly suggests to students that there are few differences among participating schools in terms of philosophy, goals, quality of student body, and approaches to settling institutional conflicts. If separation from home carries with it the desired goals of achieving sustained autonomous advances and enhanced self-regard, then, paradoxically, a large number of selective private colleges are intimating that the candidate's uniqueness and distinction will not be treated with sensitivity. Like those aspiring student applicants to public-sector institutions, often admitted by computer determination, the private-sector students will have to accommodate themselves to increased anonymity.

Actual work on the application becomes an endurance feat with the expectation of injury to the narcissistic ego. As one young woman explained it: "I feel like I'm being asked to stand naked before a gallery of judges all wearing their academic robes, with my family and friends being kept from me in the background." She was sure that her bodily defects, common to all humans, would be recognized by the impersonal judges and found unacceptable. This fantasy of exposure to critical judgment without the protection of loving and caring people speaks to the larger ambivalence of this time in the student's life—the wish to be home and nurtured versus the urgency of breaking old attachments in order to advance to a new level of self-realization.

The Interview

Even though most state universities do not offer interviews, and an increasing number of private colleges are granting group interviews for orientation purposes rather than admissions judgments, the individual interview is still a factor in the most selective schools—though it is decreasing in importance. The interview at the college is now being considered somewhat unreliable, probably because the lack of training among interviewers somewhat limits the worth of their findings and because the time constraints inherent in the admissions process do not permit reflective formulations. Nevertheless, the recommendations of alumni interviewers who are seen as discriminating by admissions offices still carry significant weight in the assessment of the student's file.

An exaggerated but discerning satire called *College Entrance*, written and published by a young man interviewed at Yale, takes into account the myriad impressions and fantasies experienced by many applicants each year. A little dulled, Mark comes to the interview, his eighth, before time, dressed in his "interview garb," carefully chosen to reflect his view of himself. He awaits the elevator impassively but it isn't working, so he leaps up the three flights of stairs. Just before rushing out of the stairwell he notices a mirror on the wall, which he guesses is a good-will gesture by the university to help him regain his composure before the confrontation with the interviewer. Anxiously he surveys his competition sunken into leather couches around him, hating their 800 SAT scores and their apparent equanimity. A lovely young woman dean invites him into her office. "Things were not going well. While I spoke of my time in Exeter she admired my jacket; the summer in Chile, 'You have a very nice tan, Mark,' she cooed; working for Common Cause, 'You certainly seem very mature.' " His story accelerates as the beautiful older woman seduces him under the watchful eyes of a portrait of Elihu Yale. He responds to her moves by becoming sexually active. She cries out, "You're in! You're in! Oh my God, this is the first time, never before, what fine credentials!" The fantasy, put to print, reveals Mark's inner feelings of awkwardness, inadequacy, and hopelessness in this unwanted competition. His anxiety is expressed through a regression to an earlier epoch in his life history with a fantasied revival of the oedipal triangle in his family. Thus, the satire depicts an unacceptable sexual connection with Mother Yale acted out under the gaze of a stern, punishing father. The passive submission,

19

an older conflict for Mark, is turned into its opposite through talents not identifiable by the most perspicacious college application form. In the real world, Mark was turned down by Yale.

After an interview at a small college, another senior, Sam, was invited to luncheon with his father by a professor friend. In a genial approach, the professor's wife asked the student about his summer experiences in Africa, his special interest in this particular college and his tentative choice of a major. His responses were incisive, adroit, and revealed some thoughtful insights about himself. On the journey home, Sam's father asked him to compare his responses in the formal college interview with his responses to the professor's wife. It was quickly apparent that the young man recalled only fragments of the formal interview and could not qualitatively assess his rejoinders to the professor's wife. Here is another common thread—interview anxiety is often at a sufficient level to repress aspects of the experience. Furthermore, the denial of competition with his peers pervades the student's interaction with the interviewer, making subsequent recall very difficult.

In the previous vignette, "College Entrance," breathless Mark tries to recover his aplomb by looking into the mirror in a stairwell, thus restoring his sense of well-being and reestablishing the boundaries between himself and the rest of the world. Given the appropriate conditions, there is a readiness among late adolescents like Mark and Sam to blur that which has been acquired most recently and most tenuously—their sense of inner sameness, their sense of the reality of the self.

College Recruitment

A brilliant black woman senior at an urban high school was invited by an Afro-American student group supported by the admissions office to spend the weekend at a New England college. The black experience at this institution was presented to the student guests in a carefully orchestrated program. The style, camaraderie, and sophistication of the approach suffused the woman's judgment, and she began to think of this college as her first choice. A few weeks passed and she visited the school once again at the behest of a former high school friend who wished to renew an old tie. In the absence of the tightly organized program of the preceding month, she was discouraged to find depressed students, beset by inordinate work obligations, who were threatening to transfer to other, less demanding institutions. Complaints of dormitory over-crowding, poor food, and uninspired teaching were aired by the same students who had been part of the earlier charade. It was impossible for her either to validate or neglect allusions to racial problems badly handled by the college administration. The young woman realized that the students' dour view of college life might be overcast by their worries over imminent examinations, but the undeniably deceptive treatment she had received earlier from her first-choice college left her skeptical about the standards and ethics of the higher educational system she had been so eager to enter.

Upon closer scrutiny, the young woman would have discovered that the selling job expressly designed for highly able black candidates also operates in different ways for desirable white candidates. As the fervor mounts for the achievement of specific recruitment goals by college admissions offices, misunderstandings, overstatements, mild deceptions, and abuses of the truth contaminate exchanges with qualified applicants. Colleges with shaky financial underpinnings have developed sleazy marketing techniques publicly exposed in college fairs. The Department of Health, Education and Welfare has, in fact, threatened increased federal intervention unless postsecondary institutions intensify efforts to assure that the student consumer is not hoodwinked. In the next few years, undergraduate colleges are going to have to give more accurate data about themselves, acknowledge their shortcomings, and indicate steps taken to improve themselves. They will have to tell applicants about the quality of academic departments, progress made in implementing affirmative-action programs, dropout rates, job placement of recent graduates, and the success rates of college seniors applying to graduate and professional schools.[5] The National Center for Educational Statistics of HEW and educational administrators suggest that the colleges' misrepresentation of themselves to high school juniors and seniors figures largely in their dropout and transfer rates.[6] Fifty percent of entering college students do not graduate because they drop out or transfer elsewhere.[7]

Symptomatic Behavior in the Winter Months

In the course of the winter months of the senior year, the external and internal pressures upon students mount. Seniors often seek help for themselves when symptomatic behavior makes them aware that their personality functioning is skewed and maladaptive. One young man referred himself for treatment when he lost all the completed applications he was delivering to his guidance counselor for approval before dispatching them to his chosen colleges. This loss permitted an inquiry into other developmental and hidden neurotic problems. Repeated challenges to vice principals in charge of discipline, school-rule violations such as smoking in prohibited areas, plagiarism, cutting classes, blatantly arrogant behavior toward respected teachers, and failure to turn in required papers are offenses committed by seniors who never demonstrated these problems before. Sudden intense heterosexual relationships with demands for mutual dependence threaten the earlier narcissistic positions of only a few years before. For many young people these intense bonds are a way of prematurely acting out their fantasies of what life will be once they are free and distant from parental oppression. These precipitous relationships often allow them to cut loose the ties of parental values without testing their capacity to move in the direction of real intimacy. It is understandable then that only rarely do these relationships survive the transition to college. Previously avoided experimental drug experiences with other young people appear attractive, as a means of warding off sexual wishes while relieving the isolation and depressive bleakness of the moment. Sleep disturbances, transitory losses of appetite, great weight gains, psychosomatic complaints, hypochondriacal concerns are some of the symptoms that may lead the senior to psychiatric consultation. There ensues for many a sense of timelessness, boredom, lassitude, and depression. Those seniors who are involved in a compelling extracurricular activity which is valued and has public character appear to manage more effectively.

Among many students there is a brittle kind of industriousness in their pursuit of high marks in the first semester of the senior year. Cajoling of teachers and grade-bargaining contribute to an atmosphere unconducive to educational inquiry. In the second semester, when the interim reports have been made by the secondary schools to colleges, a general collapse of educational objectives is widely recognized.* To deal with the expectable, many secondary schools have made it possible for qualified students to graduate at mid-year and others have planned independent projects which are ostensibly a bridge to college-level efforts. Ludlowe High School in Fairfield, Connecticut, graduated 46 seniors out of a class of 470 in January, 1977. At Phillips Academy in Exeter, New Hampshire, 37 out of 353 seniors of the class of 1977 were eligible to graduate in December of 1976. Over a 5-year period as many as 100 students in a given class at Exeter were graduated early until, out of economic and philosophic considerations (the graduates' post-Exeter experience was not being fully exploited), requirements were tightened, leading to the present decline in the numbers of students seeking early graduation. Were there no administrative interventions, it is likely that the numbers of early graduates would have remained very high, bordering on 50 percent of the class. Of the 37 Exeter seniors eligible to graduate in mid-year last year, 13 stayed to work on a project or to take post-graduate courses, essentially with a different order of motivation than if they were continuing on as seniors. Of the 24 who left the campus, 13 committed themselves to Exeter-affiliated activities

* The same phenomenon is observable in preprofessional college seniors after they submit their applications to medical and law schools.

such as Washington internship programs. A former principal of Staples High School in Westport, Connecticut, points out that with the increase in numbers of "semesterized" courses offered, there is a parallel rise in the number of mid-year graduates. Despite almost 320 full-year and one-semester courses listed in the Staples catalog, some good students seemingly exhaust the offerings which interest them by the middle of their senior year. With "semesterization," they can depart in February without damaging their academic records through failure to complete full-year courses.

Some students who are gifted but discouraged by the high school experience have been admitted to fine colleges after skipping the twelfth grade. Indeed, since 1972, Johns Hopkins University has not required the high school diploma for admission.

Yet another small and apparently declining number of high school graduates need more time to understand the critical events of the past few years and so take a moratorium by delaying matriculation at college by a year. The Yale Undergraduate Admissions Office reports that there were 1,338 matriculants in the class of 1981 and 35 more students who elected to postpone entry for a year. The possibility of deferring admission appears in the Yale Introductory Bulletin and in the material sent with the admissions letter. There are no stumbling blocks or financial penalties (except through annual tuition and board increments) for those who postpone, save the proviso that they not enroll in another institution. Hampshire College, a less structured institution whose student body is less competitive, encourages postponed entry in selected cases. Hampshire reports that 21 students deferred for one or two semesters out of a September entering class numbering 375, including 70 transfer students. There has, however, been a 50 percent decline in student deferrals over the past three years, not because of an attitudinal shift on the part of the Hampshire College admissions office, but for economic reasons. The cost of college escalates each year, even as inflation reduces the buying power of the parental dollar. There is a limited selection of job opportunities for the high school senior, and the work which can be secured often pays poorly and has little educational value.

Let us now move from educational administrative issues to psychological matters. In March, with its dark mornings and wintry blasts, students tell of anxiety dreams. One accomplished senior girl dreamt that she had died and letters from Yale, Harvard, Wellesley and Wesleyan were lying unopened on a table in her home. After her death her parents had not withdrawn her applications. Her associations revealed that in the first semester of the senior year she had not worked well, and despite her pledges to herself and to her parents, her marks were undistinguished. She worried that this downturn in her performance would eliminate her from consideration by the colleges where she had submitted applications. Thus, in the dream, she was dead when the mail arrived from these admissions offices. But now that she was lost, everyone would be sorry—colleges and parents—because she was probably admitted everywhere. The fat letters from these colleges remained unopened to spare her parents further grief. The failure of her parents to notify the colleges of her demise was a measure of their inordinate investment in her gaining admission to enhance their own conceit, rather than as a fulfillment of a goal she had sought for herself. In this light, her death served them right!

A young man with high SAT scores and in the top 2 percent of his class fretted about small dishonesties calculated to improve his candidacy at first-rate private colleges. Why did he work so hard at so many dull extracurricular pursuits which robbed important time from his genuine interests? Even with an impressive collection of merit badges he was still disconsolate, for in his quest for more "college suck" his fidelity to himself and his integrity were slipping out of focus.

By late winter he had arrived at a satisfactory position for himself through an independent study program and was feeling good about signals he received from college interviewers. But he was increasingly worried about his father. Several times in the preceding month his father had awakened him during the night saying, "Don't worry, George, I know you'll get in everywhere." The narcissistic identification of fathers with sons, surfacing in the admissions process, has been strengthened by the long-term economic and social advantages associated with a degree granted by the best colleges. The excessive participation of parents in their children's experiences repeats critical unsettled events in their own life histories. In Erikson's terms, the admissions crisis becomes for the parents a matter of establishing generativity, which is primarily the need to found and guide the next generation. If the parental effort is unsuccessful, parents often feel a sense of impoverishment or stagnation.[8] Thus, for some parents and students, failure or relative failure at different points on the spectrum of the crisis may be perceived as a mutual tragedy. The children integrate the complex parental response into the matrix of their own crisis resolutions and in every case this gives the crisis sequelae a distinctive quality.

Early Decision and Rolling Admission

Under the terms of most Early Decision Programs, seniors may be notified of acceptance as early as December 1. These students then have a moral obligation to agree to attend the accepting institution. In Rolling Admissions Programs the accepted student, having been notified anywhere from November 1 onward, must usually confirm his or her willingness to attend the college by April 15. The early filing of an application is already a distinguishing hallmark in the student's relationship with his peers and teachers. The interview experiences of early admission candidates are carefully examined by other seniors who surgically extract those aspects of the encounters which fit their own expectations, fears, and wishes. Their special stature serves as a catalyst for the inevitable fragmentation of the senior class. A senior admitted to Amherst early in the year could not express his exhilaration at school because he did not want to injure his relationships with his closest friends. He felt forced out of his group, partly because he withdrew himself and partly because of the group members' resentment of his achievement, which intensified their own concerns about their own incomplete applications. In order to regain his sense of belonging, the successful student began to deprecate Amherst silently. After all, if that vaunted institution accepted the likes of him with all of his deficits, could it really stand for excellence?* A few other successful Early Decision applicants who were experiencing the same disaffection began to spend more time together to share their feelings. In response to this development another group of seniors who shared a fear of college rejection began to meet regularly, making their domain the library's special periodical reading room. Upon testing their possession of that room filled with erudite journals, the young man admitted early to Amherst, strong and six feet tall, was hurled through a doorway by an old friend on the wrestling team. As subgroups formed, old relationships became remote, and the involvement in the school and its offerings diminished markedly. This splitting, separation, and decreased investment are unavoidable and ultimately desirable by the year's end between student and student, student and school, and student and family. However, the early notification process for some students makes for discontinuities, incongruities, and unhappiness in an already charged situation.

Anxieties and family pressures actually propel some seniors into a premature resolve to apply for Early Decision. If accepted, a number of seniors begin to reconsider their positions and discover that they do not wish to attend the institutions that accepted them. In the five to six months before April 15, transitions in their parental relationships, peer experiences, and the process of deprecating their accepting colleges lead to behavioral excesses (by parental definition, at least) which parallel the tracks taken by other students who are still in the dark about their acceptability to the college of their choice. One honorable young man, of academic

* Groucho Marx once said with bitter humor: "I wouldn't want to belong to a club that would have me for a member!"

and athletic distinction, "early admitted" to Williams, was arrested in the shoplifting of a one-dollar toy. He clearly wanted to get caught, disgrace himself and his family, and give Williams a chance to review his acceptance. His situation is repeated in many examples from this age group and others and was first classically described by Freud (1916) in a piece called "Those Wrecked by Success,"[9] which shed fresh light upon the psychology of crime.

"Bloody Monday"

Young men late in the night
Toss on their beds,
Their pillows do not comfort
Their uneasy heads,
The lot that decides their fate
Is cast to-morrow,
One must depart and face
Danger and sorrow.

Is it me? Is it me?[10]

Every year, following on the April 15th mailing, seniors urgently look for the fat envelope, the sign of acceptance. The secondary schools, because of their involvement with their students and their wish to evaluate their teaching effectiveness, the quality of their school's reputation and the wisdom and influence of their student recommendations to the colleges, are eager, too, for the results. During this day the successful students' feelings of triumph and grandiosity are muted to preserve the sensitivities of friends who have been disappointed by the thin letter. In some communities, at night, students hold bittersweet parties with the eerie yet therapeutic quality of a wake. Subtle resentment and reluctant joy make for an ambiance which many college students recall with more nostalgia than their high school graduation ceremonies. Here the stature of the young men and women is on public display and subject to more severe judgment than any admissions committee could possibly visit upon them.

For some students, the humiliation of defeat, reinforced by old memories, overcomes judgment and controls. David, a boarding school senior, talented in art and science but muddling along in the humanities, was rejected for admission at the most selective colleges. In the autumn, after his mother overrode his resistance to submitting applications to the Ivy League colleges, he had dispatched poorly drafted application forms. His unwillingness to apply was founded upon a misinterpretation of the cautious advice of a college counselor. This misreading was derived from a notion, arising in the borderlands of consciousness, that he was unworthy of admittance to an Ivy League school and that he was losing the battle for self-validation.

Since two generations before him had gone to Harvard, he lightly assumed that Harvard would be obliged to accept him as a legacy. As if to diminish Harvard's commitment to his family, his Harvard essay was insubstantial and disorganized. Given his self-defeating attitude, he failed to develop interview opportunities where his particular assets could best be displayed. He missed appointments and turned up when interviewers were on vacation.

In a postrejection, altered state of consciousness, David fashioned a slingshot, and from his room in the topmost reaches of the dormitory, he fired pellets at anonymous pedestrians and passing cars. This errant behavior repeated an early school pattern from his boyhood. When he felt unprotected (consequent to the loss of his father) and estranged from his group (associated with school bus tauntings) he became indiscriminately and dangerously aggressive to his schoolmates.

His first hit cracked the window of a car driven by a distinguished older woman from the community. When the street furor brought David to full awareness of his action, he immediately turned himself in to his housemaster. The irate master charged the student with the ploy of prompt confession in order to minimize the punishment he would have received once detective work had identified him as the culprit! No connection was made between his aberrant behavior and his rejection by colleges.

Because of his own feelings of unworthiness, David punished himself severely for his failure to gain admission to any of the colleges of his family's choice. The stormy adjudication process in his boarding school, intimately involving the school psychiatrist and his family, enabled him to restore his impulse controls through increased recognition of the meaning of his behavior. Placed on probation, David finished the year with an A average for that term (after it did not count for college admission), was graduated with honors, and went off to a second-line institution where he is excelling.

While both sexes suffer the pain of admissions rejection, why do so many young men (in contrast to young women) react with such anguish, for so long? Certainly, restitutive reactions to narcissistic injury occur in both sexes, but in young men they are often colored by maladaptive behavior. According to Matina Horner,[11] women may be protected by societal proscriptions against their being successful and competitive with men. With such proscriptions woven into the fabric of their developing self-image, their expectations for themselves are lower than those of their male counterparts. In the past, if a woman failed to reach her attempted goal she could fall back upon a family-supported position and become a wife, child-bearer, and community volunteer. But this reasoning, perhaps valid for middle-class women ten years ago, would seem to be outdated in light of the pervasive influence of the women's movement. Currently, a woman whose primary career aspirations have been blunted may move into an allied field which may carry less prestige, authority, and economic reward than her first choice.

Many young women, usually college undergraduates, but also high school seniors, explain that they can win the right to be respected only through academic and professional achievement. The more academically vulnerable they feel, the more they are driven in their work. But if this general observation is correct, why aren't women as responsive, or indeed, more responsive, than men to the humiliation of academic rejection? One answer may lie in the fact that the most blatant expressions of the competitive battle are heard from young men who have already made career choices and are driven by the fear of failure and its mortification. If they succeed they often cannot enjoy the fruits of the victory because of their uneasiness about the degree of aggression mobilized and directed against their competitive peers in reaching their goal. Another answer, suggested by women, is that men translate their feelings about admissions judgments into assessments of their manhood and their capacity to become self-supporting in a respectable occupation.

Undergraduate college women have observed that their male peers seem to have a deeper narcissistic investment in themselves than have age-comparable women friends. On a relative scale, this assessment of a lack of readiness for intimacy may be valid, yet one also sees many college women who engage in casual sex, avoid deeper commitment to men, are heavily involved in their work, and are fearful of tenderness. For this group, early marriage or pregnancy is seen as a defeat. In their career pursuits they struggle with the future problems of the management of marriage and parenthood versus their vocational development. But the intense reactions of even these women are different from those of the men previously described. Their values are not so firmly entrenched and are, therefore, subject to continuing and painful self-questioning.

Many college seniors awaiting admissions decisions for graduate and professional schools recapitulate the undergraduate admission ordeal. Old secondary school triumphs are weighed against the fantasy of impending defeat four years later. A male college senior recalled his being sent around the world after high school graduation as a Presidential Scholar. Now, with a 3.2 GPA and 720 LSAT's, he was rejected by seven law schools. Another college senior who had never written for college publications was dejected that a famous graduate school of journalism would not consider the merit of his secondary school editorial experience. A Yale woman, living near four competent male seniors awaiting Judgment Day, was perplexed because her men friends were openly mourning their rejections by Harvard College four years earlier. All had temporarily vacated any sense of the shape or meaning or history of their Yale experience.

The Senior Year Ends

In the last two months of secondary school there is further progress in attempting to give up some aspects of the loved other self of the past, with its backpack of doubts and infantile conflicts. The battle in which many have suffered during the past academic year begins to yield gently to enhanced self-regard, a renewed sense of direction and a readiness to leave home for a summer job, which for many is clearly understood as the real departure. Surely, the continuing issues of late adolescence are not wholly relieved but, nonetheless, a profound shift in the ego structure gradually becomes recognizable with an increase in the youth's capacities for adaptation. Even for those who are disappointed by their college acceptances, the process of separation moves forward inexorably despite the fact that their diminished self-regard may not allow them to make the fullest use of their adaptive capabilities until they embrace the freshman identity in the college they will attend. In psychoanalytic literature, Loewald points out how separation spurs on advances in ego development, resuming the advantageous after-effects of earlier life separations, processes which are necessary for growing maturity and individuation.[12]

Leaving Home

In 1973, *American Graffiti*, a Universal film production, depicted the plight of the adolescent departing his home for college. The film deals with four high school buddies, but chiefly with two of them, in a California town in the early 1960s. At the beginning, in the dusk of evening, two friends are presumably bound East for college together, one reluctantly, and the other eagerly. By morning, the roles are reversed: the first young man leaves, and the second stays with his hometown cheerleader girl friend. The young man who departs is told by his high school teacher during dusk-to-dawn revelries of the time when he left home for college but returned after one semester: "I wasn't the competitive type." On departure, the central character climbs aboard his airplane bound for college but still carrying a radio tuned to his local station. The radio plays until he is in the air and finally out of range—and the crackle of the static is a symbolic statement of his separation from the familiar.

The movie was a financial success (grossing $52 million) in part because of the large numbers of high school students who saw it more than once, identifying strongly with the principal theme. It depicted, in a twelve-hour period, regressive and impulsive behavior symptomatic of the struggle to separate from home and family. Yet we never see any of the youths' families until the hero boards the airplane. The young man who stays behind succumbs to the infantile dependent tie encouraged by his cheerleader girl friend and abandons his hesitant steps toward emancipation and mastery.

The Educational Hothouse

The present system of college admissions in the first-rank schools of the private sector and the most-selective schools in the state university systems can be traced to the effects of the population proliferation since World War II and the nation's answer to Sputnik I, the first man-made satellite launched by Soviet scientists on October 4, 1957. That major scientific advance made for convulsive changes in the mathematics and science curricula of our primary and secondary schools and caused delayed but necessary

33

accommodations to burgeoning new information. The late Dean William Clyde DeVane of Yale College once quipped that if there had only been a Soviet threat in the humanities, our universities could have equally enjoyed major expansions in the arts. In retrospect, we see that there was, at the same time, expansion in departments such as English, Philosophy, and History; only the teaching of the Fine Arts did not appreciably benefit from the increased availability of funding.

Secondary school curricular changes, dictated by government policies and faculty decisions and endured by students, have built a great educational hothouse in which there is a forcing apparatus incessantly at work. In 1848, Charles Dickens, in *Dombey and Son*,[13] tells of Doctor Blimber's secondary school for ten young gentlemen. The doctor had ready a supply of learning for a hundred, and it was at once the business and delight of his life to gorge the unhappy ten with it. In Dickens's hothouse, as in our own, 130 years later:

> Mental green peas were produced at Christmas, and intellectual asparagus all the year round. Mathematical gooseberries (very sour ones too) were common at untimely seasons, and from mere sprouts of bushes under Dr. Blimber's cultivation. Every description of Greek and Latin vegetable was got off the driest twigs of boys, under the frostiest circumstances.

Dickens goes on:

> The young gentlemen were prematurely full of carking anxieties. They knew no rest from the pursuit of stoney-hearted verbs, savage noun-substantives, inflexible syntactic passages, and ghosts of exercises that appeared to them in their dreams. Under the forcing system, a young gentleman usually took leave of his spirits in three weeks. He had all the cares of the world on his head in three months. He conceived bitter sentiments against his par-

34

ents or guardians, in four; he was an old misanthrope, in five; envied Curtius that blessed refuge in earth, [*] in six; and at the end of the first twelve-month he had arrived at the conclusion that all the fancies of the poets, and the lessons of the sages were a mere collection of words and grammar and had no other meaning in the world.

Plus ça change, plus c'est la même chose

Thus Dickens satirizes the terrible losses incurred in the promising young by the forcing system of modern education. More than a century later we learn to live with our own special losses. Undergraduates, especially in their freshman and sophomore years at first-rank institutions, complain that there has been no time to meditate, to enjoy the breadth of nonacademic life in the college, as professors increase the work load and administrators try to shrink the duration of the semester. Most will not dare to explore areas of study foreign to their immediate interests for fear of receiving a fatal grade. Academic activity must be negotiable in the market-place.[14] Personal relationships with faculty mentors become a bit tainted by concern with self-aggrandizement. Dormitory over-crowding and the encouragement of off-campus living diminish morale and a sense of community and purpose. The decline of the quality of the food makes the dining room less appealing as a place for coming together to establish and renew friendships. Student forebodings and joylessness are epitomized when return from vacation is referred to as "back to the slammer."

But despite these costly and dreadful parameters, there is the uplifted spirit of students that comes with the mastery of what was not known before. There continue to be teachers whose character

---

* In 362 B.C. a deep gulf appeared in the Roman Forum which seers declared would never close until Rome's most valuable possession was thrown into it. Curtius, a legendary hero, aware that nothing was more precious to Rome than a brave citizen, leaped fully armed and on horseback into the chasm, which immediately closed.

and scholarship are models for future undertakings. Academic institutions still strive to foster a sense of values, provoke informed skepticism and encourage disciplined creativity.

So often in the histories of achieving young adults in trouble—graduates of this system—we find little or no adolescent turmoil or at least too easily accomplished compromises which fend off conflict and trade off symptoms, but which are essentially maladaptive. When they were secondary school adolescents the work obligation and evidences of accomplishment loomed large and they fiercely guarded any avenues which might admit consciously experienced conflict, deflecting and avoiding issues which might divert them from their central commitment to studenthood. Their excessive defenses against adolescent drives led them to be deemed "good children," considerate of their mothers, submissive to their fathers, wrapped up in family relationships and imbued with the atmosphere, ideas, and ideals of their childhood backgrounds.[15] On the surface these students exploited the hothouse system, thrived in the artificial climate of academe and marched on to undergraduate, postgraduate, and professional schools in sizable numbers. Dickens, in speaking of the consequences of the educational hothouse, warns us about its crop, "There was not the right taste about the premature productions and they didn't keep very well." The thrust of their intellectual ambitiousness, combined with internal struggles against their drives, cause failures in clearing developmental hurdles. The demands for achievement in the outer world combined with their inner restrictions ultimately contribute in no small measure to untimely and unwanted psychological problems. Marital and parenthood problems and work difficulties are familiar complaints when these students reach their mid-twenties.

We now turn to a student group which has not been considered earlier. There are secondary school students who "take leave of [their] spirits" by Dickens's description, and who cannot be made or helped to fit into the system. They require alternate means of education in the community, upgraded technical schools, programs of internship in business and professional enterprises in the real world, or just jobs with a future. Such work will necessitate statutory changes such as lowering the minimum working age from sixteen years. Some of these students may later be able to return to the educational production line with a new direction; others may not return at all. With the incipient introduction of bills in state legislatures removing status offenders* from the jurisdiction of the juvenile court, education laws will have to be amended to permit the states to abandon compulsory education up to the age of sixteen. This development may exact the best creative ideas from the educational bureaucracy if it is to discharge its societal role. No longer will the bureaucracy be able to duck behind the crusty excuse that it cannot do its job well because it is encumbered by too many youths who are in school only because of legal constraints.

Dickens's splendid portrayal of the hapless secondary school students underscores their natural limitations and causes us to consider his observation in the light of the admissions theme of this chapter. In Dickens's hothouse, "Nature was of no consequence at all. No matter what a young gentleman *was intended* to bear, Dr. Blimber made him bear it to pattern somehow or other." (Italics mine.) Dickens's caution follows by almost ninety years upon the revolutionary book *Émile* wherein Rousseau claims that the salient biological and psychological features of child development pursue certain laws whose natural progression must be respected. The teacher's first responsibility, Rousseau emphasized, must be to keep in contact with the students' developmental realities.[16]

Certainly educational competence and talent, and the capacity to exploit one's gifts, are not distributed equally to everyone. Through Augie March, Saul Bellow tells us, "I have always tried to become what I am. But what if what I am by nature isn't good

---

* In most states, a status offender is a juvenile under the age of sixteen who can be charged for offenses not applicable to adults, including incorrigibility, truancy, running away, and immorality.

enough?"[17] Because they recognize these elemental facts, the most-selective colleges must seek to maintain admissions criteria without qualification in order to sustain their high standards of excellence.

Institutional versus Individual Aspects of the Admissions Process

John Silber, President of Boston University, makes a strong case for elitism in universities.[18] He avers that as long as intelligence is better than stupidity, knowledge better than ignorance, and virtue better than vice, no university can be run except on an elitist basis. He is opposed to university acceptance of the commonplace and contentment with mediocrity. Silber's argument ultimately leads to the emergence of a national group of well-educated affluent leaders, which has political and social ramifications. Affirmative-action policies, loans, and scholarships ensure that this leadership will come from a cross-section of our society. But it is clear that if his argument were pursued to the end, most universities could not survive and the nation would not then be served.

Josiah Bunting III, former President of Briarcliff College, points out that it is precisely from the ranks of young people who attended "second-rate" colleges, whose class rank and poor SAT scores excluded them from the elitist institutions, that will come the greater portion of future leaders who will guide us in the year 2000.*[19] He pleads the case of young people imbued with the idea of service to their communities, prepared to efface personal egoism in larger causes, to do the drudgework that does not bring public recognition or financial reward, who are not cynical and who understand that the "college decision is the most overrated decision in their lives." But the experiences shown in this chapter do not give support to Bunting's view about overrated college decisions. Surely

* This projection is only impressionistic and is not based upon any study data.[20]

38

the decision, its handling by parents and teachers, and its consequences, are important in giving direction to the vicissitudes of the self-concepts of young people. Bunting's argument takes flight as he asks: "Could Picasso ace his math SAT? Could Lincoln recognize the subjunctive voice in Latin? Could Churchill make sense of differential calculus? Did Martin Luther King know Hopkins from Keats?" But his argument suffers from this laundry list of the virtues of students who attend "second-rate" colleges, virtues which can also be immediately identified in a superficial look at students in any elitist private or public college. Further, most first-rank colleges endeavor to identify extraordinary student talent not determinable by the usual measures of admissability. Failure is inherent in the effort, and this failure might well be valuable to the "second-rate" schools which are helped by the infusion of intellectual leadership from students who were late-bloomers, people with skewed hypertrophied interests, and the like, who can arouse some teachers to produce and whose accomplishments become challenges to some of their more sanguine peers. But too often, in the swift current of student opinion in "second-rate" schools, the provocative students are isolated and their influence swept aside. Nevertheless, when talented but less confident students attend these schools they may be uplifted by the recognition of their giftedness when their work is contrasted with the performances of their less talented peers.

Findings

In this chapter two major positions have been developed. What ameliorative possibilities exist in the complex field of college admissions? In the prior discussion and in the positions which follow, if there is a clear choice to be made between the requirements of the college-admissions community and the developmental needs of the student applicants, I have come down on the side of the student.

There are few issues, unfortunately, that are so easily explicated, so lucidly presented, that such a choice can be made.

I. THE PRESENT SYSTEM OF COLLEGE ADMISSIONS TENDS TO DISREGARD EDUCATIONAL PRINCIPLES AND IS OFTEN INSENSITIVE TO WHAT WE KNOW ABOUT ADOLESCENT DEVELOPMENT.

Generally, the admissions mechanisms in universities are controlled by dedicated administrators who try to be responsive to the wishes of presidents and boards of trustees.* The latter, in turn, have to consider alumni, faculty, and state policy directives (in the case of the publicly supported institutions**). In the private sector, it appears that the more prestigious the college, the more funding is invested in the admissions office. When there are necessary university budgetary cuts, the admissions office frequently feels the pinch early. Policy implementation by the admissions administrators has led to the emergence of a managerial cadre which is isolated from the academic community, without a professional identity that merits the regard of the university at large. The cadre's recognition of its influence, the need to maintain its integrity and still be accountable to superiors in the president's office, encourage it to make elliptical judgments. The admissions cadre is disturbed by the imprecision of its decisions and worried about how to bring together the perceived requirements of the college and the attributes of a plethora of applicants. It evolves a shorthand in candidate selection which does not admit to scrutiny that large middle group of "possibles" after inclusion of the "clear accepts" and the exclusion of the "clear rejects."

The admissions managers enhance their sensitivity to the

* The following comments flow from modest inquiries of the admissions offices at five private eastern colleges of the first and second rank, each having fewer than six thousand students. Similarities and parallels were distilled from the responses, giving rise to condensed and slightly overstated opinions which, however, bring the issues into relief.
** For a discussion of public-sector institutions, admissions policies and mechanisms, refer to David Tilley's essay in this volume.

changes in values, cultural shifts, and newly established traditions of the candidates by employing recent graduates and students as interviewers. Thus, the median age of most admissions communities is usually in the range of mid to late twenties, the salaries are quite low and there is a significant turnover rate of personnel outside of the core group.

Influential faculty input is highly desirable but difficult to attain. Untenured faculty members recoil from the four-week stint of round-the-clock work which takes them away from research, teaching, and families. The senior faculty is reluctant to invest in an undertaking where many decisions have already been shaped by the admissions managers who, in most settings, can outvote academic committee people. Only when student enrollment in specific departmental majors is diminishing might professors in those fields express interest in joining admissions committees in order to advocate qualified candidates who declare for those fields on their application forms.

Faculty prerogatives ought to be asserted on every level of the admissions process with the intent of wedding educational principle to admissions policy. Participation in this arduous activity might be weighted as much as inspired teaching for purposes of considering junior faculty for promotion and tenure. Informed faculty who have served for at least two years on such a committee could contribute to evolving admissions policy and guidelines through recommendations and advice to the office of the president and the dean of admissions. Finally, the faculty members of the admissions committee should cast the majority of the votes in balloting on candidates.

Research sponsored by admissions offices is often myopic, and while its results may point to advisable shifts in a college's admissions policy for the next year and provide clarifying data to the alumni, such research rarely has national significance.* As such,

* Notable exceptions include a recent Harvard study of the fate of the class of 1971 demonstrating a trend toward almost universal graduate education[21] and a Yale study defining the successful student.[22]

institutional research does not contribute significantly to future planning or policy-making, especially in the private sector's relationship with the federal government. The skills of university research methodologists in sociology, psychology, and political science should be diverted to creative enterprises in the admissions office, much as economists and others from the faculty are deployed by some institutions to solve operating problems and to write position papers for contingency planning.

There is heuristic opportunity in conducting national pilot projects to test modifications of the admissions practices which might reduce the intensity of the crisis and at the same time enrich educational prospects. But there is no proposal which I have studied that is not rife with major difficulties. Several alternative possibilities follow:

Student notification of college acceptance should be made on November 15 of the senior year. Colleges would have to either accept or reject, eliminating the "deferred" category. This proposal compels greater risk-taking on the part of the colleges, since the earlier SAT and achievement test scores would be less reliable indicators and fall semester grades would not be available. Given the inexactness of the present system, however, it seems unlikely that there would be a significant diminution in the quality of the accepted candidate pool under this system. The rejected student, on the other hand, would have enough time to seek out another institution and could make an unhurried decision. The splitting and fractionation of the seniors would occur earlier, but since it is an expectable process and ultimately necessary for separation, secondary school administrators and counselors could be helped to manage its manifestations.

Another drawback of this system is that it would militate against consideration of marginal applicants who have an extraordinarily successful fall semester in their senior year. But slots could be saved for these late-bloomers. There would also be serious problems for students, who would have to file applications by May of the junior year, as well as major disruptions of the admissions calendar in both secondary schools and colleges. Of course, acceptance to college on November 15 would be contingent on the evidence of successful completion of the senior year and a review of the secondary school interim reports by April 15.

A new Early Action Program option of admissions has been adopted by Harvard, Princeton, Brown, MIT, and Yale with the class of 1981. Applications must be completed by November 8 and notifications of decisions are mailed in mid-December. At Yale, 45 percent of the prospective students were accepted. In all, 386 of the 839 applicants were accepted, 315 were rejected, and the remainder were deferred consideration until the spring. A laudatory feature of this program is that accepted early action candidates are not asked to respond until the usual reply date in early May. From the viewpoint of this chapter, this development is an advance because it allows the accepted student to make his or her own choices in good time and gives the rejected student the opportunity to make other plans.

This option skims off the most qualified candidates from the applicant pool and assures that the participating private institutions will have a clear shot at eminently admissible high school seniors. In the spring, under the regular admissions routine, with little more than two weeks to render a decision, accepted but hesitant seniors bothered by economic concerns may resolve these questions by turning toward public institutions. Under the new option, with four and a half months to make inquiry, to respond to parental questioning, and to gauge more accurately the long-term financial considerations, there is a greater likelihood that they will opt for a private institution.

While easing the task of the admissions offices, however, this program does not confront the dilemma of the broadest mass of applicants (most of the participating institutions have 9,000 to 11,000 applicants each year), and largely benefits the recruitment needs of the first-rank private sector institutions.[23]

* * *

Student notification of college acceptance should be made on June 15 of the senior year. In this way, the educational virtues of the senior year would be preserved. It would mean, however, that the college admissions community would have to be beefed up with knowledgeable personnel to process the returns so as to guarantee the presence of a full complement in the entering class. Colleges in the private sector who are laboring under financial duress would be further strained by the hazard of a fall-off of candidates who agree to matriculate. In addition, the rejected student would have less time to make other arrangements for the academic year commencing in September.

Colleges should have a rolling admissions program with the schools choosing different deadlines for submission of application forms and different notification dates. Thus, a given college might have headlines of October 1 for applications, with notification on November 15; November 15 for applications, with notification on January 1, etc. Another college might have deadlines of September 15 for applications, with notification on November 1, and so on. The "deferred" category would be eliminated. Colleges seeking the best candidates would have to take greater risks in offering early acceptance to students because the same students might be applying the next month, for instance, to a similar-level institution which might offer them places. The students would have the privilege of either securing acceptance upon notification or waiting until April. This process has the virtue of reducing shotgun applications to as many as a dozen institutions and offering both college and student a less ambivalent marriage.

A sizable percentage of high school graduates could defer application to college for a two-year period. These students would apply to a national service program for work with social value in this country or overseas. Upon completion of this endeavor, supervisory reports of the students' performances would be submitted to the colleges considering them for admission. The national service

44

program would represent an opportunity for the federal government to fund colleges based upon a GI Bill model of compensation.

Problems include the difficulties in assessing recommendations from field supervisors and evaluating the meaning of the two-year hiatus from high school. This proposal would place a heavy burden upon high school counselors to reconstruct salient features of a graduate's past performance and to integrate that impression with the developmental changes accruing from the field work with its opportunity for growth.

II. THE CRISIS OF THE HIGH SCHOOL SENIOR IS A NORMATIVE DEVELOPMENTAL PHENOMENON.

The emancipation experience mediated by the admissions crisis is a rite of passage. This developmental hurdle seems to be so necessary in our society today that if the institution of college did not exist, it would have to be invented. This phenomenon is observable in all social classes: for example, in trade school graduates who seek union membership and plan to leave their parents' homes. Many believe that the boarding school experience relieves the crisis of emancipation, since boarding students are obviously already away from home. Boarding schools, however, are very much *in loco parentis*, and, thus, the crisis is still intensely felt. Boarding school students, moreover, are eager to gain entry to the best colleges and when the results of the admissions procedure are known, they profoundly question whether they have done well by their parents or have fulfilled their own expectations for themselves.

Parents can and should be helped to understand the character and dynamics of this crisis. With an improved grasp of the issues, they might better judge when to stand aside and when to provide support. Increased knowledge would enable parents to assess what level of help, if any, to seek for their children and themselves, in order to deal with these issues. Such judgments are indeed difficult for caring people to make. How many parents, for instance, proud of the glowing academic record of their high schooler who exhibits no visible evidence of turmoil, would decide that expert consultation is in order?

More sensitively trained college advisors are needed to prepare the candidates for success or failure in their quest. The college advisory functions of secondary school counselors must be upgraded with sophisticated training and seminars on adolescent development, annual in-depth visitations to groups of colleges, and with tenure guarantees which would establish their professional identities. The advisors would have the obligation of clarifying the perils of rejection to all candidates and of emphasizing to them the nature of the national lottery they are playing. After Judgment Day, instead of investing time and energy only in those with no acceptances, consideration should also be given to the responses of those who failed to gain admission into their primary-choice colleges, and of those who succeeded.

Expert consultation for students, if indicated for any reason, should be sought only from professionals specifically trained and experienced in working with children and adolescents. If high school seniors only partially succeed, or fail to reach their desired goals, the anticipatory guidance of parents and counselors, combined with the increased self-awareness of the late adolescents, will help them to cope more effectively and to achieve the essential separation with the least cost and the greatest benefit.

REFERENCES

1. Erik H. Erikson, *Identity and the Lifestyle: Selected Papers. The Problem of Ego Identity*, Psychological Issues 1:1, 1959, pp. 101–165.
2. Wystan Hugh Auden, *Collected Shorter Poems, 1927–1957* (New York: Vintage Books, 1975), p. 15.

3. Anna Freud, "The Role of Bodily Illness in the Mental Life of Children," *Psychoanalytic Study of the Child.* Vol. VII, 1952, p. 79.

4. The New York Times, September 22, 1976, p. 26.

5. The New York Times, October 11, 1976, p. 12.

6. The New York Times, October 13, 1976, p. 48.

7. Lewis Mayhew, The Carnegie Commission on Higher Education, *Education: A Critical Analysis of the Reports and Recommendations* (San Francisco: Jossey-Bass, Inc., 1975), p. 42.

8. Erik H. Erikson, *Childhood and Society* (New York: W. W. Norton and Co., Inc., 1950), p. 231.

9. Sigmund Freud, *Some Character Types Met With in Psychoanalytic Work, II, Those Wrecked by Success,* Standard Edition (London: 1916), pp. 316–332.

10. Wystan Hugh Auden, "The Witnesses," 1932, from W. H. Auden, *Collected Poems,* ed. by Edward Mendelson (New York: Random House, 1976), p. 71.

11. Matina Horner, "Femininity and Successful Achievement: A Basic Inconsistency," in Judith M. Burbank, et al., *Feminine Personality and Conflict* (Belmont, Calif.: Wadsworth Publishing Co., 1970), pp. 45–47.

12. Hans W. Loewald, "Internalization, Separation, Mourning, and the Superego," *The Psychoanalytic Quarterly,* Vol. XXXI, 1962, pp. 483–504.

13. Charles Dickens, *Dombey and Son,* 1848 (Oxford; Clarendon Press, 1974), pp. 142–144.

14. Leon Botstein, "College Could Be Worth It," *Change,* Vol. 8, No. 11, December 1976, pp. 24–29.

15. Anna Freud, "Adolescence," *Psychoanalytic Study of the Child,* Vol. XIII, 1958, p. 264.

16. Jean Jacques Rousseau, *Émile* (London: Everyman's Library, 1969), p. vii.

17. Saul Bellow, *The Adventures of Augie March* (New York: Viking Press, 1949), p. 504.

18. The New York Times, September 1, 1976, p. 35.

19. The New York Times, June 28, 1976, p. 27.

20. Josiah Bunting III, Personal Communication, December 10, 1976.

21. Francis D. Fisher, *One Thousand Men of Harvard. The Harvard College Class of 1971 Five Years Later* (Cambridge: The President and Fellows of Harvard College, 1976).

22. Judith D. Hackman and John H. Hoskins, *Patterns of Successful Performance in Yale College,* Yale University Office of Institutional Research #OIR 75R009 (New Haven: Yale University, August 28, 1975).

23. The Yale Daily News, January 20, 1977, p. 8.

PETER WELLS

Applying to College:
Bulldog Bibs and Potency Myths

Peter Wells, from his position as Dean of Students at an independent day school (secondary school) whose students fall within the top 10 percent in the nation, identifies the confused American aspirations for higher education, our muddled understanding of its nature, and the complacency with which we permit our enthusiasms for it to serve as a vehicle for damaging our young. The secondary school ambiance suggests that the reality of college admissions denies the critical needs of adolescence. Wells worries about young people who succeed at clearing hurdles on the cinder track of education only to discover at age thirty that they have not achieved Elysium. Alarmed by the admissions industry's incursion into the purposes of education, he calls attention to options other than the race for college entry.

I N THE CENTER AISLE of the Yale Co-op, the small department store that caters, by subscription, to the Yale community, between the rack of Lacoste shirts and the stacks of handballs, are the bins of Yale's children's wear. Assuredly other colleges have their kiddy togs, but Yale scions can dribble their beef purée on bulldog bibs, squirt peanut butter and jelly on a T-shirt blazoned with "Yale 19??," or skin their knees wearing the heroic mantle of a Yale football jersey.

Although it would be captious for me to inveigh against Yale kiddy clothes as a frivolous scapedog for all that is wrong with college admissions, nevertheless I find in those stacks of bulldog bibs something symbolic of confused American aspirations for higher education, our muddled national understanding of the nature of education, and the complacent way we permit our enthusiasm for higher education to act as the vehicle for doing psychic damage to our young.

The bulldog bib bought by the reunion grad, stylishly Yale in his blue-and-white-striped blazer, and proudly presented to an infant in Scarsdale, Shaker Heights, or any of the other enclaves of affluent, college-educated professionals, bears a message. The message, however unconsciously conceived, states the value of Yale (in this case) and the broader assumption that the infant will go to a good college. Many overt and covert communications will, in time, accumulate, reinforcing the expectation that college will follow high school as the only acceptable and rational course of action.

Invested with shamanistic powers socially, financially, athletically, and, at times, educationally, college has become part of our national myth, a ritual of such potency that when college students a few years ago did question its relevance, their elders frequently manifested the quality of outrage and confusion that properly should accompany sacrilege.

As a nation we have, for the last decade, at staggering public cost and private sacrifice, sent an unprecedented number of our young to college, raising (despite skyrocketing population growth) the total of college-educated Americans from 10 percent to 22 percent in just thirty years. Even with current economic debacles threatening to cut enrollments, between 40 percent and 50 percent of this year's high school seniors will attend college, a figure significantly higher than in the most technocratic European countries and more than five times the percentage in this country fifty years ago. Given the statistics, which can be trotted out between halves like the "World's Largest Marching Band" as reason for national pride, what does one then make of the substantial numbers who drop out or interrupt their studies.[1]

According to many of the drop-outs with whom I have talked, the major reasons seem to be that they were emotionally unprepared for college; they did not know what they wanted to know and thus could not decide what to study; they had no idea college could be so much like high school in terms of its academic demands and drudgery; the institution did not provide the courses they wanted or meet the needs they had. Despite our national compulsion to send children to college, despite the national myth that it is a good thing, it is the children turned young adults, dropping out, "taking time off," who are really indicating by action as decisive as it is often desperate that college may not be the answer for everyone, particularly at age eighteen.

Caroline Bird observed:

> All across the country, I have been overwhelmed by the prevailing sadness on American campuses. Too many young people speak little, and then only in drowned voices. Sometimes the mood surfaces as diffidence, wariness, or coolness, but whatever its form, it looks like a defense mechanism. . . . So we may be systematically damaging 18-year-olds by insisting that their proper place is in college.[2]

Even among those who stick it out, many tell me of disappointment or a sense of malaise. How can this often mundane life be the goal for which they and their families strained every nerve?

Nevertheless, out of what are invariably impeccable intentions, parents and some schools very successfully condition (and perhaps "systematically" damage) their young to believe, without fully understanding why, that they will go to college. Parents share their bright college days if they had them, promise an opportunity they never had if they did not; assure their children they are scrimping (killing themselves is better) so that there will be enough money for a college education; urge older children to work harder, take away privileges if they do not; open a savings account so the child can from the first grade on, with Granny's Christmas check, help afford a good college; or suggest in varieties of ways that the only people worth knowing, the only professions worth entering, come at the end of college and professional training. Teachers help in countless ways, as well. I had a colorful colleague who flailed sluggish minds with the threat that they would end up piloting a beer truck. In ways usually more subtle, and thus more insidious, I share the guilt for pushing students to assume their karma is college. Indeed, the unstated but understood *raison d'être* of my school is that it will train very bright young people, future college students.

Consequently, each September, all my seventh graders "know" that they are going to college, and that it will be (because we are mostly New Haveners) Yale, or as one put it, the "Ivory League." Even though none of them has any real idea what going to college or getting in might involve, going to college acts as a given in their lives; the idea gives their future some comfortable, name-able shape; in fact, for them, it is such a certainty that they need never contemplate the future in a way normal to adolescent development.

So it goes. The passing years continue to reinforce the assumption without casting much light on the reality. Little wonder that many students, particularly those in affluent suburban high schools or private schools, arrive at their senior year with a large, undifferentiated yearning for college, never having considered or dared to consider that there might be alternatives to college. As one thoughtful student assured me, to ponder not going to college meant thinking about unthinkables, about chaos, about the negation of his whole life and of his *parents'*.

I teach in a school whose students, according to national tests, fall within the top 10 percent of the nation, a statistic which is a matter of abstract pride and teaching pleasure for me. Every student is not only college-capable but, by dint of rigorous training, well equipped to deal with college. Despite their training and their capabilities, however, most do not, even as seniors, have coherent notions about why they are going to college. That they are going, that they must, is predetermined. But where, and what will they study, and what will it be like—these are the questions that suddenly become important and for which most have few answers.

The occasional student says, "I don't know what I want to do, but I like knowing things. I want to take psychology, religion, history, sociology, and the classics; the works." That kind of uncertainty, the raw intellectual speculation, promises well. But what is one to do with the majority who do not know what they want to do, who even in our rarefied community may not be very interested in ideas, study, books. Suddenly asked what their intellectual interests are, where they would like to be in a few years, they grow flustered, as if to say, isn't it enough to want to go to college. Sometimes one encounters a student who says with enthusiasm and forthrightness, "I want to be a——." When one knows the capability and deep interest are there, that conviction can make a teacher feel good, but it can also stir concern that with limited academic experience the student has made a premature closure of available options. Some students say with assurance, "I will be a doctor" (or lawyer), disregarding the glut of students whose passion to be doctors and lawyers has made professional school admissions even more frenetic than colleges'.

My former students returning on holidays speak wearily of cut-throat competitions to maintain grade point averages that might qualify them for medical school, remark with mixtures of worldliness and indignation that sabotage by and of premeds is commonplace scandal, and express deep, gnawing anxieties about the round of LSAT's or MCAT's ahead. One wonders if the obsession to go to law or medical school is just another unexamined assumption, like going to college, perhaps a subliminal reaction to seeing few professions glorified on television as medicine and the

52

law have been. Many preprofessional students manifest little surge toward vocation; more than one fiercely eager premed I have talked with has expressed revulsion at the idea of patients—they would, please, be researchers.

I wonder what happens to the teen-ager who squelches some of the natural impulses and experiences of adolescence, turns into a Maalox-eating academic machine, and carries the anxiety of his worthiness around like a rock, just so he can achieve a good college, a good medical school, a good internship, a good residency. Then at thirty, having worked like a demon for half his life, all the clearly defined plateaus scaled, he discovers he has not achieved Elysium.

Several years ago I visited a new dentist, the date on his diploma just a month past, and was having one of those one-sided chats that occur when ten fingers, a drill, a suction tube, a water jet, and seven wads of pressed cotton fill the mouth. "I really envy you," he said. "I always wanted to be a high school teacher, a basketball coach, actually. I always wanted to coach. I go to all the games in town, coach a team at the Boys' Club, but my mother wanted me to be a doctor. I couldn't get into medical school, so I am a dentist." After my first wave of panic ebbed—what was the implication of his ambivalence on my leaking inlay—and prayers were said to St. Appolonia, I could feel terrible sadness for him. So much time committed to an undesired end from which few men could beat an honorable retreat.

That was perhaps just an isolated example, but one wonders how many other young men and women are being pressed toward good colleges and careers they do not want; the Carnegie Commission has variously estimated the dissatisfied, and one can choose to believe that between 12 percent and 34 percent may not be happy, may not want to be in college at all.[3] It requires, however, more ego strength than most young people have to say "no" to the family dream, to accept the guilt of disappointing hopeful parents.

In any event, few parents who successfully condition their children to see college as the only acceptable goal ever entertain the possibility that the thumb-sucking infant who inspires their aspirations may not be bright enough to go to college, might not want to go to college, might not get into the favored college of dear old Dad.

If parents had good educational reasons for wanting their progeny to go to college or knew clearly what they expected that college experience to provide, then one could say that someone had rational control over the college process. Unfortunately, people who have spent umpteen years dreaming about their offspring hanging around the tables at Mory's often lack a clear eye when college admission time arrives. Unless they have many children, most parents usually approach admissions with great naïveté about the process, knowing little about the reality of getting into a college, partly because college admissions have a quality of the surrealistic and partly because no one who went to college five years ago—much less twenty—has any inkling of the new demands placed on the student. Finally, even when parents *can* articulate why they want their children to go to college, most of their reasons have very little to do with education.

The primary parental priority appears to be that their child go to a good college. I hear a lot about "good colleges," much of it stated as if there were fifteen good colleges, hundreds of bad ones, and another two thousand that do not exist. Given that it is virtually impossible to evaluate the quality of the undergraduate experience anywhere, in this area of the country the major criteria for goodness seem to be that it be Big Ivy, Little Ivy, the Seven Sisters—other regions have their own prestige schools. Why the mystique hangs on tenaciously baffles me, particularly since at least some of the Ivy League schools provide such a thoroughly average undergraduate experience. As Daniel Moynihan put it: "In writing of 'quality' in higher education, it is fundamental to make clear that educational research has cast the most awful doubt on whether there is any such thing with respect to student achievement, especially, perhaps, undergraduate achievement. . . . What is transmitted differentially at, say, Harvard, is not learning but influence."[4] Nevertheless, the critical determinant of college choice in many families hinges on whether parent or child has heard of the institution. Numbers of times my colleagues and I have suggested a distinguished undergraduate institution, perhaps a small college dedicated to teaching, and have been rebuffed with a "but I never heard of that; what about the Ivies?"

In college selection, the name, the reputation, the "influence" of a particular school should be the last items to consider. More important is the institution's commitment to postadolescents as real, not surrogate, people. Better to investigate whether a student will be cared for as an individual; whether the institution will fit program to personality; whether the student will learn and will know his teachers in a way that inspires him to learn more. These, however, all too often figure as irrelevant questions when defining a good college. How frustrating it is to see a student with distinct personality needs or a clearly defined career preference applying to a college that cannot possibly serve him because his parents will not permit him to apply to the less prestigious university that could. Somewhat vexed, they assure me, when questioned, that they did not pay all that money for a private school so their child could go to a land-grant college.

Often it seems that college choice can be traced to a parental wish to bask in the reflected importance of having a child bright enough to go to a college that is superselective. I know one mother who threatened to move because of the shame that resulted when unrealistic hopes were not realized. Sometimes, even, it seems that pride in being able to afford, each year, a $7,000 education provides a motivating thrust.

Most often, the reason stated for wanting a child to go to a "good" college is that it leads invariably to a "good" job, the crown of goodness gracing every move all the days of your life.

Unfortunately, recent statistics and clever arguments by writers like Caroline Bird suggest that the edge college graduates once had in earnings has dulled considerably.[5] Professions, one by one—teaching, social work, law, medicine, and countless others—

have become overcrowded; the trained and hopeful cannot find jobs; the percentage of students who find jobs in their majors is ever more slender. Bird surprises us with the finding that the tuition, fees, and normal expenses of a Princeton education, invested at 7.5 percent interest, would produce a millionaire at age 65—a more conservative but higher-yield investment than putting the money into Princeton tuition.[6]

A recent study argues against the Bird viewpoint, "Measured by the likelihood of becoming unemployed, by earnings, or by the increases in earnings with age and experience, college graduates continue to make up an economically favored group." The author acknowledges a decline in income differentials between college and high school graduates from 1969 to 1974, ascribing it to a high proportion of young people in the population, with the supply of graduates outstripping the growth of new jobs. The study data refers exclusively to males but the researcher claims that income differentials between college and high school educated women have narrowed at only half the rate for men.[7]

So, college does, in unmitigable reality, furnish working papers, and any review of the *New York Times* listing of job opportunities indicates altogether too many starting positions for which a degree is required even if none is needed.

Trapped by their own version of the American myth of college and the practical reality of what to do with their child if he does not go to college, parents must bear the responsibility, if not the blame, for what happens to their children. Two active, intelligent parents complained to me about their bright but academically unmotivated son. The boy was not happy in school; prior conversations with him had suggested that he had no idea why he was going to college, and his anger could only express itself by his not doing the assigned work.

When I posed the question to all of them, "What about a year off; forget about college for next year?" the whole family answered simultaneously: the father an emphatic "No"; the mother a worried "He might never come back to education"; the son, "What could I do?" He went to college and dropped out, but it seemed to me that in that exchange lay the dilemma of many an American family. Parents who want to provide the best for their children understandably fear unknowns, and the children, protected for so long by people telling them what to do, lack the capacity for effective action. Easier to go the next step, sliding into college, knowing it is the wrong move, yet following it as the line of least resistance, for a while staving off the difficult contemplation of self.

If an entity called "college" could be readily defined by goals and understandings replicated by all colleges, however much their methods might differ, then there might still exist a chance for coherence in the admissions process. Unfortunately, however, the system defies definition or description. Roughly 3,000 colleges and universities exist in the United States and its possessions. Some can be entered if one has the tuition, some if one happens to live in the area; others screen candidates according to rigorous or not-so-rigorous standards that they alone understand. Some are two-year, most are four. Some are technical, some liberal arts, others both. Some offer a curriculum, except for the sciences, not much changed in the last fifty years, perhaps a hundred. Some have rigorous distribution and course requirements; others boast they have none. Some have a few hundred students; others tens of thousands.

It *is* possible to earn degree credits at various institutions in courses like:

Welding and Power Shop Equipment
Selection of Meat
Pleasure Horse Appreciation and Use
Intermediate Circus Arts
Puppetry
Elementary Typewriting
Tailoring
Great Adulteresses in the Novels

School Greenhouse Operation
The Career Criminal
Fishing Gear I

In American colleges anything has become possible reason to give a student a diploma; a Wellesley student I know leavens a demanding academic program with a course in Easter Egg Decoration. Then there is always the Evelyn Waugh character from *The Loved One* whose remarks some might take for satire, although more likely they could be fact:

> "Art in College as my second subject one semester. I'd have taken it as first subject only Dad lost his money in religion so I had to learn a trade."
>
> ". . . And what else did you take at College?"
>
> "Just Psychology and Chinese. I didn't get on so well with Chinese. But, of course, they were secondary subjects, too; for Cultural background."
>
> "Yes. And what was your main subject?"
>
> "Beauticraft. . . . I wrote my thesis on 'Hairstyling in the Orient.' That was why I took Chinese. I thought it would help, but it didn't. But I got my diploma with special mention for Psychology and Art."[8]

If college embodies all these diverse courses, approaches, majors, philosophies, and degrees of difficulty, what then is a college and what does it mean to go there? Clearly, there are thousands of possibilities, but if there is no unanimity of opinion among the colleges about what constitutes a college degree, then one can be certain that neither is there among the high school students, their parents, or the guidance counselors who are charged to place them in college.

How does one equate a program in the liberal arts with a specific degree program in something like physical therapy; how does one evaluate the graduate of a school that can be walked into on the strength of a high school diploma with one that selects from the top 3 percent of the nation? How does one weigh the quality of the education in a school where the median SAT score is 400 with one whose median is 700; big school against small school; college against university? Little wonder that students conditioned to think that finding the right college constitutes a major decision frequently experience panic.

The huge college smorgasbord provides reason enough for confusion, but add to that the fact that vast numbers of high school students have little or no idea what they want to do with their lives, frequently have few specifically intellectual interests, and often have such narrow experiences in the world that they do not even know what they do *not* want to do. And it is no wonder they panic, make wild choices seemingly at random, suffer epidemics of procrastination about filling out the applications, join lemming-like migrations to certain schools and areas (Boston being the current Mecca in the Northeast), without much regard for what they may find at the college. A good interview, a pretty campus, or other adiaphora bring on an unwarranted surge of enthusiasm.

Add to all the variables what is called the "new professionalism," a national response to cries for relevance in the shape of dramatically increased vocational programs, programs that require students to know what they want to do on the first day, because they have four carefully programmed years ahead of them. What is a senior, glassy-eyed with the little he comprehends of the options, with no sense of academic focus, to do? He can always, as one optimistic mother assured me, find himself by "taking a nice liberal arts program." Five years, two colleges, three majors later, and two semesters off, he still does not know what he wants to do—too many options—and the only thing he enjoys, making furniture, is not a profession his parents regard as a college man's.

I am not arguing that people should not go to college. Obviously an advanced, complex society needs advanced education; indeed, if American high schools continue to teach as little as they do, any motivated student may require higher education if only to read and write coherently. In 1974 half the Berkeley freshmen

59

failed the English competency exam, as did 42 percent of Rutgers freshmen. I am, however, trying to suggest that the process of going to college is mired in unconsidered assumptions which have profound implications for individual and national life. Nevertheless, if choosing a college seems confusing, the process of getting in somewhere (anywhere) is even more confusing and hazardous to sanity.

Although it is sad when students apply to colleges where they have little chance of admission, it is disheartening for me and devastating for the student when colleges with one hand turn down students who can do the work, and with the other accept students who cannot. Those powerful athletic teams, however, do not just happen, and most schools would be embarrassed to publish the aptitude scores of their football teams. The recruiting practices of some colleges are venal and well-publicized enough, but what is one to make of the distinguished and "pure" universities that also recruit athletes who are less academically able and steer them toward carefully selected courses in which they can succeed and which will not overly tax minds busy learning the playbook. A student at a *prima* institution swears to be in a motor mechanics course that meets at night in a garage, a large portion of the football team in attendance; his term paper on "My Carburetor" was received with pleasure. A former student of mine, with average intellectual powers, was admitted to an Ivy League school on the strength of a rather remarkable athletic talent and glided through his major without taking some of the courses basic to serious work in his field because they were too difficult and would conflict with his athletic schedule.

How does one explain to the eager youth who asks, "What are my chances of getting in?" the Eleusinian mystery that governs the selection process at the more competitive colleges? The admissions committee creates a class. Functioning on the supposition that the university needs many specialized people to make up its rich life—oboists, Slavonic choristers, computer wizards, lethal linebackers, barrel-jumping tricyclists, etc., etc., the committee finds the people to fit the slots. Thus, a brilliant student and middling violist may lose out to the middling student who is a brilliant violist; six creative-writing geniuses may fall so the math department will get the ace they need to keep functioning. Those universities with five or more applicants per space can afford apparently capricious decisions, but it is painfully hard to explain to a superior student that his less able classmate was admitted because he could fill the Serbo-Croatian quota.

How does one explain that the enrollment pictures and financial postures of some excellent colleges have changed so drastically in recent years that almost anyone can get in? Even more curious, how does one explain that demographics and student faddism have turned a number of rather second-rate institutions into altogether quite snobbish establishments who pick and choose with all the elitist care of a Princeton, so assured of the validity of the SAT's that they no longer bother to interview candidates? Or how does one explain the mystery of overacceptance, whereby a school gambles that some, perhaps 50 percent or more, of their acceptances will turn them down? Since some colleges have, from year to year, wildly fluctuating yields on their acceptances, the rate of acceptance fluctuates with equally unpredictable wildness.

In this maelstrom it is difficult to explain how little idea admissions committees, under complex pressures from all sides, have of what they are doing. They rarely know much about the schools from which their applicants come and have little way to compare their diverse academic experiences; they are under fierce pressure to admit alumni children, rich children, alumni children, minority children, alumni children, bright children, and in any event fill the school with a large enough percentage of paying customers to keep the school in business. More and more colleges express concern or are frankly desperate about this last item as population figures decline.

Admissions personnel have precious few gauges to measure

future academic success or failure. The admissions office frequently functions as an arm of the school's public relations efforts, not as an agent of its educators, and one senses that in many instances admissions officers neither understand nor are understood by the academics of their community. As William Ihlanfeldt notes in the *College Board Review*, college admissions pose a marketing problem:

> As an institution approaches its various markets, there are three basic concepts that should be part of its thinking: service, involvement, and openness. Higher education is a service industry; in fact, it is probably the largest service industry in the world. . . . It is primary to a successful marketing program to have as many faculty, alumni, and undergraduate students involved in the student recruitment effort as wish to be. Every time we say "hello" and shake a new hand, we are communicating what we do. . . . As long as a college is able to generate a large enough critical mass in the candidate file from the primary market early enough in the processing year, a college can feel reasonably comfortable that the enrollment objectives for the next year's freshman class can be realized.[9]

It all sounds rather like big business, like Madison Avenue and its environs, and why not: colleges and universities are budgeted for more than $30 billion a year.

Under the circumstances it is remarkable that anything rational ever occurs during the admissions procedure, and it is not surprising that most extraordinary injustices abound. With all this confusion of purpose, institutional and educational, an outsider certainly cannot predict who will actually get in.

One wonders whether parents sending children to good public and private schools, those applying subtle pressures or some not-so-subtle threats upon the high school counselor, realize what a mug's game it is. Having been assured countless times that a powerful trustee, alumni, athletic connection would grease admissions wheels, and seen it fail, I question whether anyone on the outside has absolute power to get a student into college. A counselor might keep a student out of college if his own self-interest were not so much at stake, but like many other teachers I have little confidence that anything affirmative I say on behalf of the school or as a teacher has significant bearing on the admissions process. I have heard too many admissions people in their cups speak with contempt of teacher comments.

This year, for a class of one hundred seniors, I estimate that by January first I wrote forty-three essays on behalf of the school and eighty-six personal teacher recommendations. It depresses me to think that those efforts may not count for much, and even more to wrestle with the question of what constitutes honest disclosure. The colleges encourage "candid" statements, yet I have acquired sufficient distrust of admissions committees to wonder what they would do with a fully candid statement. Shall I admit, in some year in the future, that we have reason to doubt the academic integrity of our star athlete, or that our top student has a repellent personality? Honesty makes little sense if no one else in the process is honest, if candor simply provides an easy reason for rejection. A tacky business, often, but the admissions process threatens to become even less honest under the pressures of the Buckley Amendment. How much candor can result from a recommendation the candidate can see, contest, and against which he can bring suit if he so pleases?

The real victims of the apparent assumptions that getting into college has a rational basis are, naturally, the students. Growing up with the unexamined conviction that they must go to college, they usually follow academic tracks which will qualify them for nothing but college. Worse, however, for some is the early and unrelenting pressure parents put on their children to perform, "so that they can go to a good college." I have had tearful seventh

63

graders assure me that a poor test grade would prevent them from going to college, and if that were not ridiculous enough, I have had parents of seventh-grade students ask whether a mediocre set of grades was projectible in terms of the types of colleges their child could apply to.

Obviously not everyone is hysterical so early; typically, students go their ways assuming that they will go to college—a good one, naturally. Unless their grades are catastrophic, most of them tend to see themselves as being on a par with most of their classmates. Although they can identify brighter and less bright peers, I think most students feel rather above average. When we rank our college preparatory class by grade point, those at the bottom are almost always surprised to find themselves there—it had felt as though they were doing better.

Grades are important to colleges; most of them assure us they cannot conduct a fair evaluation without them, and thus they form the central focus of student anxiety. The cruel little games of "wadja-get," the course loads rigged to improve class rank, the grade bargaining, the ugly confrontation in senior or even junior year when a teacher has the courage to call failing work by its name— all erode the purpose of education. "Why did I spend all this money," said one parent, "if he couldn't get into Yale?" That the child might have gotten an above-average education was not regarded as sufficient reason.

No matter how damaging grades can be in terms of the pressure they put on students (one wonders how adults would like "objective" evaluations every day on their job, quarterly report cards on their performance as mother, husband, party-giver), students learn ways of cushioning their egos. The real crunch comes when the Preliminary Scholastic Aptitude Tests (PSAT's) are taken. The day we hand out the explanatory booklets with their individual, pre-gummed Princeton stickers, their neat computer statement of Verbal and Math scores sends the eleventh grade into a state of shocked and quite unnatural silence. For once, the "wadja-gets?" are muted as they contemplate the digits they have been led to believe contain the shape of their future.

Having been conditioned to believe that if they do not get into a good college they will ruin their parents' lives, mark themselves as failures, and have a horrible life, no wonder adolescents (1.5 million took the test last year) quail before their SAT scores on whose stark numbers they have always assumed all happiness to depend.

The most damaging effect of the SAT's stems from the belief that they really mean something about a person, that the 20 to 80 scale constitutes a definitive statement about intelligence and worth. Not so long ago I tried to comfort a girl clutching her College Board explanatory folder. "I'm not that stupid, am I?" she asked, pointing tearfully at the 38–42 on the cover. In fact she had always performed near the top of her class, far better than such scores might indicate possible, yet while reassuring her that she was much brighter and we all valued her, I could not help thinking that it would be very hard indeed to convince most colleges that she was, in fact, brighter than the scores would indicate.

As nearly as I can judge, most colleges, despite disclaimers that they look at the whole record, all too often regard the scores as more significant data, more authoritative than such scores really are. Even granting the College Board's validity studies (although I am still skeptical about validity studies conducted under the auspices of a virtual monopoly), there are still variables which do not make the test a true prediction of a student's success in college.

For one thing, the tests do not measure motivation, desire to learn, creativity, imagination, or intellectual curiosity. They militate against slow, thorough readers, children whose parents are not native-born, and in some instances against those who are truly thoughtful. On any number of occasions, students of unique intellectual powers have scored poorly because they read more subtlety into the questions than was there.

My impressions of the SAT's are reinforced by the findings of

Michael Wallach, a Duke psychologist whose findings were summarized by *Saturday Review/World,* from a speech he made to
the Graduate Record Examination Board (GREB):

> Three major conclusions emerged from the survey: First,
> that SAT scores offer virtually no clue to capacity for
> significant intellectual or aesthetic contribution in mature
> life; second, that the best predictor of creativity in
> mature life is a person's performance record during youth
> in independent, self-sustained ventures; third, that admis-
> sions deans, for all their claims "to be moving away from
> total dependence" on the SAT's and toward concern for
> "whole persons" and early achievements, in fact appear
> to be increasingly reliant on the tests.[10]

Whatever the imperfections of the test, I have yet to meet a
college admissions officer who did not know the mean SAT score
of the entering freshman class, and few did not regard the mean as
a reflection on them and their college. A number of them refused
to consider seriously students who fell below the cutoff point set
within the university.

It is infuriating when some colleges dupe students into believing that SAT's are not important, and yet year after year post a
freshman profile that looks the same. More infuriating and
demoralizing for students and counselors are the schools that process applications by computer or a committee triage system, students with less than the right cumulative SAT score fall into the
instant reject category. It depresses me to tell that student who has
high motivation, fine skills, a splendid academic and extracurricular
record that he cannot go to the college to which he aspires, not
because he cannot do the work but because his SAT's do not add
up to a large enough total. As one student put it, "Tell me why I
worked so hard, when the only schools I can get into I could have
gotten in without working?"

Even within quite homogeneous groups, substantial differences in SAT scores can exist between one student and the next,

and even relatively small differences, exceptionally small considering the College Board itself says that an individual can vary as much as 6 points (60 on the 200–800 scale) from one testing session to the next, are understood as demarking the applicant to the prestigious college from the one who had best try for something less ambitious. Surely, it is not healthy to be forced into confrontation with the quantitative terms widely regarded as the definitive statement about one's capabilities. Few adults could accept a world in which their potential for success was so measured, and forever codified (SAT scores factor in some law and medical school admissions), yet we allow our children to undergo a system that spits them out as a 61–54, 50–47, 55–77, or whatever.

The collective worship of the SAT's, of course, has some economic implications. In an effort to gain practice, or in the hope they may get lucky, quite a number of students take the tests over and over. At $7.25 and $12.50 a throw (in the 1977 to 1978 academic year) it is an expensive proposition that makes that elegant establishment in Princeton, with its $55.9 million revenue derived from testing activities,* slick publications, and high salaries, even more princely. The spin-off cram-school industry has also emerged as a lucrative business, and although the advertised promise of increased SAT scores bubbles with optimism, the results do not generally seem that remarkable. They probably help students with less than the right cumulative SAT score falling into the multiple-choice tests; but they probably do little in a crash program of vocabulary memorization. They are for the most part a temporary tranquilizer, offering a sense that something decisive is being done—only when the money is paid, the course over, and the magic numbers return little changed, does the student realize that once again in the great college free-for-all he has been suckered.

The charade works both ways. Sometimes, usually in the

---

* For fiscal year 1976, total testing activities of ETS yielded $55.9 million out of the total revenues of $63 million. In fiscal year 1972 total testing activities earned $41.7 million out of total revenues of $47.9 million. Thus over five years there has been a 34 percent increase in testing revenues representing close to 90 percent of the ETS total income.[11]

junior year, students undergo a curious transformation. People who never had an academic interest suddenly acquire one; those without a generous impulse all at once can be found tutoring an inner-city child; chronic miscreants suddenly become publicly respectable. To some of my colleagues it appears to be maturation, and some of it undoubtedly is, but a large part results from the realization that an image must be constructed. There is a student joke about the need to gather credits in the yearbook, credits for college applications, and so clubs are joined, mythical clubs invented (I knew one bibulous student who claimed to be president of the Canadian Club) and facsimiles of identity are painstakingly constructed. Students know intuitively what Michael Wallach has validated through research:

> The key feature of the admissions picture . . . is the consistent preference for students who might almost be said to lack a personal style; figures marvelously adaptable but often deeply uninteresting.[12]

And one wonders what it means to adolescent development, if not the development of a national identity, when there are tangible rewards for being good and colorless.

Any activity such as the college-admissions process, which involves so many millions of people and billions of dollars, cannot be taken for granted. Any activity which so consumes the attention of our young and to which so much of their late adolescence is directed, or which causes so much fear and anguish, cannot just happen, willy-nilly, without some reflection about what we, as a nation, want to happen.

Certainly in this world of complexity, distinct advantages may befall a nation whose populace is made up of large numbers of thoughtful, literate, broadly experienced people. To read, write, and think with some degree of precision often proves a necessity in a complex world, and yet too few high school graduates possess these skills. Perhaps we would be better to follow the Finnish model and upgrade elementary and secondary education, paying teachers at lower levels the best salaries to attract the best people to the time when the best education is really needed. Perhaps we might try to discourage the notion that high school is simply a way station on the track to the big apple. Adolescence *is* a critical developmental reality, and yet the current ambiance of schools suggests that the needs of adolescence be denied for the college reality which will be more intense, more important.

I have always been intrigued by John Gardner's argument in *Excellence* that we might prosper as a nation if we encouraged people to do something well, rather than cleave to the narrow definition of success implied by the college myth.[18] Watching my students tinkering expertly with a beloved car or performing brilliant repairs on hi-fi equipment, I can only wonder if they would not be better off directing their energies to being superb auto mechanics or competent TV repairmen who found satisfaction in their work, rather than going off to college and getting a degree in some overcrowded profession like social work or teaching. Perhaps the nation would profit if more skilled and ambitious mechanics enjoyed their work rather than promulgating a white-collar work force sighing through jobs that have parental or social-class approval. As many young people have discovered in recent years, not enough "college-type" jobs exist for college graduates; perhaps we would be better off not feeling that people who get dirty doing their work are less interesting or capable than those who do not. Does the growth of the hobby trade suggest that many people are not really happy in jobs with a high abstraction level where effort produces no noticeable effect beyond an interoffice memo?

If our society has removed so many responsibilities from the young that it takes longer to grow to adulthood, and, therefore, the four college years fulfill a maturation and socialization function, an opportunity to be independent of parents and to meet different people, then other, less costly alternatives perhaps could serve as well. A mandatory tour with a VISTA-like organization working on rural or urban problems might not only be good for the countless ills of this country but might also be a lot better education than sending a kid off to college to get his or her head together. At some point it might prove an exhilarating experience to test theory against practical application. It might not hurt some of our children who hurtle toward college immersed in a world of abstractions to rub elbows with the social calamities of this world. If in time they decide to be teachers, social workers, politicians, or businessmen, they might be wiser for the experience.

Nothing I have ever seen suggests that adolescents abhor work. Most of them would rather be busy and useful than not. But like most of us, they would prefer and would be more industrious in situations where they felt there was some tangible reward. So many professions such as journalism, stock brokerage, insurance, and management could be so quickly learned if they were taken out of the colleges, removed from the anachronistic stimulus to unreality and conducted as high-powered apprenticeships.

Although the job market could probably not stand an influx of young people into the work force, most young people would enjoy learning more, if it had some practical connection to something they thought they wanted to know. The charge that college work is irrelevant, made during the student rebellions in 1970, is not radical folly. A liberal education is often an irrelevant experience at a time of life when many people would rather be learning a skill whereby they could actually earn a living and become adults, rather than being stuck in the adult-child limbo of undergraduate life. I would prefer to see more legitimate institutions in which one could learn a useful set of skills and which might siphon off many students who currently aim for college.

I would also prefer to see some greater interest on the part of our educational institutions in the minds of adults who, having learned the skills needed to perform a job, find they have other diverse curiosities, both vocational and cultural, that require satisfaction. If there were more national interest in the continuing cultivation of the adult mind, if advanced education were easier to acquire without worrying about degree requirements, SAT's, et al., then perhaps we would have a populace that would be more

70

broadly educated, rather than less. For my part, I have always found study more exciting when it was clear how I could use the information I was acquiring. Figures as diverse as Gerald Ford and Steven Muller, President of Johns Hopkins, have also commented on the need for more useful adult education. Ford said at Ohio State in August, 1974:

> Why can't the universities of America open their doors to working men and women, not only as students but also as teachers? . . . What good is training if it is not applied to jobs?

Muller argues that:

> Probably our greatest error has been the blind perpetuation of the traditional continuum directly from secondary to postsecondary education. We should now make it possible for most of our young people to enter the labor force at high school graduation, and then go on with postsecondary education whenever they need to do so for a well-defined purpose, not only once but perhaps several times. Lifelong continuing learning in our society is a practical need, not merely an idealist's vision.[14]

What of a liberal education? I have already said that I thought it an "irrelevant" experience, providing that one assumes, as so many Americans do, that the value of education is only to be measured in quantitative terms, that the goal of higher education is to prepare the student for a good profession, and a significant yield on tuition investment. Preprofessional education strikes many as useful, even though many professionals, in journalism and teaching, for instance, would testify that the only education worth having is to be found on the job. I once supervised a teacher whose academic schedule had been so jammed with mandatory teacher certification credits in such courses as history of education and philosophy of education that he had insufficient subject background to teach high school English.

I continue to believe, despite the fact that the tide of student opinion has turned against them, that the liberal arts furnish an important experience. It would be well in this country if we recalled that once upon a time all higher education was liberal, and that its function was to cultivate the mind along essentially humanistic lines. One can turn to Cicero or to Newman and find the careful distinctions made between useful knowledge and that which enriches and graces public or private life by its elegance and humanity.

Although most colleges periodically sound calls for the liberally educated person, there is little to suggest that colleges are really designed to cultivate him. As stated by Gary A. Knight and Peter Schotten in the *College Board Review:*

> Given the heightened pressure to attract 18–22 year-olds, colleges must mold their academic programs to meet these students' varying needs, which often means catering to their most superficial and immediate likes and dislikes.
>
> In order to construct a program of studies relevant to this increasingly diverse group of students, universities have subtly redefined the very idea of what constitutes the purpose of the university. . . .[15]

Thus colleges, to a great extent, have become credentialing institutions, and in all the dialogues I have had with parents and students over the years, the notion that education might ennoble, enrich, and make more beautiful the mind has rarely occurred.

Studies in the curriculum of the liberal arts, of course, do not qualify one for anything, but they do provide the kind of training and breadth of view which are useful in many professions, and may still be the best training for positions of responsibility in management or government. Thus, parents and students should understand that a course of study in the liberal arts is an investment in *education*, not necessarily in future earning power.

Even as I write the above encomium I feel a little silly, for why should I speak of the cultivation of the mind, of humane impulses, of the best ideas the world has had, when we are in an intellectual climate that has made college admission a dehumanizing experience, that promotes college football as the most tangible of college images, that sends to college large percentages of people who are not much interested in things of the mind.

Fifty years ago, less than 10 percent of the nation had ever attended college. Those who went were either very wealthy, very bright, or very determined—or some combination of those qualities. And more likely than not they succeeded in the world of fifty years ago, not because they had gone to college but because they had one or more of those qualities. However, in the intervening decades, many Americans have made the assumption that going to college magically confers success and status. Unless one is planning to join one of the brokerage firms that hire only Ivy League athletes, there is probably not much truth in the assumption. If, in the old days, college graduates got better jobs, it was probably not the result of their college education. That they were older, perhaps motivated to seek better jobs, perhaps connected with friends and relatives in prestigious positions, probably had more to do with their ultimate success in life. Yet, now, we send to college countless young people who are neither rich, particularly bright, nor overly determined to partake of the educational opportunity we believe guarantees so much.

At any rate, 1984 is approaching and we have created a monster, which because it is of our own devising will not in all likelihood destroy us, and that is an argument for not tampering with it. On the other hand, it is a monster which makes many unhappy, destroys egos along the way, sometimes ruins the relationship between parents and child, gobbles up personal funds, and distorts the relationships between work and the products of the mind.

What could be done to make it a better system? Perhaps colleges could reform themselves. I notice that as enrollments drop, colleges become more concerned with individuals. When the population crest passes, perhaps even the most popular colleges will

73

consider people and not statistics. The real key lies, however, in the home, in the messages that parents send children. College may be a good postsecondary option, but children should be told there are other options equally attractive; it is not just: "Go to college or get a job pumping gas." Parents could also look more carefully at their children to determine whether they are people who really want more formal education. And finally, everyone might give more thought to the value of education, at all ages, not as a stepping stone to something else, but merely as a power that is good to have, for its own sake.

REFERENCES

1. Lewis B. Mayhew, *The Carnegie Commission on Higher Education: A Critical Analysis of the Reports and Recommendations* (San Francisco: Jossey-Bass, Inc., 1975), p. 42. Another commission report, p. 58, proposes that one million college students may be dissatisfied with their experience.

2. Caroline Bird, "College Is a Waste of Time and Money," *Psychology Today*, Vol. 8, No. 12, May, 1975, p. 31.

3. In *A Digest of Reports of the Carnegie Commission on Higher Education*, ed. Michael Hennelly, Hanine Parson, Nancy Tressel (New York: McGraw-Hill Co., 1974), 3 percent described themselves as being "very dissatisfied," 9 percent as "dissatisfied," 22 percent as "on the fence" —in short, 34 percent unenthusiastic about their college.

4. Daniel P. Moynihan, "The Politics of Higher Education," *American Higher Education: Toward an Uncertain Future II*, S. R. Graubard, ed., *Daedalus, Journal of the American Academy of Arts and Sciences*, Winter, 1975, p. 137.

5. Caroline Bird, *The Case Against College* (New York: David McKay Co., 1975), pp. 62–70.

6. *Ibid.*

7. Leonard Lecht, "Grading the College Diploma," *Across the Board*, Vol. XIV, No. 4, April, 1977, p. 25.

74

8. Evelyn Waugh, *The Loved One* (Boston: Little, Brown, and Co., 1948), pp. 90–91.

9. William Ihlanfeldt, "A Management Approach to the Buyer's Market," *College Board Review*, No. 96, Summer, 1975, pp. 22–24.

10. Benjamin DeMott, "Beyond the SAT's, A Whole Person Catalogue That Works?" *Saturday Review/World*, May 4, 1974, p. 68.

11. *1976 Annual Report*, Educational Testing Service, Princeton, N.J., p. 16.

12. DeMott, *op. cit.*

13. John Gardner, *Excellence* (New York: Harper Press, 1961), pp. 128–134.

14. Steven Muller, "Colleges in Trouble: Expand Them, Don't Fold Them," *Psychology Today*, Vol. 8, No. 12, May, 1975, p. 81.

15. Gary A. Knight and Peter Schotten, "Reader Forum: Illiberal Education," *College Board Review*, No. 97, Fall, 1975, p. 8.

DAVID TILLEY

Opening Admissions and the Postselective Era: A View from the Public Sector

From the public sector, David Tilley views opening admissions as a step along the road to universal higher education which, he feels, will mark the decline of high selectivity in all but a few private colleges. For disadvantaged students, the traditional selection procedures have been inadequate and have compelled a reassessment of the validity of testing and the establishment of support programs to remedy earlier educational losses.

All who want to go to college in the public sector can gain admission somewhere in the system, especially with the growth of open access, geographic convenience, and the availability of financial aid. Nonetheless, student competition, poignant and ruthless, endures for higher levels of status and confirmation. Tilley explores the dynamics of college choice for students, demonstrating that their selection is not free, simple, or rational.

Opening Admissions

One of my favorite college admissions anecdotes involves an interview between an admissions director and a nervous applicant

76

shortly after the end of World War II. The student, worried about his qualifications and the competition of returning veterans, asks how he might get into the college. The director, with the college's priorities clearly in mind, promptly replies that there are at least three ways that the student can get to this school—by train, by bus, or by car. In those days such a college would be said to have a low threshold admission policy. Today it would be called open enrollment or free access.

In the mid-forties, when this encounter took place, some institutions acted in the belief that selection was a flawed art and that opportunity should be provided those with the motivation to try. More realistically, the adoption of a low threshold policy for most educational settings was inspired by economic needs. The ability to pay, with GI Bill benefits for example, often was *the* important admissions consideration. It is no surprise, therefore, that researchers more than thirty years later still find the ability to pay to be the strongest predictor of who will go to college. Today, free-access programs commanding government financial support assure college attendance for population groups which would not necessarily have been able to use the GI Bill a generation ago.

Concepts of equal opportunity, compensatory education, and affirmative action that grew out of the civil rights movement of the fifties and sixties are not now widely embodied in current free-access/open-enrollment programs. But in the early equal opportunity days colleges were not always very clear about which issue they were addressing. Equal opportunity guidelines tended to define target populations by economics—family income at or below "poverty" level, legal residence in a designated "impacted" area—and by academic performance. But if students met normal academic admissions standards, they were explicitly disqualified for economic assistance—an educational Catch-22. The emphasis was on expanding access and did not address disadvantaged students and their families who were making it through their own effort and sacrifice. The definitions carefully avoided racial criteria, although for many equal opportunity meant affirmative, compensatory ac-

77

cess to higher education for those racial minorities traditionally ignored in college recruitment selection programs.

Open-enrollment or free-access admissions will prove to be a major development in higher education. Already it has inspired a bitter battle over the educational and social objectives of colleges. Resistance has been most resolute from the academic center, and support most substantial from those faculty, administrators, students, and trustees who see higher education as a vehicle for social change. Among supporters are many pragmatists who have little interest in the issue itself, but who recognize that their special interests can be served by broadening higher education's enrollment base, by increasing education's political constituency, and by the inevitable public monies that will be appropriated to support politically popular objectives. Implementation of open-admissions programs in this atmosphere of conflicting beliefs and expectations, combined with the wary skepticism of those whom the programs seek to help, has resulted in profound changes in the technology of selection and in the administration of access to college. The success of these programs promises to evolve into the realization of universal higher education and very likely will mark the end of educational policies based upon high selectivity in all but a few, primarily private, institutions.

Many state university systems will point out that the law in their state requires that they enroll all high school graduates who complete a specified college preparatory program. In this sense open enrollment is not new. There are, however, subtle differences that move current programs well beyond earlier versions. The mandatory enrollment laws characteristic of many university systems in the Middle and Far West were designed primarily to facilitate the movement of traditional college-going students directly from high school to college. Operationally, students were still sorted by traditional techniques and standards (high school performance and entrance tests) and allocated accordingly. Those with marginal credentials were typically placed in a probationary status and often were required to qualify for regular registration status by proving themselves academically during the preceding summer session or in some other off-time period. In effect, admissions selection was accomplished on the basis of performance during these special sessions or during a first probationary semester. The high attrition rates of the marginal students gave this practice its "revolving-door" label.

There is a simple-minded justice and logic to the "shape-up or ship-out" quality of "revolving-door" open enrollment. Advocates of contemporary open-enrollment planning, however, feared that the "revolving door" offered only token access. Those typically excluded from higher education, and by virtue of race or poverty often denied an adequate preparatory education, would continue to find higher education unresponsive to their needs. In the search for alternatives to the "revolving door," many approaches have been attempted, and many lessons have been learned over the past decade of trial and error.

Fits and Misfits—Students and Institutions

The most selective institutions, those whose early leadership offered opportunity to disadvantaged students and gave legitimacy and impetus to the movement to expand access to those previously excluded, have come to realize that they are not satisfactory educational settings for many disadvantaged students.

> To succeed at Swarthmore, students must not only be endowed with innate intellectual abilities, they must also be educationally qualified. Students who are very bright but poorly educated are difficult to assimilate into a high pressure system like Swarthmore's. We regretfully conclude that for many such students Swarthmore is the wrong college, and that this important social function can be better performed at institutions with greater resources and facilities, though we hope that the admissions office

> will continue to seek the sort of disadvantaged students
> who do seem capable of succeeding at Swarthmore.[1]

Educational opportunity for disadvantaged students—with obvious individual exceptions—is best provided by schools with academically diverse goals and programs, with well developed remedial programs, and other student-support services.

The Swarthmore experience illustrates the importance of the student-institution fit. In the most selective undergraduate colleges, students equal in capacity but deficient in performance readiness find that they cannot participate as full members of that community. When differences are compounded by economic and/or racial factors, the colleges' good intentions offer insufficient support to repair the mismatch.

Dysfunctional mismatches are not limited to academic performance. Many urban streetwise students find the rural campus a frightening, disorienting experience, especially if the culture of the campus and the surrounding area are alien to the student. Far from feeling their lives opened by this environment, students often feel like freaks on display, fear being manipulated for the benefit of the educational establishment, are socially and culturally suppressed, and cannot be open and trusting.

Not long ago I talked with a friend who had gone from the inner-city to attend a small rural Midwestern college as a participant in an equal-opportunity program. He and his companions felt severe social limitations. As a result, some in the group were challenged to see how much they could shoplift from local shopkeepers they regarded as rednecks. The purpose was not profit but the development of self-esteem and status by creating an alienated, anti-hero ethic among peers. The activity both stimulated and frightened them. Fear of the consequences even led some members of the group to return, undetected, the boosted trophies.

On another campus, noted for its academic standards and social conscience, concern mounted over the breakdown of its self-imposed community behavioral code. Student interviews revealed that those who had been recruited as disadvantaged felt that the community code reflected the values of a white, upper middle class culture. These students could not identify with the code, nor could they conform to its expectations. They regarded themselves as different from the regularly admitted students since the alternative to college for them was poverty and failure with little prospect for a second chance. Consequently, they saw survival as their primary value and group solidarity as important to preserving their cultural identity. A white, upper middle class code that called on peers to place responsibility to the code above friendship and group solidarity simply did not serve these disadvantaged students. They said it meant self-destruction and that was just more dues than they felt sensible to pay for equal opportunity.

Campus Planning for New Learners

Every campus has similar anecdotes to tell. Pressure to provide opportunity for new learners caused many campuses to initiate programs before fully understanding their implications. Admissions officers not infrequently found themselves expected to implement enrollment policies adopted by governing boards, policies which were deficient in fiscal and operational planning. Usually in these situations admissions officers were expected to identify and enroll college-ready students whose earlier circumstances had caused them not to plan for college study. Many colleges thought that the disadvantaged students suitable for recruitment were replicas of traditional middle class students, only economically and/or racially different, and for whom little or no adjustments were required. In retrospect, one could claim that unconsciously, these colleges were seeking students who would be the same as their traditional applicants.

This belief was reinforced by some of the precollege talent search and development programs. The assumption of these programs was that the impediments to student educational development included a lack of information about opportunity, a limited world and cultural view, and general inexperience. This conception was not wrong, and certainly perceptions of the real world have expanded for populations typically excluded from higher education—but a new educational system, the community college, was required to cope with the complex problems involved. The universities and four-year colleges that dutifully pledged access opportunities to good-hearted enterprises such as College Bound, Inc., needed only to experience one College Conference Day before realizing the massiveness of the undertaking, and their inadequacy for the task.

The memory of the first such event I attended is seared into my consciousness. The location was a Manhattan public high school and the time a Saturday morning. Even before I entered the school, the full dimensions of the day began to manifest themselves. Bus load after bus load of students were being unloaded at the school gate. Most of the young people were dressed in their best clothes. I could sense the intense eager expectations of the group—this was to be an important day in their lives.

The program was broken up into a series of time slots. Students scheduled their day to visit a different college representative during each interval. When I entered the room assigned to me for the first session, I found at least one hundred students waiting for what they promptly informed me were to be interviews for college. Most expected personal time and a definitive assessment of their qualifications. There could have been no more mutually frustrating arrangement, nor a more cruel demonstration of the odds facing these students. As I imagined the college's glowing press releases testifying to its vigorous support of equality and social justice, and the equally self-serving reports to funding sources, my anger grew. Toward the end of the day, and hundreds of students later, I asked several how they felt about the event. To my surprise, they responded positively. Most felt that it was important for the college representatives to come and to experience an intense group of motivated but poor students. They believed the College Conference Day would help to improve their education since their secondary schools no longer could ignore and abandon them in dead-end programs. The event also helped to sustain the specific secondary-school support programs, which contain both academic and social work dimensions. Despite the dehumanizing scale of the day's "conferences," there was status in participation. Students felt that they had exerted some political power and in some way contributed to their futures, to their communities, and to the struggle for equal opportunity.

Political and Cultural Impact of the Working Class Student on the Campus

Colleges have learned that equal opportunity—open-access enrollment—not only requires an accommodation of new academic goals, but also of new cultural and political interests. One faculty member of a committee planning the initiation of an equal-opportunity program confided that his support was based on the hope that bringing a critical mass of working class youth to the campus would provide an easily radicalized militant faction to shake up the administration and bring about what the faculty member believed to be needed educational and campus-life reforms.

Admissions personnel frequently found that it was necessary to deal with the political agendas of faculty, students, community groups, legislators, trustees, and administrators. Some campuses were known as "good or bad" for specific ethnic groups as a consequence of the movement of admissions control for the disadvantaged away from the established admissions mechanism on campus. The admissions system for disadvantaged students was removed from the mainstream process, often to a freestanding office, where, for practical purposes, it was accountable only to a coalition of campus (faculty and student) and community minority leaders.

83

Testing for Diagnosis and Student Placement

The usual strategies used to assess eligibility or academic promise symbolized the inadequacy of traditional selection procedures for the admission of disadvantaged students. The most direct outcome of the observations of admissions programs for the disadvantaged has been the reassessment of the use of testing. Entrance tests long have been regarded as an unfair measure of academic ability of disadvantaged students, of those with a nonwhite, non-middle-class cultural orientation. With the stimulus of consumer-constituent sentiment, testing and other traditional measures of academic ability are now used in these programs primarily as diagnostic tools, and for the placement of students in appropriate academic or support programs. The most important admissions criteria have been found to be motivational willingness to work at studies, and having a goal in mind.

Contemporary observers of open-enrollment/free-access programs stress that access opportunity shifts the emphasis on standards from student selection to the ability of the learning environment to support students with disparate backgrounds and to enable this group to eventually perform on a par with the general student population. Thus, the congruence of the advantaged and disadvantaged student groups does not occur at the entry point of undergraduate education, but at its exit. Selective institutions still screen for intellectually developed students whose already substantial skills will be polished further in a community of scholars but institutions serving disadvantaged learners play a larger remedial, transitional role in helping students to recognize and develop their talents. While many free-access students will not aspire to the same academic goals as students in selective institutions, the relative gains of these new learners very likely represent a greater increment in their academic levels (even if programs are not completed) than in those of selectively admitted traditional college students. Understanding the importance to disadvantaged students of

84

the initial enrollment encouraged admissions programs to make the process as attractive as possible. Special consideration is given to individualized assessments which diagnose and attempt to resolve personal and family complexities (e.g., loss of income to family unit, child care). This process enables admissions personnel to understand and to accept the consequences of a high risk enrollment policy. Colleges have learned that even students who are academic failures very often profit in personal development and occupational opportunities. As one student put it, "I'm better off saying that I went to college and flunked out than some of my friends who didn't go to college or finish high school, but did go to jail."

Minority Students versus Women, the Aged and the Lifetime Learner

The striking effect of these more than minor changes in admissions is that while access has been expanded broadly, the chief beneficiaries appear to be less the ethnic minorities than other groups. After an initial surge, minority enrollments in higher education have leveled off and, in the fall of 1976, declined somewhat, even though the minority college-age population is increasing and the white college-age group has plateaued. Similarly, the proportion of students in the lower family income categories has not increased significantly. The primary beneficiaries of open-enrollment programs, therefore, appear to be women, older students, and lifetime learners—those seeking intermittent part-time career and personal development programs. For the most part, they are very similar to the white middle class students who make up the traditional college population. They have established constituency power which has secured for them relatively nonjudgmental access policies, and have created educational programs with personal and goal-oriented performance standards. Again, in many of these programs the admissions process has been decentralized and converted into an advisement and registration process.

85

The simplification of enrollment access makes considerable sense in implementing policies which encourage universal higher education. The gatekeeper function with its mystique of exclusivity evokes an era when higher education served technological and meritocratic ends rather than broad human-development objectives.

Performance and Goals of the Nontraditional Student

Institutions that have opened their doors to nontraditional students now have had enough experience to show that most are capable of satisfactory performance given the appropriate academic and personal support. These institutions have found that the majority of new learners come to college to improve the quality of their lives and to demonstrate that the label of academic inadequacy given them in previous schooling was, as they suspected, an inaccurate assessment. They seek an identity that they feel has been denied them; they seek to correct an injustice.

For the most part, the goals of the nontraditional student are not academic but vocational (practical) and personal. Many are unhappy about their interpersonal relations, level of maturity, and ability to cope. In college they hope to find the skills to help them secure a stable economic life and personal growth that will lead them to a satisfying family life.

Traditional admissions programs cannot serve such needs. Change is inevitable and will be made more swift as a shrinking traditional applicant pool creates practical pressures on colleges to broaden the search for students.

The implications for change will go beyond the techniques of enrolling students. Admissions practices reflect institutional goals, standards, and style. As admissions becomes an information assessment and guidance function—consumer oriented and socially determined—of necessity, institutions will find that faculty roles will change and student performance assessment will begin to evolve along individualized patterns. Thus, the goals of higher education will expand to embrace human growth needs, to meet the objectives of our changing society, and to fulfill the visions of the American Dream.

The American Dream and Historic Changes in Access Policies

The American Dream has always been at the heart of higher education in this country; most particularly the development of public higher education. Public higher education in its earliest forms provided the technological and professional skills needed by a developing agricultural and industrial nation and, through policies of open access or low threshold admissions practices, offered the access to opportunity sought by an upwardly striving people. Public higher education also reinforced the twin national objectives of a free people: the democratization of knowledge and the improvement of the quality of life.

In the movement of students from high school to college, our society long has instituted passport controls. The required documents reflect subtleties of the dominant values of the period. In the colonial era religious concerns, mirrored in the curricula, emphasized classical orthodoxy and gave college-entrance selection a pastoral character. Students were expected to "supply the churches in this colony with a learned, pious, and orthodox ministry.[2]

As orthodox classicism gave way to the academic developments of the Enlightenment in the eighteenth century, notably in the sciences, the shape of both society and higher education changed. A more rationalized and scientific approach to religious, social, political, and economic issues promoted a secular view of the world and a general sense of progress and perfectability. Secularization of academics led to intellectual professionalization and new, more strenuous, academic criteria for student selection, governed

87

by the faculty through its creation of the enigmatic "committee." The secularization process also enhanced the development of public higher education through the democratization of access to knowledge.

In recent years academic professionals have lost much of their control over student access to college. Legislators, through fiscal allocations (including massive debt service for campus facilities that administrators now are expected to keep fully occupied) and human-rights statutes, have given impetus to a movement for universal and lifetime higher education by providing extended learning opportunities, open admissions, and free access. Student selection, once determined by the interests and values of the dominant religious or academic guild, with the understanding that some students, if not most, would be *excluded* from higher education, has been transformed by the introduction of policies of broad inclusion and the allocation of students seeking postsecondary education to programs suitable to their level of readiness. As the public mission of higher education has increased its influence, admissions decisions have moved from the aegis of the faculty (guild) into the hands of administrators accountable for fiscal prudence and the achievement of political goals, and of the students upon whose preferences and initiative enrollment patterns actually depend.

More recently, the courts have been called upon to adjudicate conflicts between legislative intent and institutional policy and capacity: The Allan Bakke and Marco DeFunis, Jr., cases describe the principal conflict born of special-admissions programs and affirmative action—compensatory fairness versus equal treatment.*

* In the fall of 1977, the Supreme Court heard a suit brought by Allan Bakke against the Regents of the University of California. Bakke, who is white, charged that he was rejected twice for admission to the Medical School of the University of California at Davis, while minority applicants with lower qualifications than his were accepted under special programs.

In another case, the University of Washington was sued by a white law school applicant, Marco DeFunis, Jr., who claimed that the affirmative action admissions program made him a victim of "reverse discrimination." The Supreme Court, in 1974, declared the case moot—no decision on the merits of the case was taken—because DeFunis had eventually been accepted to the University of Washington Law School.

The issues go beyond traditional questions of the admissions process, such as the usefulness of grades and test scores in predicting college performance. Universal access to knowledge is the new mandate, requiring new concepts and skills in the management of college admissions.

The rapid build-up of public higher education following World War II has removed the practical meaning and status of admission to undergraduate study. For example, a larger percentage of the population now goes to college than has ever flown in a commercial airplane. The goal of 50 percent college attendance by high school graduates envisioned by the Truman Commission in the 1950s, and regarded by many as an optimal hope, has been achieved and surpassed. In one representative suburban-rural county, Suffolk in New York State, 70 percent of high school graduates go on to postsecondary study. Less than twenty years ago fewer than half that proportion went on to college from the same area. Going to college today is the mundane norm.

The Job Market and Postgraduate Education

With so many young people entering the system, there are problems in absorbing graduates into the jobs and careers for which they train. So, while the question of "will I be admitted to college," may not be in doubt very often today, the anxiety once reserved for freshman admission is now displaced by worry about access to graduate or professional school, or a good job, or any job. To be sure, some students still face competitive admission at some prestigious and selective institutions. Enrollment at these institutions, however, represents only about 15 percent of the total undergraduate population. The majority of students seek and enter institutions where access is relatively assured, given a reasonably realistic self-assessment. The point is that access to undergraduate study is sufficiently open so that few students doubt that they will be able to go to college should they want to. Most states by policy

89

or by statute assure college access for high school graduates. In our study (Human Development and Educational Policy [HUDEP], 1975)[3] of students who applied to one particular public university, less than a fraction of 1 percent did not go on to any college. Those who did not attend a college did so by choice. The annual American Council on Education (ACE) Freshman Survey study, which is widely reported each year in the media, shows a high proportion of students saying that they attend the college of their first choice, and the proportion has been increasing in recent years. There are some who will suggest that students tend to upgrade the rating of the college they actually attend, and for this reason the ACE data may be biased. Nevertheless, the fact remains that while there may be tension among some students competing for the most selective colleges, there is little concern about being shut out of college attendance altogether, and students in general seem to be satisfied with the colleges in which they enroll.

Postbaccalaureate study is another matter. In some fields (the most popular), applicants far exceed openings—medicine, law, clinical psychology, veterinarian medicine, for example. Also, at this level the status of programs is regarded as critical to professional futures. The high cost of postgraduate training has put the support of many programs in jeopardy as funding becomes more difficult. Recently it was reported that cuts in the City University of New York (CUNY) budget have resulted in a 25 percent reduction in graduate enrollments. Clearly, graduate and professional programs are not able to satisfy the enrollment demands.

The full dimension of the situation is obscured by the self-selection and counseling-out that occurs prior to making application to graduate or professional school. Students who perform below the expected competitive levels in freshman and sophomore courses often drop out of preferred career patterns (but not college) or are forced out by prerequisite standards needed for upper division courses and by committees whose recommendation is needed for advanced study. Frequently these decisions are not based on student potential but on the ability to perform tasks regardless of readiness. My own study of the inorganic chemistry course showed that while this subject "guarded" access to upper division courses in the sciences and engineering (including pre-medical studies), success in the course was not related to aptitude but to specific training in mathematics and to being male.

Almost twice as many students enter college expecting to go on to graduate or professional school as actually do go on, if Stony Brook is at all representative. Our studies (HUDEP, 1973)[4] suggest that the implied goal change tends to be accompanied by feelings of depression. The majority of upper-division students found to be mismatched with the institutional environment are those whose original postgraduate goals have been abandoned. Our data show that the frequency and severity of concerns that students have about postgraduate plans increase as students approach graduation, and that the anxiety is quantitatively and qualitatively greater than in high school "senioritis," particularly feelings of being alone and powerless. Often these feelings are personified in the lives of friends a year or two older who are observed drifting, unemployed or underemployed.

Postbaccalaureate study today is carried on largely in the public-education sector. While many private institutions are struggling with the burdensome costs of educating graduate and professional students, there has been compensatory growth in graduate opportunity in the public sector, especially in distinguished programs at institutions such as the University of California at Berkeley, the University of Michigan, and the University of Texas. In the East, private colleges and universities are still the academic status leaders and historically have been the academic innovators in the nation. But the early signals of change are apparent: the more able students look at undergraduate programs as preparation for graduate and professional schools, hence there is a tendency for them to select for undergraduate study universities that also offer graduate programs in which they are interested. Therefore, the status of undergraduate colleges (and enrollment in them) is increasingly determined by their graduate and professional schools. Public institutions now enroll the overwhelming proportion of college attendees. Students (head counts, FTE's*) are a major source of institutional capital and capital is the life-blood of institutional development and of the maintenance of quality. It is therefore inevitable that enrollment numbers ultimately will determine where academic quality and status can be maintained.

The Public Sector versus the Private Sector

Admissions officers, in an effort to balance the impact of education's social missions, institutional economic needs, and the faculty's concern for academic quality, attempt to preserve the traditional façade of the selection process.

There are many differences that distinguish the student selection policies and processes in the public sector from those in the private-university sector. While private colleges are found throughout the United States, their frequency and status are related to the setting, development, religious, and economic character of the area. The original colonies in the East naturally have the oldest and most highly regarded private institutions. As the frontiers pushed west, settlers brought with them their religion, schools and colleges to supply the churches with clergy and the schools with teachers. As technological needs grew, the government, through subsidies and land grants, helped initiate state public higher education systems. Today, outside of the Northeast, college students enroll overwhelmingly in public institutions. In Missouri, nearly 70 percent of enrollments are in the public sector and in Texas almost 90 percent. Massachusetts, however, enrolls more than 55 percent of its students in private institutions. Similarly, while there are distinguished private colleges in all areas of the

* Full Time Equivalents: a budgeting term used in the public sector.

country, other than in the East, large public universities are considered to be at least equal in status to the outstanding private institutions. Recently, some prestigious private institutions have been absorbed by state university systems in order to preserve their quality and, in some cases, to assure their survival.

Prior to joining a new public college as its admissions officer, in the late 1950s, I had never worked or studied in a public institution. My admissions colleagues and I were called coordinators of field services then, since it was believed unseemly for public colleges to have directors of admissions, implying to legislators the need to recruit students for tuition-free programs. I was aware that in some states the public university was its academic pride. In New York, however, pride and prestige seemed to reside in the private sector, City University of New York (CUNY) notwithstanding. I was eager to discover how the public sector leaders regarded themselves and the role of the emerging state university system.

Public Education and Political Ends

Those faculty on the local campus where I served were also products of private institutions. They felt that their goal was excellence in the traditional model of the most selective institutions. This view was sharply challenged, however, when in a meeting of state college admissions officers, a state university executive chastised the group for an increase that year in the proportion of freshmen who ranked in the top quarter of their high school graduating class. The official went on to point out that the state system was not for "geniuses" who could go elsewhere, but for middle-range-ability students of middle class families needed to staff the state's schools and civil service. "Smart alecs" were described as a threat to the stability of middle class institutions, especially the public school systems, since they would not be satisfied to "leave things alone."

93

His commentary was not intended to be humorous, but derived from the view that public education is for the middle class and those likely to sustain middle class roles and values. If private educations served the goals of change and meritocracy, public education addressed mediocrity and the preservation of the status quo.

Public education, of course, serves political ends. That an enlightened citizenry is required in order to preserve a free and democratic nation is a Jeffersonian article of political faith. The public-education system also serves as a sophisticated vehicle for influencing public policy. Access to higher education is believed to be the best route to economic opportunity, status, and power. Access to college also can be offered as a surrogate for the jobs and political power sought by the economically and socially disadvantaged.

Open enrollment and other free-access programs are clear cases in point. Similarly, the impact of equal rights legislation falls most heavily upon the public colleges and universities. Financial aid to selected populations, grant support for outreach to women, the elderly, and other nontraditional "new students," and improvements in the convenience of access can be used to "cool out" the bread-and-butter issues, and to experiment with emerging social changes. These processes essentially manipulate who attends college and who ultimately enters the social mainstream of American life.

The State University of New York (SUNY) has come a long way since the day of its institutionalized inferiority. Its political and educational self-image has changed from that of a Sancho Panza to the private sector to one of substance and vision which recognizes the leadership role public education must play to assure both educational opportunity for learners and the perpetuation of a healthy balance among public and private college programs and services. This new vision embraces a consortium concept featuring increased interinstitutional cooperation within regions, the movement of faculty and students from institution to institution and

94

between the public and private sectors that has fascinating implications for college admissions in the future.

Credentialing and the Pursuit of Education

One of Robert Hutchins's more memorable suggestions was to award the bachelor's degree at birth, thus freeing people to get about the business of becoming educated. "Credentialing" still gets in the way of education today (but not the support of education), although some curriculum reforms in recent years have encouraged more program variety and more student identification with learning. Given the current trends in career opportunity, it is likely that there will be an increase rather than a decrease in "credentialing" as vocational competition increases. One can anticipate the emergence of a new educational pattern which separates "credentialing" (certification of competence) from the delivery of educational services (learning). Further, the new pattern may eliminate the "credentialing" function of admissions selection as we know it. We expect the evolution of free-access policies with assessments based upon performance *after* entry, passing over the college-gatekeeper function to the applicant.

The Right to Education and the Absence of Selection—Undergraduate Education in the Public Sector

A principle of most public higher educational systems is that it is a person's right to pursue as much higher education as he or she can master and afford. Access is limited only by practical constraints such as space and budget. Admissions assessment is less judgmental than advisory. Even high risk students, if they wish, are given an opportunity to try.

Students today may enter most public state systems at any one of a variety of institutions, such as two-year colleges or universities. The politics of free access have helped promote the two-year community colleges and their linkage to upper-division institutions. As four-year colleges and universities have examined the costs and academic impact of serving academically disadvantaged students, there has been an increasing interest in tilting admissions programs in favor of upper-division transfers. This tilt effectively forces students in the direction of community colleges, where costs are lower and services can be concentrated. Theoretically and, in some public state systems, actually, credits are banked in a central data system after course completion, examination, evaluation of life experience, or independent study. Once in the system, students may utilize resources wherever they are. Movement from one level to the next is thereby facilitated. The price of directing students toward the community college is their guaranteed admission to an upper-division institution with full credit for courses completed, the transfer being little more than a bureaucratic ritual assuring that passports are in order. The needs of our democratic society are well served when students who would not qualify for freshman admission into four-year institutions become university juniors after the successful completion of a two-year community college program. Regional cooperation among institutions gives promise of expanding this public system to include the private sector.

The Beginning of the Postselective Era

What happens to academic communities under such an open-access arrangement? Probably nothing. The traditional public sector selection practices have only a small role in creating an academic environment. Institutional style, growing out of faculty teaching-learning priorities and socializing forces, is much more important. Academic communities very likely will grow stronger from the broader base of membership and from the natural affiliation of academic interests. These systems, largely as a result of the need for tax-dollar support, will almost all be administered by the public sector and be responsive to broad social and political interests. Admissions committees, as standards setters and gatekeepers, will pass into history as access to higher education and knowledge is democratized.

Already, the difficulty of selection for undergraduate study in the public sector is largely a myth. Virtually all who want to go on to college are able to gain admission at some point in the system. Only in the most select institutions (largely private), enrolling about 15 percent of the college population, is the competition such that entrance is seriously in doubt. Many institutions labeled as selective are not. SUNY—Stony Brook, for example, is regarded as selective. It does enroll students primarily from the top quarter of their class. But after a measure of self-selection, virtually all who complete applications are accepted because of a low yield from admissions offers. Since only 30 percent of admissions offers result in enrollment, over three offers must be made to achieve one enrollment. To enroll a class of 1,500, for example, almost 5,000 offers must be made. By the time incomplete applications are purged from the process, an applicant pool of several thousands boils down to about five hundred rejections, which is well under 10 percent of applications. It is not unknown for an admissions director to re-open some of these cases if enrollment targets are raised late in the year as new operating funds materialize or if additional enrollments are needed to justify existing funding. This phenomenon is typical of good-sized public institutions.

Selection in public colleges really is done in advance of application, by the candidate, the family, school counselors, college personnel, and by the weight of public opinion. Somehow this haphazard process manages to join the students' and the institutions' expectations with a minimum of application trauma. Students sort themselves in terms of anticipated selection probability and institutional academic level. Since the future forecasts an insufficient number of students to support institutional needs (dormitory debt service requires full occupancy; academic diversity needs certain minimum enrollment), it is probable that admissions pains will soon be on the institutions' rather than the students' side. Students will select among colleges which are competing for survival enrollments.

The era of the admissions mystique is ending. It's a big business now with professionals working at the key transaction points and pressuring to maintain, if not increase, the flow of students into their institutions. For the most part, student intake is geared to institutional economic concerns. The "keeper of standards" role traditionally associated with selection has been returned to the faculty in the classroom.

The Place of College in Our Society— Selection and Acceptance

What place does going to college occupy in the lives of high school students and their families? The evidence is that the majority of high school students today plan to go on to college. The probability of actual enrollment, however, is greatly influenced by family economics (the higher the family income, the greater the enrollment probability), father's occupation (the more prestigious, the greater the chance of a son's and daughter's college attendance). Other enrollment factors include nearness to a college (not necessarily the one attended) and sex. Males still go on to college more often than females. Presumably, this latter circumstance will change as more women appear in traditionally male career roles and family-care patterns change.

Family income, father's occupation, and sex also tend to define the enrollment pools for public versus private institutions, and the candidates for institutions with more and less prestige. Only the exceptional individual with potential for college breaks the pattern by not enrolling—and often not for long, as is witnessed by the recent influx of older students at many institutions. Today, young people are programmed for college. Parents and secondary schools require college acceptance as validation of their nurturing, and as good children, our daughters and sons dutifully go about their college-attending occupations.

The bottom line of college-going is acceptance. Those of us who have paid our dues at endless numbers of College Nights know that the first question asked of college recruiters invariably is "What's the average?" or "What does it take?" Vague descriptions of flexible "individualized" judgments across a range of criteria seldom satisfy the inquirers' need for certainty about their selection. The answer often determines who in the audience stays for the remainder of the presentation.

The significance of acceptance undoubtedly contributes to the absorbing interest and energy given to the process of selection by applicants, parents, and schools. Even though admission is not much in doubt, the importance of the prize makes it necessary to enhance its status by embellishing the game. The focus is on strategies that attempt to "psych out" interviewers, application readers, and entrance examinations, strategies which order credentials in as favorable a competitive position as possible. "Winning" involves the number of acceptances, high College Entrance Examination Board (CEEB)/ACT scores, invitations to join the college board, and so on. The status of some guidance counselors is based on their effectiveness as applicant advocates (e.g., securing an early decision or verbal assurance of selection or the special review of a complex application). Since follow-up studies are seldom made, or, if made, given much publicity, and the payoff is too remote, it is understandable that college-acceptance rates become the measure of admission success rather than college graduation or some other more distant and difficult-to-measure developmental goals.

The apparent artlessness of this passive approach to selecting a college is unsettling. I have always felt that the consumer should test the character and quality of the institution first, before submitting to the institution's assessment. But that is to miss the point. Acceptance is an affirmation of the value of the student, the parents, the secondary school, and the community. The quality of secondary schools often is measured in terms of the percentage of graduates who go on for postsecondary study and the prestige of the institutions entered. Somehow admission of the valedictorian to an Ivy college validates secondary school quality more than a reduced drop-out rate. Schools with a high college-going rate translate into a good real estate values, a generally stable local community, and an improved local economy.

College acceptance also is a major social dividing line. For many families it defines parenting success and values. Peer friendships tend to divide into college-bound and non-college-bound groups. Few friendships which cross this boundary persist very long after high school, particularly for those who go away to college. Acceptance to college, in a sense, is a major assessment of the success of parent-school-community stewardship in the development of its young people. College-going is a testimony of continuing adult care for the welfare of youth.

The development of public-education systems with open access policies, geographic convenience, and financial-aid packaging have taken much of the risk out of the admissions game but, surprisingly, have altered its ambiance very little. Acceptance may be assured, although recent budget constraints suggest that in some areas (for example, CUNY) open access is threatened (a potential social flash point), but competitions for high levels of status and affirmation go on.

FTE (the full time enrolled student) generates and validates school budgets especially in the public sector and is the basis of predicted enrollment. If there is a reported shortfall of students after registration, the states may adjust the budget downward, probably cutting positions. To get budgets approved and planning accomplished, institutions may inflate their expected FTE's. In some universities, to achieve required research-funding levels, the states will require certain FTE levels (undergraduate and graduate students). If they are not met, it is often the undergraduate funding that is cut, leading to the view that in some state institutions graduate education is built on the back of undergraduate education. So we see that enrollments generate funding but later in the process enrollment targets may be reached to validate the funding. In this complex series of events, enrollment shortfalls activate a pecking order for survival, bumping the less-valued institutional programs.

The competition for college admission is both poignant and ruthless. High school grading systems are "weighted," failed courses suppressed, rankings manipulated so that in some secondary schools the college bound arbitrarily are ranked ahead of the non-college bound. Confidential memoranda attribute low grades, especially on standardized tests, to experimental curricula and every once in a while to teacher failure, which is usually punished by reassigning the teacher to an administrative post. Some schools and counselors assume an aggressive, almost threatening posture, claiming that their excellence and/or uniqueness defies comparison with other institutions or even the comparison of students in the institution with each other. Occasionally advocacy verges on coercion with veiled threats of law suits, letters to political leaders, and leaks to the press charging unfair and discriminatory practices. Each year admissions directors can expect calls hinting that the delicate health of one or both parents might not survive the disappointment of their child's rejection. In some cases the school's response to the plea for expediting a child's admission has nothing to do with the student's merits and everything to do with the parents' status and the school's image of itself.

Several students have told me that they might as well be admitted because they were going to attend regardless of the admission decision. This bravado, and ploy, always appealed to me. I wondered if these students really were sophisticated enough to know that a student probably could enroll in certain large institutions without being admitted and not be found out for some time —if ever. One student told me that a rejection notice would be my death warrant. He pointed out that not going to college would condemn him to a life without hope. He wanted me to experience the reality of what he was feeling.

Getting the fat envelope is important. Curiously, the admissions office usually is seen as an obstacle to admission. Every selection policy tends to be viewed as a device to *exclude* the candidate. This attitude of suspicion and its resultant demand for explicit fairness frequently results in too much rigidity. Strict actuarial selection by the use of objective criteria uniformly applied threatens the consideration of such nonmeasurable criteria as motivation, leadership, and the late-bloomer phenomenon. And even objective selection, regardless of regression study data, carries an enormous error factor on its back.

There is a large body of literature addressing the prediction of student performance in college. Typically, these analyses are based on regression studies of the influence of selected variables (e.g., grade performance, testing scores) on some performance criterion (e.g., freshman grade average, persistence). Both CEEB and ACT have been proponents of these prediction techniques as important aids in the selection and advisement of college students. As a result, most colleges have built a prediction formula into their admissions assessment program.

The issue often in conflict is the relative advantage of professional judgment, with its capacity to consider impressionistic data and to read behind grades and test scores, versus the consistency of statistical prediction. Prediction formulae typically achieve a correlation quotient of about 0.5. (Some researchers claim that stronger results can be achieved through more careful partitioning of groups.) This still leaves a large error factor which inevitably will exclude potentially successful candidates and include some who will fail. Professional judgment, it is argued, is no more precise. Comparison tests tend to show that formula selection outperforms individual assessment and certainly is less costly. A combination of formula and human judgment, however, tends to exceed the accuracy of either system taken alone.[4] The price of objectivity is an arbitrary setting aside of the known error, sometimes as much as 50 percent. Prediction formulae are a marginal improvement over a coin flip. They are uniform, however, if not fair. But in the age of accountability, being able to demonstrate consistency is important, as least to administrators.

Decisions about going on to college are made during important developmental periods for both the student and parents. For students, going to college coincides with and symbolizes the transition from late adolescence to young adulthood. For parents, it marks the approach of mid-life, the flight of offspring from the nest. It marks a change from a parent-oriented home to one centering on the marriage partnership. Often for parents it is a time of summing up and, not infrequently, making a decision to change career, to separate, or to make some other major shift in life style.

Admissions and financial-aid officers are familiar with the unique pressures on parents' lives. For example, many families find themselves facing a profound dilemma when their children's college entrance suddenly comes in conflict with an opportunity for a profitable financial venture such as the opportunity for the father to buy into the business where he has worked for many years or to open his own business. The funds needed are those that have been set aside for college. The conflict is clear—the child's college opportunity versus the parents' economic opportunity.

The advent of state and federal loan programs, work-study programs, and other financial-aid resources has made the conflict resolution easier, as has the development of low-cost public higher education facilities such as the two-year college. Some middle-income parents discover that they can take advantage of funding agencies by divesting themselves of assets such as savings, reducing salaried income (often possible in partnership or private business), and seeking financial aid. They can thus maintain a comfortable life style and either defer the costs of their children's education or have them subsidized.

Selecting a college is not as simple, as free, or as rational as the American Dream would have it. In our discussions, students often claim the ideal of free choice. "The decision is up to me," they say, "and I want to pick the best place for me." Our data and the literature agree, however, that choice generally occurs within economic and geographic constraints. We find, for example, that students tend to draw up their college lists into either public or private sector groupings. Students who are admitted to Stony Brook but don't attend, for example, overwhelmingly enroll at another unit of the State University. Also, while these students claim that their college choice was their personal decision, over two-thirds agree that consultation with parents was a very important consideration. It is clear that parent economic support establishes the limits of choice and that parent opinion, often the mother's, is profoundly influential.

The influence of adults is significant, matched only by the influence of reports from students already attending the institutions being considered. Parents obviously help define the practical limits on college options—money and distance—and very likely contribute to the nature of academic and career goals. Furthermore, college-going in general is related to parental approval of post-secondary education. This may account for the differential in college-going patterns for men and women. People tend to behave in ways that replicate success and gain approval while avoiding the risk of failure and disapproval.

The emergence of the suburban culture and the decline of the power of the family unit create new and important adult figures in most adolescent lives. Typically, these are active and caring teachers, employers, or leaders of youth-oriented community activities (music, athletics, politics). While it is popular to bad-mouth guidance counselors, a high number of students indicate that they have turned to such counselors and found their help useful. My own efforts to find and recruit able students who were turned off by the formal school organization led me to discover that police-men patrolling youth-hangout areas are often sought out by young people for help. Other students use bartenders, shopkeepers, vir-tually anyone who is accessible, open, but not a pushover for youthful manipulation. There is a constant search for adult rela-tionships and leadership.

Faculty-Student Interaction in the Public University

This search for adult relationships is demonstrated by the impor-tance applicants give to the quality of faculty they expect to find at institutions of their choice and the expected quality of interaction with faculty. In the minds of many students, no interpersonal ex-pectation is more important.

High faculty quality and faculty-student interaction are char-acteristics widely attributed to private institutions, where overall enrollments and class size are lower than in public institutions. Stu-dents entering public universities accept the fact that they are likely to be large, that there is a risk of being lost, and that the management styles probably result in minimal institutional caring for students as individuals. Even as public sector students resign themselves to these drawbacks, they hope for relationships with a small number of faculty in areas of key career interest.

Students recognize that getting ahead in life requires ability, effort, and breaks. Middle- and lower-class youth understand dis-advantages and the politics of opportunity allocation. As potential Horatio Algers they have studied "making it." Most know that admission to the prestigious Ivy, Potted Ivy, Seven Sisters, or their Midwest and West Coast equivalents would mean that they would have more going for them: more breaks, a better address than those attending most public colleges. But if they enter college where the institutional label isn't enough, then most students hope to find a faculty "hook," one of the "stars" lured to the state campus by money, facilities, and, unknown to the student, a minimum undergraduate teaching load. Students hope this mentor will sponsor them on the road to professional school where they anticipate meeting and conquering their privileged prestige-school rivals.

Institutional Choice and College Expectations

Public university entrants don't so much make free choices as they make the best of limited options. Institutional choice is based first upon the quality of students' academic records. The best credentials are directed to the universities, the rest to the four-year colleges, and so on down the line. Other factors include geographic proximity, that is, in families that can afford it, children go away to college; educational-career goals, and personal and social agendas. Of these factors, career goals and social goals are most important.

Once the practical decisions about college-going are out of the way, college selection is very much tied to the expectations students have for college. The poles of choice are: college as a social experience, and college as preparation for postgraduate professional study or career. The majority of students, at least, say that they are motivated by postgraduate professional ambitions. Some men and women view college as an end in itself and anticipate their undergraduate years as a time for making good lifetime friends, being in a stimulating social, cultural, intellectual environment, and, in general, experiencing what is thought of as a liberal arts education. These students often say that they do not seek a competitive or rigorous academic environment, and consequently they tend toward the four-year colleges rather than the universities.

The majority, however, especially the men, seek training for a postgraduate school or occupation. For these students, undergraduate school is instrumental to their life plans. Choices are evaluated in terms of their contribution to meeting life-goal expectations. These students are success oriented and identify with the status of anticipated goals (doctor, lawyer, scientist, scholar) and the symbols of achievement (grades, honors) leading to these goals. Such students, therefore, are impressed by institutions with professional programs in the fields to which they aspire and faculty with national or world reputations in those areas.

In conversations with students they expressed the concern of many that they had had no significant contact with mentors and doctoral candidates in the field of their choice. They felt their choices of university program and career to be reasonable, based on comparisons with other students before them, but they still lacked a sense of authenticity, of legitimacy. By being in an academic environment where their chosen field is visible and contact can be made with experienced faculty and advanced graduate students, the beginning students feel they can gain a sense of reality and socialize more appropriately. Thus, they can more directly pursue their goals by curricular and extracurricular activity or change their direction early enough so that college does not cost more in time and money.

Students in the public sector particularly face both the traditional maturation process, and a social-cultural transition. Just as one develops personally through experience, there is a need for young people also to connect themselves directly with the social-cultural ideas and roles they are considering.

Such contact, however, can be a two-edged sword. Many students are disappointed to discover that most distinguished faculty are human, complete with warts, often self-centered, and disinterested in eighteen-year-old friends. It is easy to understand, therefore, how the frustrated expectations of bright young people seeking adult leadership can be turned on by virtually any aggressive, assertive adult willing to share his or her passion, be it a Ralph Nader, a Mahareshi, or any number of trendy politicals or cultists.

The Microcosm of Freshman Studenthood

The reality of studenthood for the freshman is often disheartening. The anticipated reinforcement of self-regard, success, leadership, the certainty of knowledge, does not materialize as expected. Grade-getting and adult-pleasing are neither satisfying nor sufficient activities. Students recognize that they must risk suffering through changes and accept the structure of their own resources, or buy the illusion of security through dependence on the structures of others.

Some students entering the public sector anticipate its disappointments and prepare themselves to be as invulnerable as possible by making a minimum investment in the life at the university. The year becomes simply a sequence of classrooms and impersonal relationships with teachers and peers and no commitment to extracurricular activities. There is little chance for internal change, just a credential for time passed.

Our studies (HUDEP, 1974)[5] show this grim scenario to be most characteristic of transfers and commuters, almost half of whom, in our sample, expect to be elementary or secondary school teachers, and almost half of whom are married.

The American Dream As a
Developmental Opportunity

If the majority of students see in the public or private college any particular developmental opportunity, it is to escape what their parents have settled for. We find that the college plans of peers exert a negative influence on college selection. Obviously most students from any given group do attend the same cluster of institutions, but there is little indication that they expect to maintain precollege friendships, or even sexual partnerships. College is a break from the past and the start of a new life, with new friends and new social-cultural patterns.

The American Dream for parents is that their children will reap the benefits of opportunities the parents were unable to realize. This was somewhat more the case for parents who reached adulthood during the Depression and went to work rather than to college, or, in many cases, to complete high school. The parents of 1975 to 1976 college freshmen were born in the Depression, and reached adulthood during World War II or the Korean War. Many fathers did use GI benefits to attend some college, but the pressures of marriage, children, and an expanding economy often drew them into the labor force, and into what many find now to be an economic treadmill.

Parents want a better life for their children, and the professions are their ideal. The professions provide credentials that will assure material well-being and remove children from the rat race their parents find themselves in. Time and time again in interviews, students express their desire to escape the life style of their parents. This is not a repudiation of their parents, but a fear of experiencing the same dependency on and exploitation by political and economic forces.

Women often comment on their mothers' undeveloped talents, and what they have given up by accepting the role of housewife and mother. In reviewing the educational histories of the parents of Stony Brook students, we often find that the mothers have had more education than the fathers but have not gone on to satisfying careers or life activities. Daughters see their frustration and don't want to repeat that pattern.

Sons see the drudgery, boredom, and in some cases, the indignity of compromises between their fathers' work ethics and personal values. It makes them angry, afraid, and motivated. Success in education is the way out; success is important.

Those who seek a public higher education do not appear to overlap very much with those who go to private colleges. The groups are separated by economics and by attitudes toward the purposes of higher education. Public higher education sustains the reality of the American Dream as it democratizes access to knowledge and provides the means for many to enrich the quality of life.

REFERENCES

1. *Critique of a College* (Swarthmore, Pennsylvania: Swarthmore College, Nov. 1967), p. 257.

2. Ernest P. Earnest, *Academic Procession: An Informal History of the American College, 1636–1953* (Indianapolis: Bobbs-Merrill, 1953), p. 22.

3. Group for Human Development and Educational Policy, *Freshman Admit-Declines; Where, Why: A Study of Freshman Applicants Who Decline Offers of Admission*, Working Paper No. 8 (Stony Brook: State University of New York at Stony Brook, 1975), p. 4.

4. Group for Human Development and Educational Policy, *Academic and Non-Academic Student Life at Stony Brook*, Report No. 1 (Stony Brook: State University of New York at Stony Brook, 1973), pp. 4–5.

5. Group for Human Development and Educational Policy, *A Preliminary Study of Transfer Students at Stony Brook*, Preliminary Working Paper (Stony Brook: State University of New York at Stony Brook, 1974).

PHILIP R. REVER

The Dynamics of Admission to the
Less-Selective Public and
Private-Sector Colleges

Philip Rever, as Director of the Washington office of the American College Testing Program, is a national observer of the dynamics of admission to the undergraduate college. His analytic review of the admissions process in the less-selective public- and private-sector colleges places in perspective the chapters by Herbert Sacks and Peter Wells, who have written about entry into the highly-selective institutions, and the piece by David Tilley who has addressed broad admission issues, largely in the public sector. Rever's discussion focuses upon the rational processes and irrational impulses that affect the problem of choice, and he emphasizes the fact that students do not apply for admission willy-nilly despite the suggestive evidence that one-third of student applicants make an inappropriate choice.

He identifies the apprehensions of applicants to the less-selective institution as part of their movement toward independence and emancipation. Even though there are psychodynamic parallels, the anxieties described by Rever are not of the same intensity as those discussed by Sacks and Wells or even by Tilley. He raises the interesting possibility that the relatively low level of anxiety experienced by students expecting admission to the less-selective institu-

tions may limit the evolution of the process of separating from home, and thus may contribute to the high attrition rates in college and to the large numbers who seemingly make an inappropriate choice.

APPROXIMATELY ONE million students leave their families each fall to begin baccalaureate studies at the 1,900 or so four-year collegiate institutions in this country. Their matriculation will be the culmination of the lengthy process of choosing a college. Though simply stated, choosing a college is in reality a series of decisions that are incredibly complex for a number of reasons. First, choosing a college is not a unilateral decision. Second, college-admissions policies and past academic and nonacademic accomplishments limit students' freedom to choose. Third, a large array of people from parents and peers to teachers influence the choice. Fourth, the decision involves a myriad of questions about the future such as: What do I want to study? Will I like the dormitory? Will I fail? Can I get a good job if I graduate? How much financial aid will I be able to obtain? Uncertain answers to these and other questions can produce considerable apprehension about which college to attend. Fifth, choosing a college is an integral part of the emancipation of students from parents, and, for about three-quarters of them, precedes the first extended separation from their families.*

It is clear why considerable effort has been spent identifying who and what forces are responsible for the decision to attend college.[3] But it is not clear why less effort has been spent studying

---

* About one-quarter of all first-time four-year college and university students live at home while attending college[1] but the more selective the institution the fewer entering students live at home.[2]

who and what forces are responsible for the choice of a *particular* college. This oversight may be corrected somewhat by this chapter, which focuses on why and how a particularly large group of students seek admission to and enroll at "less-selective" colleges and universities.

Less-Selective Colleges and Their Students

There is no question about the existence of a hierarchical prestige structure among four-year collegiate institutions in this country. At the top of the hierarchy are a relatively few highly ranked undergraduate schools that attract a national student body, have more applicants than places in their entering classes, and can only admit a few from among the thousands who apply for admission. On the other end of the scale are the indispensable colleges that use what is known as the "98.6° F. test" for admission. Between these extremes are institutions of greater or lesser selectivity which require applicants to meet or exceed criteria of differing degrees of difficulty. The prestige of an institution is largely determined by its selectivity.

Selectivity, however, is a relative term since even the "98.6° F. test" institutions employ some criteria when judging the admissibility of a candidate. This relativity is apparent in the definitions employed to classify colleges. Besides using a ratio of admitted students to applicants, a ratio that could be quite misleading, two approaches have been most common. One, favored by Alexander W. Astin's Laboratory for Research in Higher Education, is based on the average college admissions test scores of entering classes.[4] The higher the average test score, the more selective is the institution. Astin's definition yields three categories of selectivity for colleges and universities: high, medium, and low; to which he adds a fourth category for some four-year colleges: very high.

Another definition of selectivity reflects a different emphasis in admissions policies. The American College Testing Program uses a five category definition:[5]

1. Open	all high school graduates are accepted.
2. Liberal	some accepted students are from the lower half of their high school class.
3. Traditional	all accepted students are in the upper half of their high school class.
4. Selective	majority of accepted students are in the upper 25 percent of their high school class.
5. Highly Selective	majority of accepted students are in the upper 10 percent of their high school class.

About one million students who enter college for the first time each fall undertake studies leading to a baccalaureate degree at four-year colleges and universities in the above five categories. What follows is a description of colleges and universities with selective, traditional, liberal, and open admissions policies; their students; and the process that results in the enrollment of these students in these kinds of colleges.*

The Institutions

According to the American College Testing Program about 95 percent of all four-year colleges and universities have less-selective admissions policies. And, although precise figures are not available, it is estimated that over 90 percent of college entrants each fall begin their studies at less-selective colleges. Consequently, the bulk of our

* This emphasis on four-year colleges and universities is not intended to overlook the important role community and junior colleges play in baccalaureate education.

baccalaureate education system is composed of less-selective colleges and their students.

Characterizing less-selective colleges and universities is problematical because they vary in size of enrollment, baccalaureate programs offered, sources of operating funds, and admissions processes. Entire books, including *Colleges of the Forgotten Americans* by Dunham,[6] *The Multicampus University* by Lee and Bowen,[7] *Institutions in Transition* by Hodgkinson,[8] *The Regional State Colleges and Universities* by Harcleroad, Molen, and Rayman,[9] and others, have been written about them. Since, however, it is not the purpose of this essay to present a comprehensive portrait of less-selective institutions, only a sketch will be provided here.

Type of Control and Geographical Location. Colleges are divided into public and private categories that connote their tradition and denote their governance structure and primary sources of operating funds. Although all colleges receive funds from a variety of sources, public institutions typically receive direct subsidies from state or municipal treasuries and are governed by boards appointed by elected state or municipal officials. Private institutions are financed by tuition and gifts, although some also benefit from federal and state taxes. Moreover, private institutions, traditionally, have been subdivided into those with governance ties to churches (sometimes called private–church related) and those independent of any church.

Not all private colleges have highly-selective admissions policies nor do all public institutions have less-selective admissions policies. But can you, the reader, answer the following true–false questions correctly?

1. T or F?   Relatively few private colleges accept students from the lower half of their high school class.
2. T or F?   More than half of the selective and highly-selective colleges are public.

3. T or F?   More than half of the highly-selective colleges are located in the northeast region of this country.

4. T or F?   Every state other than Alaska and Hawaii has at least one highly-selective college.

Answers to the above questions can be found in the data contained in Table 1 which was compiled from the *College Planning/Search Book*.[10] Statements 1, 2, and 4 are false and statement 3 is true. Fifty-three percent of the private colleges listed in the *College Planning/Search Book* admit students from the lower half of their high school class. Less than 25 percent of the selective and highly-selective colleges are public. If Pennsylvania, New Jersey, and New York are included as being in the Northeast, about 52 percent of all highly-selective colleges and universities are located in that area. There are only two highly-selective institutions among the eight states of Alabama, Arkansas, Kentucky, Louisiana, Mississippi, Oklahoma, Tennessee, and Texas. From the data in Table 1 we can see that (a) highly-selective institutions are concentrated in the northeastern and western regions of the country, (b) private colleges outnumber public colleges in all categories of selectivity, and (c) states with relatively large numbers of highly-selective *private* colleges and universities also contain relatively large numbers of highly-selective and selective *public* colleges and universities.

Programs of study. Less-selective institutions offer almost all generally recognized major fields of study. But selectivity may not be directly related to the numbers of fields of study offered by the college.* Some open-admissions colleges offer very few majors, others offer a large number. In general, it appears that private colleges and universities have fewer major fields of study than do their

* No definitive data were found that express this relationship, although Minter and Bowen[11] report that among private four-year colleges, highly-selective colleges offered an average of 294 courses while less-selective colleges offered an average of 186 courses.

116

TABLE I

Institutional Selectivity and Geographical Dispersion by Type of Control

Selectivity	Open		Liberal		Traditional		Selective		Very Selective	
Control	Public	Private	Public	Private	Public	Private	Public	Private	Public	Private
Region*										
Pacific and Mountain	19	27	21	50	17	20	21	27	7	8
North Central	22	12	20	52	6	24	2	17	3	1
Great Lakes	15	19	26	92	17	49	8	36	1	7
South Central	52	24	38	73	7	29	3	16	0	2
South Atlantic	12	10	40	70	18	39	9	40	4	5
Middle Atlantic	7	2	24	67	9	47	21	56	3	23
New England	3	5	10	49	11	24	5	20	0	17

* Pacific and Mountain = Alaska, Arizona, California, Colorado, Hawaii, Idaho, Montana, Nevada, New Mexico, Oregon, Utah, Washington, and Wyoming

North Central = Iowa, Kansas, Minnesota, Missouri, Nebraska, North Dakota, and South Dakota

Great Lakes = Illinois, Indiana, Michigan, Ohio, and Wisconsin

South Central = Alabama, Arkansas, Kentucky, Louisiana, Mississippi, Oklahoma, Tennessee, and Texas

South Atlantic = Delaware, District of Columbia, Florida, Georgia, Maryland, North Carolina, South Carolina, Virginia, and West Virginia

Middle Atlantic = New Jersey, New York, and Pennsylvania

New England = Connecticut, Maine, Massachusetts, New Hampshire, Rhode Island, and Vermont

Source: The American College Testing Program, 1976 to 1977.[11]

public counterparts. The number of majors offered by colleges and universities is probably more related to their purposes and therefore their size than to their degree of selectivity. But some major fields of study, such as agriculture, engineering, and home economics, are simply not widely available. These majors are most likely found at traditional, selective, or highly-selective universities. Otherwise the more popular fields of business, education, the fine and applied arts, languages, humanities, mathematics, natural sciences, and social sciences are offered at both highly-selective and less-selective colleges and universities. Hence, except for those seeking a few particular fields of study, college-bound students have little difficulty finding institutions that offer their intended major.

Costs. The cost* of higher education has skyrocketed in recent years.[12-14] The absolute dollar charges for room, board, tuition, and fees at private institutions have risen faster than charges at public institutions even though, as Minter and Bowen observe, private institutions' charges, where seen as a percentage of disposable per capita income, have remained somewhat constant.[18] Nevertheless, the National Center for Education Statistics reported that for the 1974 to 1975 academic year, it typically cost $1,903 to attend a public university, $1,682 to attend a public four-year college, $4,193 to attend a private university, and $3,419 to attend a private four-year college.[19] Therefore, it is clear that private universities have the highest charges, private four-year colleges the next highest, public universities the next highest, followed by public four-year colleges.

Do average charges for room, board, tuition, and fees vary with selectivity? Do average expenses for books, supplies, transportation, incidentals, and so on, vary with selectivity? Unfortunately, these and other important questions cannot be answered with certainty. The reviewed literature on comparative costs at

---

* Costs, as used here, refer to out-of-pocket costs to parents and students. More technical discussions of costs to society, cost net of taxes and financial aid and opportunity cost can be found elsewhere, e.g., Van Alstyne,[15] and Bowen and Minter[16] and Leslie and Johnson.[17]

different kinds of colleges focused on cost differences between public and private institutions rather than on relative selectivity. Consequently, only uncertain responses can be made to the often heard "I can't afford to send my kid to a private college." Where combined student grants and loans are substantial, parents' net cost (after tax, out-of-pocket expenditures) for a son or daughter might be lower at an "expensive," highly-selective private institution than at an "inexpensive," less-selective public institution. Intuition suggests that net out-of-pocket cost to parents and students varies directly with selectivity, but until appropriate research is completed, the relationship cannot be firmly established.

The Admissions Process. The admissions process at less-selective institutions differs from the process at highly-selective colleges and among the less-selective institutions themselves according to their organizational structure and purposes.

The admissions process at the majority of colleges requires considerable paper work. Admissions offices have to collect, assemble, file, and review applications for admission; letters of recommendation from teachers, principals, and others; high school transcripts; college admission test scores; and advanced-placement test scores. In addition, many highly-selective colleges require a personal interview conducted by a staff member of the college or a graduate of the university, if the candidate lives quite far from the campus. Unlike the highly-selective institution, less-selective institutions tend not to require an admissions interview. Those that do may conduct interviews for purposes other than selection. If, for example, the college is struggling to fill its entering class, the interview may be used as a recruiting device. All in all, the admissions process itself is formidable, and its complexity is largely determined by the size of the institution.

Institutions offering relatively large numbers of programs of study often use a two-step admissions process. First, the admissibility of the student to the institution is determined. Then the admissibility of the candidate to his or her expressed program of study is decided. The second judgment of admissibility may not be made until after the student has completed general studies, and then applies for admission to a special program of study after the sophomore year. Nevertheless, the smaller the institution and the more selective it is, the fewer are the admissions decisions.

Also, large less-selective institutions often use tests to place students properly once they have been admitted. Students with better academic records and test scores are allowed to enroll in higher level, more advanced courses during their first year than students with poor academic records. Other students are required to take remedial or refresher courses in areas such as English composition and mathematics. Thus less-selective institutions, particularly large universities and colleges, attempt to introduce some homogeneity of educational development into their classes.

Virtually all colleges and universities, regardless of their selectivity, allow students to earn credit toward graduation by taking examinations such as the College Level Examination Program (CLEP) and the Proficiency Examination Program. Moreover, many offer their own challenge examinations.

There is one major area in which the less-selective institutions' admissions process differs from the admissions process at more-selective institutions. Less-selective institutions (and some public highly-selective institutions) use a "rolling admissions system." Admission is granted to every applicant whose academic record meets or exceeds the minimum criteria, and the decision is made as soon as the candidate's application materials are available for review. Rolling admissions are possible because the criteria for admission at these institutions are often based mostly on the empirical data of rank in class, and minimum admission test scores.* In contrast, test scores and rank in class do not automatically determine who will be admitted to highly-selective private institutions where virtually all candidates have exceptional test scores and high school grades. Consequently, the marginal determining factors in admis-

---

* Public institutions usually must place a limit on the numbers of out-of-state applicants who can be admitted. Hence, less-selective institutions may become highly selective for out-of-state applicants.

sions decisions at highly-selective institutions frequently include the intended major field of study, extensiveness of out-of-school activities, among others. To be sure, outstanding high school records and admission test scores are necessary for consideration by highly-selective colleges, but they are not always decisive in admissions decisions. In this sense, academic records and test scores are given more weight in the admissions decision at less-selective institutions than at highly-selective institutions. Moreover, because admission to a less-selective college is primarily based on high school records and test scores, students who apply to such institutions are better able to judge their chances of being admitted, thus reducing the apprehension that can result from the uncertainty about being admitted to a highly desired institution.

The foregoing discussion of the admissions process, costs, fields of study, and the definition of selectivity offered is important to the understanding of why and how students apply to less-selective institutions. Characteristics of the less-selective institutions play a major role in the process of choosing a college. But before this role is described, it will be helpful to provide a profile of the students who enroll in less-selective colleges and universities.

The Students

The most recent profiles of students who enter less-selective institutions were published by the Laboratory for Research in Higher Education. Its report, *The American Freshman: National Norms for Fall, 1976,*[20] and other sources of information reveal how students in institutions of varying selectivity differ on measures of academic achievement, family background, and levels of aspiration.

Demonstrated achievements. Students demonstrate their abilities three ways. They are (a) rank in class or high school grades, (b) college admissions and placement test scores, and (c) participation in activities such as student government, athletics, art and science fairs, debate and public speaking contests, writing, music camps, and so on. Students with differing levels of achievement in these areas enroll in institutions of differing selectivity.

Obviously, the more selective the institution, the higher the average admission test scores as shown in Table 2 and the higher the average high school grades of the entering class.[21] But average scores and grades do not reflect the complete picture. The less selective and the larger the institution, the greater the diversity of

TABLE 2

Institutional Selectivity and Typical Admissions Test Scores

Selectivity	Typical Test Scores Averages Reported by Colleges*	
	ACT	SAT (V+M)
Open	16–20	750–950
Liberal	18–22	800–1000
Traditional	19–23	850–1050
Selective	21–25	950–1150
Highly Selective	25–29	1100–1350

* ACT = The American College Testing Program's Assessment
  SAT = The College Entrance Examination Board's Scholastic Aptitude Test. (V+M) is the sum of the verbal and mathematics test scores.

Source: The American College Testing Program, 1976, *op. cit.*, p. 11.[22]

measured abilities and achievements among students (which is the reason for the post-acceptance "placement" decisions discussed earlier). Accordingly, larger, less-selective institutions not only tend to enroll students with lower average test scores and high school grades, but there is also greater diversity on these measures among enrolled students.

Little is known about the relationship between an institution's selectivity and its students' out-of-class accomplishments while they were in high school. It can be guessed that the relationship is a weak one because academic accomplishment and out-of-class accomplishments of college-bound high school students are not related.[23] Students with unexceptional admission test scores and high school grades may have excelled in student government, athletics, science fairs, art, debate, and so on. Therefore, it is probable that in many cases the less-selective institutions enroll substantial numbers of students who excelled in extracurricular activities.

Level of Educational Aspiration. Students entering less-selective colleges and universities typically have lower levels of educational aspirations than students entering highly-selective institutions as shown in Table 3.[24] Moreover, students in private institutions are more likely to aspire to an advanced degree (Ph.D., Ed.D., medical degree, or law degree) than students at public colleges and universities. Additionally, these tendencies are more pronounced for women than men. However, students with all levels of educational aspiration can be found in every college and university regardless of its selectivity.

TABLE 3

Institutional Selectivity and Level of Educational Aspirations of Fall 1976 Entrants

	Proportion Desiring Degree Beyond the Master's			
	Universities			
	Men		Women	
	Public	Private	Public	Private
Low Selectivity	28.5	40.0	17.5	30.3
Medium Selectivity	29.1	55.0	19.7	37.4
High Selectivity	41.1	64.8	30.5	53.1
	Four-Year Colleges (Men and Women)			
	Public	Private Indp.	Private Cath.	Private Other Sect.
Low Selectivity	18.0	25.1	21.1	18.7
Medium Selectivity	21.2	22.9	28.2	24.5
High Selectivity	27.4	39.0	33.6	37.7
Very High Selectivity	*	55.5	*	*

* No colleges in this category.

Source: Astin, et al., *op. cit.*, pp. 65 and 79.[25]

Family background. There is a direct relationship between selectivity and various indices of family background. For example, the more selective the college, the higher is the average income of parents;[26] the more advanced is the educational level of parents, and the smaller is the proportion of blacks or American Indians among entering students.[27] However, the greater the selectivity, the greater the proportion of Asians among entering students.[28]

None of these observations are particularly startling in light of the historic and well-documented relationship between socio-economic status and college entrance.[29, 30] Apparently, some changes in these patterns are occurring;[31] however, the social class structure in this country continues to be directly reflected in the hierarchy of selectivity of collegiate institutions.* Even so, the less selective the institution, the larger is the array of social class backgrounds among its students.

Several generalizations can be drawn from the preceding descriptions of students at less-selective institutions. They can be summarized as follows:

> The less selective the college the lower (a) the average measured ability levels, (b) the typical parents' socio-economic status, and (c) the level of most students' educational aspiration; and the greater the variability of these same attributes among enrolled students. Thus, the less selective the institution the greater the diversity among the enrolled students, and the greater the emphasis on rank in class and test scores in admissions decisions.

Applying for Admission

The foregoing description of less-selective colleges, their admissions processes, and their students provides some obvious clues about how students decide which colleges to apply to. But the relationship between institutional selectivity and certain student

---

*This reflection occurs not because highly selective institutions exclude students from lower class backgrounds by intent. But income, parents' education and other indices of socioeconomic status have a positive relationship with the indices of achievement used as criteria for admission.

characteristics oversimplifies the dynamics of the process that culminates in a matriculation decision. For example, some exceptional students from lower-class backgrounds are admitted to and enroll in highly-selective institutions and some exceptional students from high socioeconomic status backgrounds enroll in colleges with an open-admissions policy. Why do these and other deviations from the typical patterns of enrollment occur? Moreover, given the large number of less-selective colleges to attend, how and why do particular students choose a particular institution?

Choosing a College as a Decision-Making Process. The phrase "choosing a college" implies that someone has the authority and responsibility for making that decision. It implies that there are alternative colleges from which to choose. Lastly, it implies that there is a "right" college or a collection of "right" colleges for each prospective collegian. Each of these implications is inherent in decision-making theory and career planning.*

Who Chooses? Although students who responded to Astin's survey[33] indicated that relatives, teachers, counselors, peers, and college representatives influenced their choice of a college, it appears that students typically have the authority and responsibility to choose which colleges they will apply to and attend. Some support for this conclusion comes from the respondents' indications of their reasons for going to college and for selecting the college in which they ultimately enrolled. Depending on the selectivity of the colleges and universities in which they were enrolled, between 25 and 32 percent of the students reported that one of the very important reasons for attending college was that their "parents wanted me to go." In contrast, less than 10 percent of the same students reported that a very important reason for selecting the particular institution they ultimately attended was that "relatives wanted me to come here." But this is scant evidence about who makes the choice.

---

* Readers interested in learning more about various decision theories as they apply to vocational decision-making are urged to read Jepsen and Dilley's review of such theories and their cited sources.[32]

Parent-child relationships are important determinants of who makes the decision. Sons and daughters who have established or are establishing their independence from their parents and are progressing toward "mature heterosexual and peer relationships, confident pursuit of a vocation, or a sense of identity,"[34] are likely to be allowed to make their own choice. In turn, establishing independence or self-identity can be either impeded or facilitated by autocratic,* democratic, or laissez-faire parents.[35-37]

Authoritarian parents would be less likely to allow students to choose their college. On the other hand, laissez-faire parents would be more likely to allow their offspring autonomy in the process, whether or not the child was capable of or ready to make such a decision. Democratic parents would play an important role in the process, trying to help their child make the correct decision, but retaining ultimate authority over the choice. It might also be speculated that both laissez-faire and democratic parents would turn authoritarian if their offspring were leaning toward a college or university that did not satisfy their expectations and aspirations for that child. It is unknown how often struggles develop between authoritarian parents and their children over who is to choose the college, nor is it known who wins such struggles and why. Also, it is unclear how often sons and daughters of laissez-faire parents experience debilitating psychological problems or symptoms because their parents will not help them or make the decision for them. The psychodynamics of strained parent-child relationships may, in fact, constitute major impediments to choosing a college.

Other conflicts between parents and children can occur. For example, the power of both parents and peers to influence educational aspirations is well documented,[39] and conflicts between parental expectations and peer expectations often develop as adolescents displace their allegiance from parents to peers. When stu-

---

* Autocratic parents "tell" their children what to do, for example, "you will go to X college." Laissez-faire parents act just the opposite. Elder and Bowerman further define "democratic child-rearing practices" as those where the adolescent freely participates in discussions of issues relevant to his behavior and may even make decisions, but where parents retain ultimate control."[38]

dents who would qualify for admission to a more-selective institution express preference for a less-selective institution in opposition to their parents' wishes, intense conflicts can occur, particularly when the students' preferences are related to the enrollment or expected enrollment of friends at the less-selective colleges. Furthermore, the intensity of the conflict between parent and child may vary according to the selectivity of the choices of the two parties. When the conflict is over two equally selective (and therefore between roughly equally prestigious) institutions, the less intense the conflict might be. But whatever the intensity of the conflict between parent and child, struggles over who is to make the decision may, for some college-bound students, rekindle psychological issues from earlier life.

Freedom of Choice. Regardless of who chooses the college, absolute freedom of choice is restricted by the selectivity of even less-selective colleges, by the cost of college, and by the location of institutions. Students do not apply for admission to college willy-nilly. For example, most students apply to fewer than three colleges,[40] and about three-quarters of all students are admitted to and enroll in their preferred or first-choice institution.[41] Of course, surveys reveal that the more selective the colleges in which collegians ultimately enrolled, the more colleges and universities those students originally applied to; some students applied to as many as six or seven. But the prevailing pattern of relatively few applications suggests that some sorting and selection occurs before applications for admission are completed and mailed.

Selectivity. Clearly, all institutions are beneficiaries of considerable self-selection by high school graduates. Admission policies, average high school grades and average test scores of previous entering classes are routinely made public by the majority of colleges and universities.[42-44] Particularly for the less-selective institutions who admit students primarily on the basis of rank in class, there is little mystery associated with the admissions decision. Consequently, most applicants to less-selective institutions are apparently able to judge their admissibility before making application.

Nevertheless, it is the rare applicant who can meet the admissions criteria at all colleges and universities. The less well candidates have done in high school academic subjects, on admissions tests, and in out-of-class activities, the greater are the effects of selectivity on their freedom to choose.

Costs. The cost of attending college places additional restrictions on the freedom to choose. Few parents and students have access to unlimited financial resources. Consequently, cost can generally be cited as a major restriction on freedom of choice.

But do students choose a less-selective institution because it costs less to attend? Or, how sensitive are parents and students to price and cost differences among institutions of differing selectivity? There is no agreed-upon answer to this question, though some students cite cost as a major consideration in their choice of a college.

For example, students who responded to Astin's survey[45] and who were enrolled in public colleges and universities were two to three times as likely to cite low tuition as a very important reason for selecting their college than were students in private colleges and universities. Even so, no more than 20 percent of those enrolled in public colleges and universities reported that low tuition was an important factor in their choice. A similar finding was reported by the American College Testing Program,[46] although, in this case, close to 50 percent of students at public colleges and universities reported that low cost was a major consideration in their choice. Still another survey of college-bound high school seniors[47] and their parents found that parents were generally unable to estimate accurately what it would cost for their children to attend college, even after a college had been chosen. The results of these surveys suggest that while financing college is a concern of most students,[48] it may not be decisive in choosing a particular college. It may be speculated that most colleges considered by students are within their parents' resources and that other institutions, some of which might be affordable when all expenses and student aid have been calculated, are excluded from consideration.

But the sensitivity of parents and students to price and cost differences within and among institutions of varying selectivity has yet to be determined.*

This exclusion process does not mean that some parents of students at less-selective colleges do not have major financial problems nor does it mean that there is almost no conflict between these students and their parents over money. Students at less-selective public colleges who reported low cost as a major reason for enrolling there may be reflecting their parents' *unwillingness* as well as their *inability* to pay for a more-selective institution or a similar private institution. It has been shown, in fact, that parents' willingness to contribute to their son's or daughter's college expenses is inversely related to income.[53] Less wealthy parents expect to contribute proportionately more of their income to student tuition, room and board than the more wealthy.** Students with the greatest need for financial assistance, those who are increasingly well served by federal, state, and institutional aid programs,[54] tend to enroll in the less-selective public institutions.[55] This means that some students who could be admitted to more-selective colleges and universities or to a private institution of similar selectivity may nevertheless enroll in a public institution because of their parents' unwillingness to make a larger contribution to their expenses. It is not certain how often this unwillingness dictates which college a student attends, but when it does, it could affect students of families on all income levels. In any case, it is safe to say that the lower the parents' income, the greater the influence cost may have on choice of a college.

Location of the College. It is not clear that the distance from the students' homes to various colleges restricts their freedom to choose a college. It is known, however, that the homes of well over 80 percent of recent college entrants were within 500 miles of the

---

* For studies of demand for higher education see Carlson,[49] The National Commission on Financing Postsecondary Education,[50] Radner and Miller,[51] and Weathersby and Jackson.[52]
** What parents *expect* to give with relation to what respected economists claim they *can* give is an index of willingness.

campus.[56, 57] Given the relative density of less-selective colleges in each state compared to the sparsity of highly-selective colleges, it would seem likely that some students who are eligible for admission to more-selective colleges may apply to a less-selective one because it is closer to their home. Even most students at highly-selective institutions lived within 500 miles of their college. This is particularly true for highly-selective *public* universities, only 7 percent of whose entering students lived more than 500 miles away. At private, highly-selective Catholic four-year colleges less than 7 percent of the 1976 entrants lived farther away than 500 miles. Between 18 to 36 percent of the students at highly-selective private universities lived more than 500 miles from the campus. Consequently, relatively few students travel farther than 500 miles to attend college, even among those who attend the relatively scarce highly-selective colleges and universities. Of course, it is not certain that students and parents limit their search for a college to those within 500 miles. It may be that they seriously consider colleges and universities farther away and simply tend to enroll in colleges closer to home for some reason other than the distance, such as expense implications, convenience, and wanting to maintain contact with friends. But, whatever the reasons, the data suggest that the location of colleges, like their selectivity and cost, limits the freedom to choose a college.

How do the limits on freedom to choose interact? Answers may be forthcoming from a study of the impact of student financial aid on choice being conducted at the Higher Education Research Institute in Los Angeles, California. C. E. Christian recently published some results of the study.[58] Among other findings, she reported that if the choice is between two public institutions, students tend to enroll at the college that is less selective, closer to home, and smaller. If the choice is between two private institutions, students tend to enroll in the smaller, more-selective college somewhat farther from home. In either case, the student will attend the college that offers the largest amount of student aid.

One from among Many. Most students can choose from a

considerable number of colleges that are within 500 miles of home, that offer their intended course of study, that are within their financial means, and to which they can be admitted. How and why is one finally selected? Most of what is known is related to the question of why rather than how, and relatively little study has been made of the process of choosing a college. Hence, the following discussion is necessarily speculative and applies aspects of the utility-expectancy theories of decision-making.[59-62] Drastically oversimplified, these theories suggest that there are three elements in every decision. The first is predicting the consequences of alternative decisions (in this situation, the consequences of attending different colleges), the second involves attaching a value to each consequence (such as determining its relative importance) and the third is choosing the alternative with the optimal combination of positively and negatively valued consequences. Each of these three elements, predicting the future, rating the importance of various consequences, and synthesizing both the consequences and their value, is troublesome to students with a choice problem.*

Predicting the Future. One of the major difficulties encountered by students lies in estimating the probability that various consequences will occur if they enroll in each college they are considering. Obviously, all kinds of things could happen to them at each college. So how do they identify the consequences of particular concern to them?

The consequences about which they express the most concern are related to their reasons for attending college in the first place: their educational and career goals, their opportunities for social contacts, financial considerations, location of the college and its size.[66] Although it is doubtful that students and parents literally sit down to enumerate all the possible consequences of attending a number of colleges, students *are* able to indicate why they have chosen a particular college.

Often cited reasons for choosing a college can be translated

---

* Each of these elements is related to diagnosis in counseling. See Crites[63, 64], and Patterson.[65]

into predictions about the consequences of attending different colleges. Earlier research by Richards and Holland[67] suggests that most reasons can be placed in one of five categories. Four of the five categories and some predictive interpretations are provided below:

Intellectual Reputation:	"If I attend I'll get a good or excellent education so I can get a better job, study what I want to study, make more money, or go to graduate school."*
Social Climate:	"I will find the social opportunities satisfactory. I can date, make new friends and so on."
Financial Consideration:	"I will not have to worry about money, or work too many hours, or take out a loan, or strap my parents."
Location and Size:	"I will feel better closer to (or farther away from) home, my parents, and my friends. I will get lost at a large university (or I will be uncomfortable at a small college)."

The fifth category of reasons cited for attending a particular college involves some miscellaneous factors that are also related to the future but are difficult to interpret. For example, "advice of parents, information provided by a teacher or counselor, or advice of someone who attends the college, or a campus visit" may mean a variety of things. But the most likely interpretation is that these factors are additional sources for predictions about the future or

* Each of these is also a reason frequently cited for going to college.[68]

for confirmations of predictions already made by the student.

In addition to identifying the consequences of attending different colleges, students estimate the probability that each consequence will occur at each college considered. For example, they may say "If I go to X college, I am guaranteed to receive some financial aid, but if I go to Y college it is unlikely I will receive financial aid." Each consequence may have a different probability of occurring at each college. Hence, the predictions can become difficult.

This difficulty may be magnified if the information on which the predictions are based is inaccurate or incomplete. That is, the accuracy of predictions may be a function of what students know about themselves and about their prospective colleges.

How much do students know about themselves? Or, asked another way, "How much progress have college-bound students made toward establishing their own identities?" Most students are progressing, sometimes not so smoothly, toward developing competencies, managing emotions, developing autonomy, establishing identities, freeing interpersonal relationships, developing purpose, and developing integrity.[69] They seem to have a reasonably accurate picture of their academic abilities, their skills, their interests, and have made at least tentative educational and career goals.

Students enrolled in less-selective institutions have rated themselves below average on various abilities, skills, and personal attributes. The more selective the institution the greater the proportion of 1976 entrants who rated themselves above average in academic ability, athletic ability, artistic ability, cheerfulness, drive to achieve, leadership ability, mathematical ability, mechanical ability, originality, physical attractiveness, popularity; popularity with the opposite sex, public-speaking ability, intellectual self-confidence, social self-confidence, sensitivity to criticism, and understanding of others.[70] Self-ratings on defensiveness, political conservatism, political realism, and stubbornness appear to be independent of institutional selectivities. Deviations from the above patterns were most likely to be reported by men at public institu-

133

tions with regard to cheerfulness, originality, physical attractiveness, popularity with the opposite sex, social self-confidence and understanding others. Of course, the actual realtionship between these self-ratings and the way others would rate the students is unknown (although the earlier discussion of academic accomplishments and aspirations suggests some degree of accuracy). If the ratings were accurate it would be possible to conclude that students bound for less-selective colleges are as knowledgeable about themselves as students bound for more-selective colleges, and, furthermore, that they are not differentially impeded by lack of self-knowledge in making predictions about the future.

Certainly, some students overestimate their abilities and skills, some underestimate them, some have diffused interests and uncertain or unrealistic goals,[71, 72] and still others have neuroses and psychoses.[73] In fact, whole groups of professionals, such as counselors, school psychologists, and some psychotherapists, are devoted to helping young people with their problems. But by and large, most college-bound youth know a great deal about themselves even though they may be uncertain about the accuracy of their knowledge. Both uncertainty and deficiencies in self-knowledge can affect the accuracy of their predictions about the future.

In addition to knowledge about themselves, students with a choice problem need accurate, reliable, and complete information about colleges for accurate predictions. According to students, colleges and universities do not always provide the information needed to make accurate predictions.[74] A recent survey by Mary Kinnick[75] found that college-bound high school students expressed a need for the following information: admissions policies and criteria, costs, financial aid available, physical surroundings, social life and activities, teachers and instructors, support services (housing, counseling, study-skills laboratories), school reputation, programs of study available, consequences of attending, other characteristics of the college, and a miscellaneous category which included the jobs and careers graduates pursued after graduating. Reasonably accurate predictions about the future must be based on information from institutions *and* students' knowledge about themselves.

Values. Students bound for less-selective institutions also face a problem determining how important the consequences of their choices will be for them. They place different values upon each of the factors involved in their choice of colleges. For example, some students would consider the location of the college more important than its academic reputation. Others would reverse the importance of the two factors. Not all consequences are equally valued by all students. Nor is the likelihood of experiencing desirable or undesirable consequences equal at all colleges. Sounds complicated? Think of the students and parents who are trying to predict the future and determine which consequences are most important to them.

These differing values are why Alexander Astin's group and the American College Testing Program, among others, routinely ask students what are the major factors or most important factors in the choice of a college. Kinnick's survey[76] revealed that college-bound students in Oregon ranked eleven factors in the following order of importance to their decision-making process:

1. Information about jobs and careers after graduation
2. Program of study
3. Costs
4. Availability of support services (housing, counseling, study-skills laboratories, etc.)
5. Teachers and instructors
6. Results of attending
7. Admissions policies
8. Physical surroundings
9. Financial aid available and other characteristics of the school (tied)
10. Reputation of the school
11. Social life and activities

Her rankings were based on averages; different students would rank different factors in different orders of importance.

Are college-bound students certain about what is most important to them? Not according to some unpublished results of yet another survey.[77] When students were asked by Mary W. Settle to rate the importance of a list of factors similar to the one above in a paired-comparison, forced-choice scheme* their ratings were inconsistent. Consequently, her data suggest that placing relative values on various predicted consequences of attending college is a major problem for most college-bound students.

Choosing One. Even when students are able to predict the consequences of attending various colleges and are able to attach a value to each, they encounter another problem when forced to identify the college with the optimal combination of valued consequences. Synthesizing these predicted consequences and their values is a problem that has been classified as "indecision" or "indecisiveness." "Indecision," used in this context, might be defined as the lack of ability to synthesize the predictions and the values in order to choose one college from among several. "Indecisiveness," for purposes of this research, might be defined as the presence of other problems, such as conflict between parents and children, fear of failure, anxiety and depression, that prevent students from making a decision. Both "indecision" and "indecisiveness" can motivate college-bound students to seek help from parents, peers, counselors, teachers, and relatives. With or without this help students may choose a college based on their "achievement needs."

Atkinson and Feather[78] and others would view the choice of a college as a risk-taking behavior, which it is, since predictions about the future are imperfect. Consequently, the choice of a college in terms of its selectivity may be determined by students' need to achieve (succeed) and their need to avoid failure. All applicants have both needs, but one need dominates choice behavior. It has been demonstrated that persons with a dominant need to achieve will choose a course of action, like the choice of a college, in which their predictions will have a 50–50 chance of coming true. On the

---

* A method of testing which compels the subject to make a choice between relatively unacceptable alternatives.

other hand, persons with a dominant need to avoid failure choose a course of action in which their predictions are either virtually guaranteed or virtually nil. The application of Atkinson and his colleagues' work to the choice of a college may partially account for the enrollment of exceptional students in less-selective colleges and may also explain why some students who barely meet the admissions criteria of a college will enroll there, nevertheless. If the needs to achieve or to avoid failure do play a role in choosing a college, these needs probably partially account for the tendency of students to apply to a few colleges with similar admissions policies.* Nonetheless, students claim that they frequently encounter considerable difficulties in obtaining the information that would help them predict the consequences of attending different colleges.

The Bottom Line. Are students able to predict accurately the consequences of attending different colleges, to place values on these consequences and to weigh all this to make a rational decision? Do students choose the "right" college?

Based on transfer rates from one institution to another and the relatively large attrition rates** among college students, it would appear that many students do not make a correct choice.[79-81] But Astin[82] has stated that "Among the four-year colleges and universities, selectivity has no systematic relationship to persistence, after controlling for the drop-out proneness of entering freshmen, their financial aid, work status, and residence." Astin reported that the most frequently cited reasons for dropping out include boredom with courses; financial difficulties; marriage, pregnancy, or other family responsibilities; poor grades; and dissatisfaction with requirements and regulations.[83] Perhaps these drop-outs underestimated the value of these consequences when choosing a college or

---

* Senior Author's Note: While this observation may be true of some groups of students, the personal experiences of Sacks and Wells suggest that those with a need to achieve, and who indeed are competent scholars, might very well apply to as many as a half dozen highly-selective colleges with similar admissions policies.

** Attrition is defined in terms of transfer and discontinuance of education. Follow-up of drop-out students has been a difficult task, but offers the uncertain evidence that within seven years most earn a degree.

made inaccurate predictions about them. It is, of course, equally plausible that these students' values and objectives may have changed[84] and that their original college choice was rational, that is, consistent with their predictions and values at the time.

According to one longitudinal study of the choice process,[85] about two-thirds of the college-bound students represented in the sample made original rational choices. That is, according to the researcher's definition of rationality, most students enrolled in a college with the optimal combination of valued consequences for them. But one-third did not. If the study is sound, about 300,000 students make the "wrong" choice each year!

Some Concluding Observations

This chapter intentionally focuses on how and why students enter less-selective colleges, and what kinds of problems they encounter in the decision-making process. However, there are several topics that were not addressed because so little is known about them. For example, how do parents with unrealistically high aspirations for their son or daughter react to the inability of their offspring to gain admission to more-selective colleges even when the institutions are not *highly* selective? Similarly, students' reactions to rejection by less-selective colleges are largely unexplored even though very few students, less than 5 percent, enroll at a college simply because they were not accepted anywhere else.[86] There is still much to learn about the process of choosing a college.

We might conclude from the information reviewed in this chapter that:

1. There is some evidence to suggest that about one-third of college-bound students make an inappropriate college choice.
2. Most students limit their applications to colleges where they will be admitted, and the vast majority of students

(over 70 percent at even less-selective colleges) enroll in the college they preferred to attend.[87]

3. The major problem—choice—encountered by students bound for less-selective institutions implies three other problems: predicting the consequences of attending different colleges, placing values on these consequences, and synthesizing the predictions and values to make that choice.

4. Most students bound for less-selective institutions do not experience considerable anxiety in the choosing process because they can accurately judge their chances of being admitted and because the institutions' admission decisions are conveyed to the student without much delay.

For some of the students, the process of choosing to enroll in one of the less-selective colleges may carry with it recognition of the fact that they will not be attending the highly-ranked institutions with their greater prestige, opportunities for learning with nationally recognized figures, implied preferential treatment later in the job market, and seemingly easier access to postgraduate education. But for most students, applying to a less-selective college is a matter of course, given their family expectations, secondary-school traditions, and the character of the community and region. Hence, most students do not compare themselves to their peers who may apply to the most-selective institutions. The self-regard of this vast majority of high school students does not appear ever to be tested since the correctness of their predictions for acceptance spares them the duress experienced by those who apply to the highly-ranked colleges, thus allowing them to adapt easily to the reality of their future early in the senior year. Yet, like the applicants to the highly-ranked colleges, they must sort out their goals and objectives and clarify their relationships with parents and peers. They make the same dynamic moves toward independence and emancipation even though the external manifestations of their conflicts may be less apparent than what is observable in aspirants for admission at the most-selective colleges. Is it possible that the process of expectable admission to the less-selective institutions associated with a relatively low level of student anxiety limits "working through" of the separation from home and contributes then to the high attrition rates in college and to the large numbers who have made inappropriate college choices?*

* Senior Author's Note: This tentative but important hypothesis seemingly contradicts Astin's earlier statement that the selectivity of the four-year institution has no systematic relationship to student persistence. However, the empiric observation of students attending the most selective four-year institutions demonstrates comparatively low attrition rates that are largely connected to internal conflict.

REFERENCES

1. *Assessing Students on the Way to College*, Vol. Two, The American College Testing Program. College Student Profiles: Norms for the ACT Assessment (Iowa City, Iowa: 1972), pp. 197–198.

2. Alexander W. Astin, Margo R. King, and Gerald T. Richardson, *The American Freshman: National Norms for Fall 1976*. Laboratory for Research in Higher Education, The Graduate School of Education, University of California (Los Angeles: undated), pp. 62 and 76.

3. Robert K. Bain and James G. Anderson, "School Context and Peer Influences on the Educational Plans of Adolescents," *The Review of Educational Research*, Vol. 44 (1974), pp. 429–445.

4. Alexander W. Astin, *et al.*, *op. cit.*, pp. 8 and 12.

5. The American College Testing Program, *College Planning/Search Book, 1976–77 edition* (Iowa City, Iowa: 1976).

6. E. Alden Dunham, *Colleges of the Forgotten Americans: A Profile of State Colleges and Regional Universities* (New York: McGraw-Hill, 1969).

7. Eugene C. Lee and Frank M. Bowen, *The Multicampus University: A Study of Campus Governance* (New York: McGraw-Hill, 1971).

8. Harold L. Hodgkinson, *Institutions in Transition: A Profile of Change in Higher Education* (New York: McGraw-Hill, 1971).

9. Fred F. Harcleroad, C. Theodore Molen, Jr., and John R. Rayman, "The Regional State Colleges and Universities Enter the 1970's," *ACT Special Report Ten* (Iowa City, Iowa: The American College Testing Program, 1973).

10. The American College Testing Program, 1976, *op. cit.*

11. W. John Mintner and Howard R. Bowen, *Private Higher Education, Third Annual Report on the Financial and Educational Trends in the Private Sector of American Higher Education* (Washington, D.C.: Association of American Colleges, 1977), p. 29.

12. *Ibid.*, p. 65.

13. The National Center for Education Statistics. *The Condition of Education, 1976 edition* (Washington, D.C.: U.S. Government Printing Office, 1976a), p. 95.

14. The National Center for Education Statistics. *The Condition of Education, 1977 edition* (Washington, D.C.: U.S. Government Printing Office, 1977), p. 17.

15. Carol Van Alstyne. Tuition: "Analysis of Recent Policy Recommendations," in K. E. Young, ed., *Exploring the Case for Low Tuition in Public Higher Education* (Washington, D.C.: American Association of Community and Junior Colleges, American Association of State Colleges and Universities, and National Association of State Universities and Land Grant Colleges, 1974).

16. Howard R. Bowen and W. John Minter, *Private Higher Education, First Annual Report on Financial and Educational Trends in the Private Sector of American Higher Education* (Washington, D.C.: Association of American Colleges, 1975).

17. Lawrence L. Leslie and Gary P. Johnson, "Equity and the Middle Class," in K. E. Young, ed., *Exploring the Case for Low Tuition in Public Higher Education* (Washington, D.C.: American Association of Community and Junior Colleges, American Association of State Colleges and Universities and National Association of State Universities and Land Grant Colleges, 1974).

18. Howard R. Bowen and W. John Minter, *op. cit.*, p. 65.

19. The National Center for Education Statistics. *Projections of Education Statistics to 1984–85* (Washington, D.C.: U.S. Government Printing Office, 1976b), p. 104.

20. Alexander W. Astin, *et al.*, *op. cit.*

21. *Ibid.*, pp. 61 and 75.

22. The American College Testing Program, 1976, *op. cit.*, p. 11.

23. John L. Holland and James M. Richards, Jr., "Academic and Nonacademic Accomplishment: Correlated or Uncorrelated," *ACT Research Report No. 2* (Iowa City, Iowa: The American College Testing Program, 1965).

24. Alexander W. Astin, *et al.*, *op. cit.*, pp. 65 and 79.

25. The American College Testing Program, 1976, *op. cit.*, pp. 65 and 79.

26. *Ibid.*, pp. 62 and 76.

27. *Ibid.*, pp. 68 and 82.

28. *Ibid.*, pp. 61 and 75.

29. Robert K. Bain and James G. Anderson, *op. cit.*

30. National Center for Education Statistics, 1976a, *op. cit.*, pp. 77–81, 220.

31. Lawrence L. Leslie, "Higher Education Opportunity: A Decade of Progress," *ERIC/Higher Education Research Report No. 3* (Washington, D.C.: ERIC Clearinghouse on Higher Education, George Washington University, 1977).

32. David A. Jepsen and Josiah S. Dilley, "Vocational Decision-making Models: A Review and Comparative Analysis," *The Review of Educational Research*, Vol. 44, 1974, 331–349.

33. Alexander W. Astin, et. al., *op. cit.*, pp. 64 and 78.

34. John J. Conger, "A World They Never Knew: The Family and Social Change," in Graubard, S. R., ed., *Twelve to Sixteen: Early Adolescence, Daedalus*, Fall, 1971, p. 1125.

35. Charles E. Bowerman and Glen H. Elder, "Variations in Adolescent Perception of Family Power Structure," *American Sociological Review*, Vol. 29, 1964, 551–567.

36. Glen H. Elder, Jr., "Structural Variations in Child Rearing Relationship," *Sociometry*, Vol. 25, 1962, 241–262.

37. Erik H. Erikson, *Identity: Youth and Crisis* (New York: W. W. Norton, 1968).

38. Charles E. Bowerman and Glen H. Elder, *op. cit.*

39. Robert K. Bain and James G. Anderson, *op. cit.*

40. Alexander W. Astin, *et al.*, *op. cit.*, pp. 65 and 79.

41. *Ibid.*, pp. 64 and 78.

42. Barron's Profiles of American Colleges, *Descriptions of the Colleges.* Vol. 1 (Woodbury, New York: Barron's Educational Series, Inc., 1976).

43. James Cass and Max Birnbaum, *Comparative Guide to American Colleges, Seventh Edition* (New York: Harper and Row, 1975).

44. The College Entrance Examination Board, *The College Handbook* (New York: 1975).

45. Alexander W. Astin, *et al.*, *op. cit.*, pp. 64 and 78.

46. The American College Testing Program, 1972, *op. cit.*, pp. 225–227.

47. Philip R. Rever, William Goggin, and Joseph Henry, *Socioeconomic Influences on the Educational Career Paths of Kentucky High School Seniors, A Report to the Kentucky Higher Education Assistance Authority* (Iowa City, Iowa: The American College Testing Program, 1973).

48. Alexander W. Astin, *et al.*, *op. cit.*, pp. 69 and 83.

49. Daryl Carlson, "Student Price Consumer Coefficients for Grants, Loans, Work-Study Aid, and Tuition Changes: An Analysis of Student Surveys." A paper presented to the Policy Development Group, Office of the Assistant Secretary of Education, Department of Health, Education and Welfare (Washington, D.C.: November 13, 1973).

50. The National Commission on Financing Postsecondary Educa-

tion, *Financing Postsecondary Education in the United States* (Washington, D.C.: U.S. Government Printing Office, 1973).

51. Roy Radner and Leonard Miller, *Demand and Supply in U.S. Higher Education* (New York: McGraw-Hill, 1975).

52. George B. Weathersby and Gregory A. Jackson, "Individual Demand for Higher Education—A Review and Analysis of Recent Empirical Studies," *Journal of Higher Education*, Vol. 46, 1975, 623–652.

53. James E. Nelson, "Are Parents Expected to Pay Too Much?" *The College Board Review*, Vol. 92, Summer 1974, pp. 10–15.

54. Lawrence L. Leslie, *op. cit.*

55. Alexander W. Astin, *et al., op. cit.*, pp. 70–73, 84–87.

56. *Ibid.*, pp. 63 and 77.

57. National Center for Education Statistics, 1967a, *op. cit.*, pp. 99 and 233.

58. C. E. Christian, "Studies of the Impact of Student Financial Aid Programs," A paper presented to the National Association of Student Financial Aid Administrators Annual Conference (New Orleans, Louisiana: July 7, 1977) mimeograph.

59. Ward H. Edwards, Harold Lindman, and Lawrence Phillips, "Emerging Technologies for Making Decisions," In *New Directions in Psychology, II* (New York: Holt, Rinehart & Winston, 1965).

60. Harry B. Gelatt, "Information and Decision Theories Applied to College Choice and Planning," *Preparing School Counselors in Educational Guidance* (New York: College Entrance Examination Board, 1967).

61. Harry B. Gelatt and R. B. Clarke, "Role of Subjective Probabilities in the Decision Process," *Journal of Counseling Psychology*, Vol. 14, 1967, pp. 332–341.

62. Eugene C. Lee and Frank M. Bowen, *op. cit.*

63. John O. Crites, "Career Counseling: Then, Now, and What's Next?," *The Counseling Psychologist*, Vol. 4, 1974, pp. 3–23.

64. John O. Crites, "Career Counseling: A Comprehensive Approach," *The Counseling Psychologist*, Vol. 6, 1976, pp. 2–12.

65. C. H. Patterson, *Theories of Counseling and Psychotherapy* (New York: Harper and Row, 1966).

66. James M. Richards, Jr., and John L. Holland, "A Factor Analysis of Student 'Explanations' of Their Choice of a College," *ACT Research Report No. 8* (Iowa City, Iowa: The American College Testing Program, 1965).

67. *Ibid.*

68. Alexander W. Astin, *et al., op. cit.*, pp. 64 and 78.

69. Arthur W. Chickering, *Education and Identity* (San Francisco: Jossey-Bass Inc., 1969).

70. Alexander W. Astin, *et al., op. cit.*, pp. 63 and 78.

71. Arthur W. Chickering, *op. cit.*

72. Joseph Katz, *et al., No Time for Youth* (San Francisco: Jossey-Bass, 1968).

73. Graham B. Blaine, Jr., and Charles C. McArthur, eds., *Emotional Problems of the Student* (New York: Appleton-Century-Crofts, 1971).

74. Mary S. Carlson with Chip Berlet, eds., *The Options Handbook:*

Communicating with Prospective Students about Postsecondary Education (Washington, D.C.: The National Student Educational Fund, 1976).

75. Mary Kinnick, *Information for Prospective Students about Postsecondary Education: A Partial Assessment of Need* (Portland, Oregon: Office of Planning and Institutional Research, Portland State University, 1975).

76. *Ibid.*

77. Mary W. Settle, *A Longitudinal Exploration in College Choice Decision-Making*, Unpublished thesis submitted to the Graduate College, The University of Iowa, 1974.

78. John W. Atkinson and Norman T. Feather, eds., *The Theory of Achievement Motivation* (New York: Wiley & Sons, 1966).

79. Robert Cope and William Hannah, *Revolving College Doors: The Cause and Consequences of Dropping Out, Stopping Out, and Transferring* (New York: Wiley, 1975).

80. Alexander W. Astin, *Preventing Students from Dropping Out* (San Francisco: Jossey-Bass, 1975).

81. The National Center for Education Statistics, 1977, *op. cit.*, p. 186.

82. Alexander W. Astin, *op. cit.*, p. 122.

83. *Ibid.*, p. 15.

84. Kenneth A. Feldman and Theodore M. Newcomb, *The Impact of College on Students. Volume 1. An Analysis of Four Decades of Research* (San Francisco: Jossey-Bass, 1969).

85. Mary W. Settle, *op. cit.*

86. Alexander W. Astin, *et al.*, *op. cit.*, pp. 64 and 78.

87. *Ibid.*

HOWARD B. LONDON

The Perils of Opportunity: The Working-Class Community College Student in Sociological Perspective

According to Howard London, students come to the community college to escape and to make it in America. He looks at the students' class culture, how they feel and live within it and the consequences of bringing those attitudes and experiences into the context of community college life. He views the discontent and seemingly deviant and recalcitrant behavior of working-class students as an adaptive response to an unhealthy social situation.

His research sheds new light on the psychosocial factors that help to determine student transitions to senior-level college, terminal vocational curriculum, or to the work force.

I N T H E F A L L of 1973, on the former site of a county prison, the doors of City Community College opened for the first time to the white, ethnic, working-class students of a major Northeastern city. Like the ancient prison it replaces, the new multi-million-dollar complex turns inward, to buffer the students from the noise of the nearby expressways, rapid-transit lines, railroad yard, and airport: the classrooms are buried, windowless, in the bowels of the building. The outside world is presented only with bleak concrete walls. Two pedestrian overpasses jut like defensible drawbridges from either side of the institution and over them pass persons who are to be changed and returned to society better, more productive citizens. School or prison, the assumption reflected in the architecture is that change requires isolation from some alien and hostile community.

Although the analogy between school and prison, if irresistible, is in some ways heavyhanded, after spending one academic year with the students of City Community College—in their classes, cafeteria, school lounges, bars, and even in their homes—I came away with the conviction that they were indeed participating in a work-release program, only in reverse. Released from their jobs (or, as with some females, from the household chores) these students were coming *to* the institution for a chance to escape and to make it in America.

To understand from what and to what students were escaping, it is necessary to grasp what it meant for them to be working-class people in a middle-class land. I am not talking here of the objective, "hard" indicators of socioeconomic status, although by all conventional standards—parents' education, father's occupation, and family income—these students were indeed working class; rather, I am speaking of class culture. The students' class culture, how they felt about and lived within that culture, and the consequences of feeling and living in that way in the context of the community college, were the "soft" data of this investigation. These data are no less important in sociological study than "hard data"; in this study they were essential to the understanding of the inner life of City Community College.

As do their counterparts across the nation, most City Community College students, whether in a liberal arts or vocational curriculum, had poor academic histories; undoubtedly many of their schools had not served them well. A school administrator estimated that 25 to 30 percent of the student body were denied admission by four-year colleges and universities and another 5 percent had withdrawn from them for academic reasons. She further stated:

> The law enforcement majors were underachievers and had a lot of trouble in high school. Their range of scores on the SAT's was from 200 to 350. The liberal arts people scored higher but the very few who got over 500 or 600 are from your suburban schools. . . . We have maybe 10 or 12 who did that well. But it's the law enforcement kids, they're the group. Most of them are young; they just got out of high school. They're psychological misfits. They mostly failed in school.

In our society, lack of intelligence as conventionally measured by IQ and achievement tests is regarded as the equivalent of personal failure, especially by middle-class teachers and school administrators. In *Blaming the Victim*,[1] William Ryan points out that even liberals, who are more inclined to see contextual effects, ultimately blame the student for poor performance:

> He (the student) is said to contain within himself the causes of his inability to read and write well. The shorthand phrase is "cultural deprivation," which to those in the know conveys what they allege to be inside information: that the poor child carries a scanty pack of cultural baggage as he enters the school. He doesn't know about books and magazines and newspapers, they say. . . . In a word, he is "disadvantaged" and "socially deprived," they say, and this, of course, accounts for his failure (*his* failure, they say) to learn much in school.

Ryan's point is that by attributing society's problems (urban decay, unresponsive educational bureaucracies, poor schools, ill-prepared and overworked teachers) to the individuals affected, these individuals are seen as inferior. They are perceived as lazy, undignified, and morally and psychologically unfit ("psychological misfits").

This is how the students of City Community College labeled themselves. Their working-class faith in the ethic of individualism told them that personal achievement was a matter of self-control, drive, and intelligence, so that what one does with one's life reflects one's personal virtues, flaws, and social worth:

> "My family is real blue-collar," says Frank. "My father works on construction. Now what the hell can he do on a day like this? On the way in, the radio said the wind chill factor is minus ten degrees. Minus ten degrees! He's fifty-five years old; he can't go on in construction much longer. And my mother's family are longshoremen. The [union] card gets passed down. It's a tradition in some families and I know some kids who took a lot of shit because they didn't want the card. Now you take me—I worked in construction for two years after I was out of the army and I'll never forget the first day on the jack-hammer. I came home, my hands all swollen and my body still shaking. After a few weeks you think nothing of it, but [he taps his chest with his finger and widens his eyes] I don't want to do that for the rest of my life! I want to better myself and I want things better for my family, so first I have to better me."
>
> "Ya, I know," says Louie. "What is there to phys ed classes? All you have to do is organize a bunch of kids. Teaching and coaching baseball, I really think that would be a great life. To have a good job, a good family, a nice car, that's all I want. I don't want to be super wealthy, just comfortable without breaking my balls. It's just those damn biology and anatomy courses—I hate those fuckin'

things. If I didn't cheat like a mother I'd never get through. Shit, it would be easy if I was smart."

"Ya, I know what you mean," replies Frank.

As Frank tapped his chest there was anger and fear in the thought that he must become a "better person" to avoid living his father's life. To have a comfortable life Louie cheats his way through examinations in courses he hates but must pass. Both blame themselves for this condition, Frank saying his difficulties stem from not being a "better person," Louie that things would be easy if only he were smart. Their aspirations, therefore, involve more than money: They seek not a job, but a position which to them confers a sense of worth and honor.

It gradually became apparent that students like Frank and Louie were not part of a "deviant lower-class culture pattern," but rather had internalized some general notions of social and economic success and of what it takes to be successful as defined by middle-class people and institutions. The students did doubt, however, that they had the necessary individual attributes to become successful. Indeed, in the following excerpts from students' essays and from my field notes of their conversations, concepts of "failure" and "personal deficiency," though not confirmed and forever ratified, are suspected, so that remorse and disquietude are common themes:

My life began July 22, 1953. I weight 6 and ½ pounds and was 21 inches long.* As a child I enjoyed playing with my playmates and growing up with my family. I started school at the age of 5. School was exciting and wonderful. I had all the friends I ever needed. Then as the years went by it started to become more difficult. It was hard for me to learn and understand the basics of educa-

---

* Errors in spelling and grammar are unchanged in all quotations from students' essays. The essays were written during the first week of school in the social science and English classes required of all students.

tion. My teachers referred to me as a dreamer always in that other world. It was hard to study and conscitrat on the exact work I was doing. I sometimes refer back to the days of my childhood. My childhood was my wonderland of fairyland. I live in a large family with one brother and four sisters. I am presently working at a supermarket where I work parttimes evenings. I have been working there for a year since last November. My hobbies include all sports, but I prefer hockey and baseball the most. I never played any sports in high school probably because I am too small. . . . The reasons I am going to college is to get a better job which pays more money. In college I hope to learn new things and ideas because there is no person that knows everything. The reason I chose City Community College is, well I am not that smart anyways feeling it would be easier to get into a community college rather than, let's say University of —— [a state university]. Another reason is that the school is nearby and is easy to get to. I am in the Business Administration course because I am interested in business. As for my future, at the present time, I am undecided, but there is some fields that interest me such as Accounting and I have always wanted to own my own business. As for my goals, hopes and ideas I have none at the present time.

(From a student's essay)

All during high school coming to college was the furthest thing from my mind. I worked for three years while I was in high school and that really screwed up my grades, but I didn't really care. The money was good, but in a way it was worthless. I still have some nice things I bought, like my stereo, but the rest was just wasted. When I graduated I didn't want to work and like I said, college was the furthest thing from my mind. I didn't do anything except swim during the summer and then I heard about this place. So I wound up here through nobody's fault except my own.

(Conversation after class)

I felt for the past year and still do feel about the uncertainty of my future. I did not think too much of what I was going to do when I got out of high school because at the time, getting out of school did not seem like a reality. I did not take my schoolwork as seriously as I should have and my attendance was poor. It finally hit me one day when I went from a B in Spanish to a F failure for the year. That is when I really started to think. I was off in another world that summer before my senior year in high school. I was thinking very seriously about that failure. . . . I then began to apply to various colleges. I went to my guidance counselor and he helped me a great deal in deciding what colleges were right for me. To five colleges I applied for admittance but all but one refused me. The one I was not rejected at put me on their waiting list. I went back to my guidance advisor and he told me about community and junior colleges and City Community College. He went on to explain that I do have abilities, but that I needed a little more guidance and help than other people which is not easily given at a four-year college but in a Community College it is a general practice. This explains the reason why I am here.

(From a student's essay)

Many students more explicitly compared themselves to senior-college students or to some vague middle-class reference group and in so doing again saw themselves as comparative failures:

AL: "Hey, I got an A on my report."
SEAN: "Yeh? So you want a star on your forehead?"
AL: "Oh man, it was great; he thought I was smart, like I was from ——— [an affluent suburb]."

TOM: "Yeh, or maybe —— or —— [two more affluent suburbs]."

They all smile at this as we enter the classroom together.

(Hallway conversation)

As the following comments illustrate, the students' circumstances and self-doubts led them to appreciate that they had arrived at a critical and fateful juncture in their lives:

Nothing but disappointment has been my past experience so City Community College is my last hope.

(From a student's essay)

Steve told me that he was rejected at two colleges but put on the waiting list at two others, both state colleges. He applied to City Community College in late August and was notified of his acceptance three days later. "Wow! I figured maybe I better not go there. If they took me that fast they're probably getting the bottom of the high school classes. But I knew if I went out working for six months it would be balls to get back in."

(Conversation in the student lounge)

I quit public high school and joined the US Navy. . . . I also completed high school while in the service. My return to civilian life was somewhat a shocking experience. In the Navy, I had not truly considered my future life, and now I was face to face with the responsibility of choosing my future life—freedom. After working several odd jobs, I entered a community college in —— [another city]. Surprisingly, I managed average grades, the first quarter, but I withdrew from the second quarter. I worked for ——, didn't like it and quit. Now I am determined to stay in school. I can't afford not to.

(From a student's essay)

In the face of their concerns and self-doubts it would be logical to expect students to work hard in order to "reestablish" themselves and thereby to maximize their life chances. They were in school, after all, because they had some awareness of the root causes of their anxieties. Yet they did not seize the hour. In class after class it was painfully obvious that reading and writing assignments were most often undone, that students were unwilling to engage in class discussions and that attendance was poor. Indeed, on a typical day more than one-half the student body of 1,103 was absent. The first edition of the student newspaper, published only eight weeks after the start of classes, featured an editorial on absenteeism, the lead sentence reading:

> Believe it or not, a college student has certain recognizable responsibilities. The major responsibility is to actually attend college.

To understand why students followed a course of behavior which diminished the possibility of success as defined by their middle-class, gatekeeping teachers, it is necessary to examine briefly the values and expectations of the vocational and liberal arts faculty of City Community College. The vocational faculty came from the work world to teach secretarial skills, law enforcement, fire prevention and protection, and an elementary sequence in business administration. As "ex-practitioners" they emphasized the memorization of discrete facts and the mastery of various tasks, procedures, and skills. The liberal arts faculty, who taught separate courses for the vocational and college-transfer students, were, in a word, intellectuals. Only three had doctoral degrees, yet almost all had at one time been formally enrolled in a doctoral program, only to withdraw due to the pressure of personal, family, and economic circumstances. It was evident in both interviews and classroom observations, however, that they retained a strong belief in the independent worth and efficacy of working with ideas, and they wanted their students to discover the usefulness and joys of manipulating and synthesizing abstract concepts. Although not unappreciative of the vocational students' aspirations, these teachers did expect students to acquire a broader, more analytic, and flexible view of the human condition and/or a more scientific view of the physical world.

The chief problem for vocational students was that the different values, expectations, and pedagogies of the vocational and liberal arts teachers exacerbated self-doubts concerning mind, intelligence, and limited social mobility. For liberal arts students, intellectualizing implied upward mobility and this status change was both welcomed and feared, as we shall see. Indeed, self-doubts among both groups of students, so intimately linked with social class, created a double bind: suspecting their abilities to work with ideas led them to suspect the worth of working with ideas, yet mind and intelligence were held to be important indicators of worth and character. Regardless of the curriculum, then, academic activity was a problematic feature of community college life, bound as it was with questions about one's fate, one's niche in the social world, and hence about what membership in a status group implied about oneself and about one's social honor. The students' dilemma then was how to define an unfamiliar institution, an institution which on the one hand might be the vehicle for a critical opportunity, but on the other hand might injure them further.

The Male Vocational Students

Vocational classes frequently corresponded very closely with textbook assignments; lectures were often taken from the text and repeated verbatim. Furthermore, in most classes students were given, in advance, the questions and answers to the multiple-choice and true-false examinations. The majority of class time, however, was given to the acquiring of the skills and procedures used in the various occupations for which the students were being trained; so mechanical were some courses that tape recorders replaced human teachers. In the humanistic sense this was not "education," with the emancipation that that implies, but rather a series of mental and physical tasks. Vocational students both liked and resented this approach: while it was a predictable and orderly system within which to work it was also one further reminder of what they thought to be their meager capacities. Students often compared what was wanting in their programs to what they believed to be wanting in themselves, drawing connections between subject matter, pedagogy, and self-definitions:

> Costello asks if Smith (with whom he team teaches) gave back their last exam. When a student answers yes, Costello asks if Smith reviewed the test in class.
>
> DAN: "It was too simple to go over in class." There is no laughter or other response from the class.
>
> As they are dismissed I hear Bob say to Joe: "They give simple tests to simple people. I knew I should have gone into liberal arts."
>
> (A law enforcement class)

These courses, then, presented a moral conflict: to do well required engaging in mechanical behavior incompatible with self, but to do poorly reaffirmed the existential *bête noire* described earlier. The common solution was for students to redefine the institutional definition of doing well in a manner which protected their sense of social honor. This code of honor was expressed through behavior which symbolically put forward to both peers and teachers a claim that one was a person possessed of dignity and self-esteem in that one's unwilling compliance was not cheaply given. Like the threats to self-determination, will, and efficacy which, according to Goffman in *Asylums*,[2] give rise to the resistance and underlife in total institutions, the students' informal code of honor redefined the official expectations "of what they should be putting into and getting out of the organization and, behind this, of what sort of self and world they are to accept for themselves." Specifically, where attendance was expected, absenteeism prevailed; where enthusiasm, low levels of effort; where honesty, cheating.

Before detailing these forms of resistance, one additional factor—the vocational students' experience in their nonvocational courses—must be examined.

By stressing the value of intellectual activity, the liberal arts teachers become, in effect, another reminder of what the vocational students thought to be their own shortcomings. They became wary, then, of their liberal arts teachers as illustrated by the discussion of these three students:

> MIKE: "Edwards is too smart to be teaching here. He should be at a real college. He should be at Harvard or Yale. He even looks that way with his sports coat and patches."
>
> HBL*: "What do you mean?"
>
> MIKE: "He's really intelligent and sometimes I can really get interested in what he's saying, but it doesn't relate to anything. Like I don't know why he's talking about it in the first place. And sometimes he'll be talking and then switch to something completely different and I don't get the connection."
>
> GEORGE: "I think he ought to be someplace else. He's even got his Ph.D."
>
> LARRY: "No, he has his doctorate. He said a couple of times that he was against the war and in radical politics like SDS and that bullshit. I don't hold that against him because he's probably over that. But that and what Mike says about him being intelligent, it just goes to show the difference between him and us."

A similar theme was struck when I asked why a group of business students rolled their eyes and looked pained whenever their government teacher mentioned one of her books:

* The author.

156

SHEILA: "At first I just thought it was interesting because I never knew anyone who wrote a book. But the more she talks about it the more I think she's putting us down. I mean I get angry. It's like saying, 'I wrote this book and you couldn't write a book so you listen to me.'"

PAUL: "It's a holier-than-thou attitude. Any teacher can make you feel that. No matter what you do they always have that over you."

HBL: "Have what over you?"

PAUL: "Their education. Most of my teachers are nice enough people, especially Huber, but they have a way of making you feel like shit at the drop of a hat."

Given these concerns, resistance to the "intellectual" teachers required additional measures: where assignments were to be read and written, they frequently were not; where discussions were anticipated, there was often silence; where classroom decorum and deference were expected, there arose incivility. Let us now turn to these forms of resistance and their functions.

Chronic absence. Absence was seen by some students as a means of dissociating themselves from slavish adherence to official expectations, and as such was often positively redefined:

Len and Don decide to go home even though they have two classes this afternoon. Len wants to work on his car and convinces Don to help him, but not without some coercion. At one point Len said it wasn't "cool" to go to class as much as Don did. I ask what he means and he tells me that if you go to every class you're seen as a "brown-nose," trying to curry the teacher's favor.

(Two law enforcement students)

JERRY: "Mr. Crane asked us how come we're absent so much, so I gave him some crap about working and Tom told him he has mono."

157

HBL: "Why, wasn't that true?"

Jerry says that he only works two nights a week and that Tom does not have mono: "Sometimes I think I don't go because they want me to go. If I went to every class I'd feel like a dope."

I ask why he would feel like a dope.

JERRY: "Nobody goes to every class. You don't have to. You can borrow somebody's notes and besides, I'd be too studious if I did." The word "studious" is said with derision.

(A business administration student)

That students stayed away from classes does not necessarily mean that they stayed away from school. As in most schools, socializing in the lounges, hallways, and cafeteria was a popular pastime; as a class hour approached and a group decided not to attend, their justifications often referred to the defiance of indignities:

After lunch a group of students decide not to go to Pierce's class but to play Ping-Pong in the "pit" (the game room).

BILL: "He's so fuckin' boring. He just stands there with one leg up on the desk and lectures. Why the hell don't he do something interesting? I feel like I'm a writing machine taking down notes on shit."

(A law enforcement student)

I sit with Steve and Ian in the lounge. We talk about hockey until the bell rings. They decide to skip Ashley's (a social science teacher) class. After a few minutes I ask what they think of Ashley.

IAN: "The first week of class she told us about her background, how she taught at some exclusive private school.

It seems the whole semester she's been talking down to us like she was on some kind of platform. A lot of guys don't like that. You can bet your ass that's why we're not in class right now."

Steve agrees.

(Two fire science students)

Alan tells Frank you have to be a "sucker" to go to Robertson's (a business teacher) class more than once a week: "It's just facts, facts, facts. Learn this, learn this, learn this. All you gotta do is find out from somebody what you have to know to pass the module test." He says again that only a sucker goes regularly and that "I'm no sucker."

(A business student)

Low Level of Effort. Not doing reading and writing assignments or volunteering for class discussions was more common in the male vocational students' liberal arts course than in their vocational courses. From their perspective, minimizing effort was not seen as laziness or indifference, but rather as the proper stance to take to avoid self and peer derogation; it was not a question of being unmotivated but of being motivated by interests at odds with teachers' expectations:

A student asks Ryan (a social science teacher) about the book report assignment. Ryan says it is not due for three weeks but he wants them to read it now.

STUDENT: "But I don't want to read it now if I have to report on it later. I'll forget it."

RYAN: "Actually I want you to read all three books now."

The class laughs. . . .

159

As I walk out with Tom and George I ask why they laughed at Ryan's request.

TOM: "I couldn't be a bookworm if I tried." He says he tried to read the first book but it was "weird" and "I didn't understand it." He adds: "So why should I knock myself out?"

I say that if he tries to read the book more slowly it might become clearer. He reminds me of the conversation we had yesterday morning about how it took him a few days to learn to properly use a lathe, and that every time he made a mistake he was embarrassed. "If you had that job and never learned how to use it, wouldn't you be embarrassed?" I say I would and he replies, "Well, I've been going to school for thirteen years and I didn't understand the first chapter of this book." He holds up the book Ryan assigned. "So why should I read chapter two?"

(A business student)

Rock shows me a reprint of an article by Bloom (an English teacher) that was given to everyone in Bloom's class. Their assignment is to read the article and grade it.

ROCK: "He's been giving me C minuses and that's just what I'm going to give him. Why should he get any better than I do? I'll get my thesaurus [he pronounces it "thesaurusis"] and cross out words left and right and use some others like he does." Rock is angry and obviously insulted. "Just look at the title and that will tell you what kind of a guy he is."

He gives me the reprint, points to the title and says, "Translate that for me!"

The title is "Linguistic Camouflage—Euphemisms Are In."

ROCK: "Now who the hell wants to do anything for a turkey like that?"

(A law enforcement student)

LEO: "It's not like I feel superior or snotty myself, but the students here just don't seem to work very hard. I remember when I was in high school we took books home and did some studying. Don't get me wrong—I don't want to give you the impression I study hard. It's like this. The teachers here have a way of emphasizing that tells you what's going to be on a test. The pressure here is minimal. You go to classes, don't you think it's easy? I think you'd find that the opinion of most students here is that it is very easy. You take Smith's class. We have reading assignments, but no one does them. Why should we? He's never asked us a question in class yet. Costello's class is one of my toughest, but even there I don't do much reading. Actually I don't know what effort is anymore. The only way I can tell what effort is, is to see what everybody else is doing and most everybody is doing nothing, so is the little I do effort? . . . I don't feel like I have to compete; the best thing to do is to just get by and to make out OK without putting yourself to the test."

HBL: "What test?"

LEO: "I don't mean a *test* test. I mean getting by without studying. Let's face it, if there was a lot of pressure here most guys wouldn't do good and would have been out by the end of the first semester."

HBL: "Do you mean that there's sort of an unwritten agreement that students won't work hard?"

LEO: "Well, I suppose, but it's not really that. It's more like most guys couldn't do anything hard anyhow. Look, none of us are what you'd call your basic bright student."

161

HBL: "In other words, if nobody really works hard then everybody's safe?"

LEO: "That's right."

(A law enforcement student)

On many occasions I witnessed students helping each other prepare for vocational tests by asking objective questions from a written list. Although this required some involvement with course material, students were careful to avoid giving the impression of being inordinately involved in their work by commenting on the mechanical nature of their preparation in a fashion that dissociated themselves from it:

> I come across John helping Mo prepare for this afternoon's test. John is asking Mo a series of questions that Smith said would be on the exam. Several times Mo answers the questions before John is through asking them. When Mo does this John says, "Holy shit" or "Jesus." At one point John comments that Mo must have read the book carefully. Mo answers he hasn't read the book at all, that he was only concerned with memorizing the answers. He adds: "So there's nothing amazing about it. It didn't take any smarts."
>
> (Two law enforcement students)

> Jerry tells Roberta and me that he is going to take his business module exam next period. I wish him good luck and he says he won't need any because he memorized the answers yesterday with another student and has gone over them again this morning. He shows me the list of questions and I ask him one or two which he readily answers. He comments, "See, nothing to it."

ROBERTA: "Pretty proud of yourself, huh?"

JERRY: "For what? Memorizing this? Anybody could do it."

(Two business students)

Cheating. Cheating was common but not universal. For those who did cheat, it was yet another way of dissociating themselves from their work; implicit in their comments is the idea that while getting by is important, one's work should not be taken too seriously:

TOM: "Man, you gotta cheat to pass this. You can't learn all that shit unless you read the textbook all day. I'll be damned if I'm going to do that."

VINNIE: "There are better ways than that to spend a day unless you're like Ralph and don't mind being a good little boy and doing your homework. I seen him yesterday in the library with his workbook. Shit, I had workbooks in the third grade."

(Two business students)

After class I hear Charlie ask Dom if he cheated. Dom says no and asks Charlie if he did.

CHARLIE: "I had to. I couldn't get into memorizing all that junk."

(Two law enforcement students)

Incivility. Approximately one month after school opened students began injecting *sotto voce* taunts into class lectures and discussions. These indignities were directed at two kinds of teachers—those who taught liberal arts courses and those who taught vocational courses but were clearly identifiable as middle-class persons. For example, law enforcement students did not harass two teachers who were ex-detectives, but they did make life difficult for the lawyer who taught the legal aspects of police work:

Costello (the teacher) begins by saying he wants to discuss a short newspaper article on the death penalty. He reads the article and says, "It would be interesting to discuss the death penalty, wouldn't it?" Three students say "No" rather loudly, look at each other and smile. Costello begins discussing the death penalty as if he hadn't heard their remarks.

A student asks if they should take notes.

COSTELLO: "No. It's not necessary for this material. Just relax."

They do relax. They make a big show of closing their books and stretching out. Costello asks if he has already explained *McCulloch vs. Maryland* to this class. Some say he has, others that he hasn't. Meanwhile they are all smiling at each other; many are fighting laughter. Later Lou tells me he did explain the case before, but that they were just razzing him.

Costello says that under the circumstances just described a suspect cannot be searched. Then he says he has made a mistake, a suspect can be searched. In unison the class says, "Oh-Oh." Their tone is derisive. One student says, "Let's stab him . . . oh!" and clutches his chest. Costello continues, although red-faced. Many of the students are smiling almost joyously at each other, as if they have just pulled a fast one.

Toward the end of the class Costello begins to discuss when a policeman can legally draw a gun. Brian interrupts rather loudly: "There are three times when you can draw a gun."

JOE: "Tell us! [very satirically]"

As Brian recites the three reasons Joe says "Uh-huh"

after each one. It seems that Joe is out to irk both Costello and Brian (who had a reputation as the teacher's pet).

Similarly, fire science students did not taunt their ex-fireman teacher, but they did ridicule their "eastern"-educated chemistry teacher, as in these representative scenes:

> As the class ends she says, "Your assignment is to read pages 129 through 139 in the text." Ron says loudly, "Ya, we'll do that." A few students snicker.

> She asks if they had any difficulty with the homework problems. Someone in the back of the room says very derisively, "Oh no, they were very easy." Laughter.

Of course, law and chemistry are related to police work and fire science, but these courses emphasized "theory" rather than practice. Similar challenging asides frequently punctuated the English, social science, history and math classes. In these classes, taunts usually came as an immediate response to a teacher who either was stressing the value of working with ideas, acting too "intellectual," or, worst of all, disparaging working-class people. In each case, the teacher's remarks were reminders to the students of what they thought to be their own limited capacities and social worth. The students became engaged in a symbolic crusade whereby they could defend their honor by attacking that of their teachers:

> They are reviewing for tomorrow's final exam. At one point Delaney (a math teacher) says: "With the exception of some multiplication problems, we didn't go beyond addition in this course. Oh well." She reviews some laws of addition and multiplication: the distributive, the commutative, the additive inverse, and the additive identity. She asks if anyone read last Sunday's *New York Times Magazine*. No one has. She says there was an article last Sunday on the new math, "which is just what

we've been doing in this course." She then returns to a problem they were working on and I can see what is coming. The students have just been told that, "Oh well, we've only done addition," and then asked if they read the *Times*. It doesn't take long. In response to one of Delaney's questions a student satirically says, "Come on, you tell me the answer. I want to learn." There is laughter from several others.

(A math class)

Palmer (an English teacher) distributes copies of a short article from *The New York Review of Books* by Alfred Kazin on the political and ideological uses made of the American flag by the working class. For the first few minutes she analyzes the structure of the essay and the writing techniques used by the author. The students (most of whom are law enforcement majors) are asked to pick out key sentences. The conversation soon turns to the substance of the article and six or seven students (about one-third of the class) begin one of the liveliest debates I've heard all year. Palmer takes a liberal stand, vehemently denigrating the United States; among other things she criticizes government secrecy, Watergate, the Asian War, the 1968 Chicago convention, and inflation. She makes her disgust evident. Four people support her statements. It isn't until she makes a key mistake that students begin opposing her. The mistake is siding with Kazin in opposing the "unthinking, fanatical working-class hard hats." She reads the following quote to buttress her statement: "This particular segment of the working class most features crane operators and other lordly specialists who from the heights of their well-packed pay envelopes look down on blacks who can't even become plumbers' apprentices." She then says: "We've been talking about the working class, but maybe we ought to get it straight what we mean by that. What would be an example of a high-status occupation?"

A male student gives a closed fist salute and says defiantly: "In my neighborhood construction workers have high status." A number of students cheer. Palmer is red-faced and agrees that status varies with neighborhood.

Another student says: "We have some rich people moving back into —— [the community where City Community College is located] and fixing up the big old houses. They're all weirdos—flaky."

Palmer asks: "Why do you feel like that?"

STUDENT: "The same reason you do. Class prejudice!"

Four or five male students cheer. The discussion quickly returns to the anti-U.S. statements made earlier. The students defend the U.S. saying how we've supported relief efforts and spent billions on foreign aid to ungrateful nations. A number of small debates erupt simultaneously. The class is out of hand. Palmer herself is engaged in a side debate. She tries to quiet the class but they act as if she is not there. One student tells her to "sit on it."

(An English class)

Foley asks the class to distinguish between reports, inferences, and judgments (terms used in their textbooks). There is no response. She calls on students and they obviously do not know the answers. One student finally offers a partially correct answer. She berates the class saying, "You haven't lived up to your responsibility as good students and as long as you don't you can expect me to be bitchy." At the word "bitchy" the class gasps satirically. She ignores this and goes on with the lesson by asking the class for descriptive adjectives.

167

One student says, "I'd like to give you one, but I can't say that," implying that his adjective is obscene.

A few male students snicker and poke each other in the ribs. She has difficulty quieting them down. Some of the students prepare to leave too early—they close their books, stretch, put pencils in their pockets. The talking continues. Foley yells, "Let me have your attention please!" I see some of the students looking at each other with impish smiles on their faces. During the last three minutes she has to speak over the students.

(An English class)

At the beginning of class a student asks Lionetti how they did on the test, to which he replies, "I think a lot of you know more than you show." He explains they are going to begin something that will be important to them— "something you will be able to use a lot." He begins explaining percentages—how they are notated, e.g., the difference between .2 and .02, how to move the decimal point, etc. Later the class has great difficulty changing fractions to percentages.

Lionetti asks: "Phyllis, how do you change ⅜ to a percent?"

PHYLLIS: "I don't know."

LIONETTI: "No idea?"

Phyllis shakes her head no. Lionetti gives the class a formula: "This formula will come back to *haunt* you." He gives the class exercises to do. After a few minutes he says, "Ellen, what are you doing?"

Ellen says sheepishly: "Nothing. I don't know how to do it."

Lionetti reexplains; his tone is friendly and patient. Then he says: "You have to learn to think about it. I can't keep on telling you how to do it step by step. You've already forgotten what we learned in the last two weeks about decimals and fractions. Is that the way you do it? Learn it and forget it?"

Steve laughs and says somewhat hostilely, "Ya!" Two others laugh—apparently at their own inability. They scratch their heads as they realize they don't know how to do the problems. In reexplaining how to change fractions to decimals the fraction $\frac{1}{20}$ is put on the board.

Lionetti asks: "Does this ring a bell?"

STUDENT: "Five percent?"

LIONETTI: "Right. What is one-twentieth of a dollar?"

STUDENT: "A nickel."

Lionetti says in an undertone: "I hate to ask real obvious questions, but sometimes I get scared." For a moment the class stares at him silently. A student flatulates very loudly and the class roars with laughter. . . . On the way out of class Tom (the offender) is congratulated by Nick and George.

NICK: "You sure got him good."

GEORGE: "Atta baby Tom, you really socked it to him."

TOM: "Oh man, it couldn't have come at a better time."
(A business math class)

Scenes such as these were commonplace, occurring daily in liberal arts courses taken by training-program students as well as in those vocational courses taught by the lawyer and the chemist. These incidents suggest that two competing definitions of the school situation existed for students. The first was that they were in school to do something for themselves, and this required cooperation with and acquiescence to the teachers' definitions and requests. When oriented to this definition, classes proceeded smoothly and without interruption. The second was the more negative definition, described earlier, in which students were induced by the machinations of the social-class system to assume responsibility for their current predicament. When oriented to this definition, often as a reaction to teacher's words or manner, students counterattacked. To the extent that students were always subject to being discredited, classes were always precarious, always potentially subject to the disruption of a competing definition of the situation which momentarily devalued the worth of what they and their teachers were doing and saying. The students, fundamentally, were expressing what was ultimately a social-class dilemma. By angrily pricking the authority of the teacher's definition of the situation, students were confirming that they all knew "something was going on underneath," and (perhaps most importantly) were upholding their honor by taking action on this collective realization. Indeed, the wry smiles, knowing looks and self-congratulations expressed both pride and joy in the momentary abandoning of acquiescence, in the momentary exercise of power, will, and autonomy. Thus, in this social-class struggle in miniature, taunts were the weapons by which minor victories of dignity could be won.

Absenteeism, minimizing effort, and cheating served a similar function, for, as seen in the remarks of students, these measures, when taken together, gave substance and a sense of solidarity to the different groups of training students. The function of such behavior was to demonstrate that each student was part of a collectivity worth belonging to because it protected the most intimate interests of its members.

The Female Vocational Students

Almost 85 percent of female vocational students were enrolled in the secretarial curriculum. Unlike their male counterparts, the secretarial students exhibited overt resistance in their vocational rather than in their liberal arts courses. The following is a typical example:

> Ajamian (the teacher) asks them to shut off their type-writers and prepare for a short quiz: "It's not on some-thing you've never heard of before. We've gone over these things numerous, numerous times. I just want to see if you know them." She asks questions.
>
> The students talk among themselves.
>
> TEACHER: "Absolutely no talking."
>
> A student asks: "Can we whisper?" Laughter and more talking. Someone makes a joke I cannot hear—more laughter. Three more times the students make jokes about the quiz questions Ajamian is asking. The students groan at some of the questions—half in seriousness, half in jest; the groans are overexaggerated.
>
> AJAMIAN: "Make sure you're doing your own work, please." The questions are all mechanical, concerning formats, spacing, fingering, etc. For the third time she says, "No talking, no talking whatever." She mentions a brand name of stationery and a student yells out from the third row, "What kind was that?" As she answers and continues her explanation of the business-letter format some students are talking.
>
> AJAMIAN: "Do you want to talk or are you going to listen to me?"
>
> The two students continue talking.
>
> She yells: "You probably want to talk, but I'll make you listen to me."

The students are quiet for a minute but again begin talking once the quiz ends and they are instructed to continue their typing. I cannot hear what they have to say over the din of the typewriters.

In their liberal arts courses, secretarial students were cooperative, attentive, polite, and, in the collective judgment of their teachers, among the brightest and most willing to do academic work of all students in the school. This inversion can tentatively be explained by noting that 72 percent of these young women came from the wealthier, more middle-class communities adjacent to the working-class communities surrounding the school. Having a higher social status (as measured both by residence and family data), the secretarial students were more concerned with detaching themselves through classroom behavior from the uncomplimentary implications of their work: specifically, that the low-status value of a secretary's "mechanical" work implied downward or no mobility.

That the threat of downward mobility was a very real concern for the secretarial students was seen in their attitude toward the male students in the school:

I ask three secretarial students if the guys in the school are the kind of guys they would like to marry. They say emphatically no.

DEBBIE: "They have no class, no sophistication. I mean, who cares about driving around in a souped-up drag machine."

PAM: "I have a word for them—gorillas. The school is full of them."

I ask if this includes the guys in the liberal arts courses.

DEBBIE: "Not so much. They're bad, but not like the law enforcement group. They're totally unsophisticated."

The three of them consider it highly unlikely that they would marry someone who had not gone to college.

MARY: "Well, you know, you're supposed to act dumb to keep a guy and I admit to doing that, but not with any of the guys here because they're not my type. Most of them are very immature."

PAM: "*Very* immature." Pam tells me she was in a two-year dental hygienist program at —— University but had to drop out because of an accident. She now hopes to get a job in a law firm or "a business with a good reputation."

I ask what her father does: he is an electrical engineer, white collar.

I ask if she would consider marrying a policeman or a fireman. She says that you never know what will happen, but she seriously doubts it.

I ask about the students in the business program, and Pam replies: "You've got to understand that most of them come from ——, ——, or —— [three nearby working-class communities]. Most of them don't know what they're doing in business and they won't go anywhere, most likely. I just can't see them really becoming anything."

I ask: "So you kind of rule them out?"

MARY: "I guess we have prejudices against them."

The strength of these "prejudices" was reflected, in part, in the seating patterns in those liberal arts classes which the secretarial students and male vocational students took together: in twenty-nine of the thirty-four such classes observed, the students segregated themselves sexually as they took their seats.

* * *

Implicit in this analysis of the relationship between social psychology and social class is a joining of the Meadian and Marxist social theories, both of which postulate the existence of a dialectic between the individual and society. In their study of blue-collar and lower-white-collar workers, *The Hidden Injuries of Class*, Richard Sennett and Jonathan Cobb have stated in this regard that the social-psychological impact of class "is that a man can play out *both* sides of the power situation in his own life, become alternately judge and judged, alternately individual and member of the mass. This represents the 'internalizing' of class conflict, the process by which struggle between men leads to the struggle within each man."[3] In playing out this drama, the students' immediate responses to the circumstances of school life had an effect upon their long-range interests, an effect that neither they nor their teachers desired, for by working at cross purposes with themselves they were assuring the very defeat they wished to avoid. On those occasions when students expressed an awareness of this paradox, they lamented their absenteeism and limiting of effort which seemed to increase the moral responsibility they had to assume for their own sense of inadequacy and frustration. In the following poignant vignette an unusually perceptive student comments on this predicament:

> I am sitting alone in the student lounge when Red, a business student, wheels in the TV, connects it to the videotape player and shows *News and Views* (a student-produced video tape announcing school events and presenting interviews with teachers). Red sits next to me and says, "It's really something how apathetic the students are here. This is the sixth week we've done *News and Views* and you and I are the only ones here. It's not as though we didn't put up posters [announcing the time and place of the showing] all over the place." I say that I agree with him, the students are apathetic, but this may not be the best example of it.

RED: "I know what you're going to say; that the attendance thing and the fact that nobody does anything are
better examples." He also mentions that the lack of involvement in student government is another indicator of
apathy.

I ask him why he thinks this is.

RED: "In America now—and the James Bond movies
really helped it along—it isn't cool to feel emotionally
attached to anything or anybody. Maybe with your
family, your girl friend or your guy, but it just isn't cool
to show any emotional involvement with a school. I've
noticed all year that the kids in this school are anti-intellectual and to be honest so am I. And I ask myself why. I
think it's because people have a need to pull others down
to their level. Working-class people are notorious for
this; they love to think that they are better than intellectuals or just plain middle-class people who don't work
with their muscles. My father's like that. That's an emotional thing, anger."

Red goes on to say that not only might there be this kind
of anger, but that the students may resent the teachers
because the teachers represent education and intellect.
He says that the most popular teachers are the ones who
themselves are working-class people. He adds, "But there
are some teachers who just talk *way* over the heads of
their students and they'd have to be really out of it if
they didn't know they were doing it." Red says he's
heard many students complain about this problem. He
then says that maybe one way to get students to watch
News and Views is to "put something anti-intellectual
on."

The show comes around on the tape for the third time.
One segment is Red himself interviewing Johnson—one

of the most academically-oriented teachers in the school. The interview concerns his western civilization course next semester. Johnson says in a very slow, methodical manner: "A lot of the course is lecture because that's still an important form of communication. But we'll also be making more use of the [video and audio] tape center." In the interview Red asks him what the class will cover.

JOHNSON: "We'll start with the impact of liberalism, the causes and consequences of the American and French Revolutions on our ideology, the scientific revolution, how World War I led to World War II and to the cold war, and whether the cold war is really ending. And I forgot to add, in addition to making use of the tape center where some people who actually acted out history can be heard and seen, we will make more extensive use of our library resources than we were able to first semester."

In the interview Red winces and says: "That sounds like a lot of studying."

Johnson twists his mouth in an effort to turn down a smile and replies, "Yes, it will be a lot of studying."

Red turns to me and says, "Did you see my face when he described the course and his smile when I said it would be a lot of studying? That's what turns me off."

HBL: "What does? The description of the course or his smile?"

RED: "Both."

HBL: "How does it turn you off?"

RED: "In a way it's puzzling, because we're here to get a better job, to make something of ourselves, but we put down the school and stay away from it. This teacher gives you a lot of reading and writing to do and immediately you're pissed off. That happened in Human Relations class, in Marketing and in Tobin's [English] class. It's biting the hand that can feed you. You'd think people would try harder, but they don't and that's bad for them, for me, for anybody."

Although he grasped the relationship between class and anger, Red and students like him believed that as responsible individuals, ideally they should attempt to make the best of an unfortunate situation. Yet meeting this responsibility would mean meeting the demands, expectations, and values of those who made them feel inferior; and so as a matter of honor it became necessary for students to resist, even if that meant feeling bad about it. They could not completely resolve this contradiction any more than they could erase class distinctions; they could only turn once again to that behavior described here which expressed their frustrations yet at the same time preserved a modicum of the integrity they needed to persevere.

The Male Liberal Arts Students

Successful completion of the liberal arts program required demonstrating both familiarity with certain abstract concepts and competence in working with them. The students in this curriculum associated such intellectual activity with upward mobility, for after graduation they could either transfer to a four-year institution or perhaps more easily acquire a white-collar position. It was not that they saw middle-class people as intellectuals, but that working with ideas was seen as necessary to becoming middle class.

In the simplest of terms, the male liberal arts students were ambivalent over the prospect of mobility and the "intellectualizing" necessary to make that prospect a reality. There were two reasons for this: (1) to enroll as a liberal arts student and then do poorly was publicly and privately mortifying; (2) to do very well called for changes in values, life styles, and self-images that were socially and personally distressing. Both failure and success, then, left these students vulnerable. Let us first examine the consequences of failure.

Like students in every school and at all levels of education, liberal arts students feared the consequences of failure. For these students, however, the prospect of failure took on an additional dimension—it could negate the prospect of mobility to which they had publicly committed themselves. They were in effect attempting to exit the blue-collar world, and in this sense they had put themselves to the test. That they were aware of this is seen in the reactions of those who did poorly:

CHRIS: "I really got myself into it this time. He's been talking about the Roman Empire and I don't know what's going on. I got a 42 on my last test. I don't care, I'm going to flunk this one too."

HBL: "You don't care?"

CHRIS: "No, I know how to drive a truck."

We both smile at Chris's gallows humor.

(A liberal arts student)

I ask George and Mike how their community problems test was. They both say it was difficult and that they did not do all the reading. Mike says that because his grades are so low he is thinking of transferring into law enforcement next semester.

GEORGE: "Hey man, stick with it. They'll help you get through. You're no flunky."

MIKE: "Well, I flunked the mid-term and there's no way I passed this." He discusses the difficulty he is having in his other courses and says he dislikes most of his teachers.

Despondently he adds, "At least I gave it a shot. Being a cop ain't so bad. It beats a lot of other things."

(Two liberal arts students)

That reaching the end of one's rope could be so humiliating was evident in a social science class where a student whom I knew to be failing and considering withdrawal complained of the overemphasis on earning a college degree:

BERT: "Why go to college if you're going into a trade? To learn thirteenth-century Shakespeare?"

GREENBERG: "Shakespeare didn't write in the thirteenth century." There is a roar of laughter from the class and comments like, "OK, Bert" and "Good goin'." The two students on either side of him rib him with their elbows. . . .

After class I talk with Bert who is obviously still upset. I ask what I think is a neutral question, knowing that Bert will know what I mean: "What do you think, Bert?"

BERT: "Fuck those guys. I'm no genius, but just because I don't know when Shakespeare. . . . Shit, if my uncle gets me an apprenticeship [in an electrical workers union] I think that's OK. That suits me just fine."

HBL: "Ya, but you sound angry about it."

BERT: "I'm just pissed off right now. That was a real put-down."

HBL: "Are you pissed off because of that or because of the whole situation?"

BERT: "It's the whole goddamn thing. . . . Every time you screw up you know you're closer to being out."

Two days later I ask Bert if he is going to drop out. He tells me he can't get into the union, they're laying off men now. He says he doesn't know what to do, since work is hard to find: "It's really bad—if you fuck up school you just hang it up and kiss it good-by. That's why I went into liberal arts."

I ask him to explain.

BERT: "Because if you make it through all four years you can get a job. You don't have to worry about unions unless you're on top and they're working for you."

On the one hand becoming a union member suits Bert fine, on the other hand he'd like to be on top. Other students similarly implied a negative view of their own working-class status. Clearly, it was respectable to be a blue-collar worker, but it was somehow better to be a white-collar worker, since that was evidence of your intelligence, drive, and virtue. As would be expected when people are ambivalent about such an important matter, the students were quite uncomfortable in this situation.

Compounding their fear of failure and the loss of mobility it implied was an apprehensiveness among the male liberal arts students about the consequences of success and the mobility it would bring. Again, this unease was a product of the students' views and behavior concerning "intellectual work," for this was the activity they saw as crucial for access to middle-class positions. The first hint of their "fear of success" came during the first week of school when a class was asked to write, in the words of the instructor, "a four-page intellectual autobiography" in which they were to describe the factors, especially the ideas, most influential in their "intellectual development." The reaction of the class was whooping, raucous laughter. One student prompted even more laughter when he asked if the report could be fiction. On the way out of that class I followed five students down the stairwell and overheard them say:

"This is a classic case of bad vibes!"

"How are we going to get rid of him? Shoot him?"

"He's gotta be kidding!"

"He's going to be too much—too much work!"

"He's a liberal."

"And probably a fag."

Earlier we read excerpts from some of their essays. Despite their protestations the students did write them; it was, after all, the first week of school and there was a modicum of initial enthusiasm. Although none were over three pages, their essays were serious and, as we have seen, the students were not unaware of the importance of the next two years. Writing an intellectual autobiography, however, was not something they had thought they would ever be asked to do, even in school. In the essays, students referred to the circumstances of their lives, rather than crediting ideas *per se* in the formation of their consciousnesses or behavior. (As the teacher consented to share the essays with me, he remarked that they were "social autobiographies" and not "intellectual" ones.) The assignment was as unusual and humorous for these students as asking Harvard women to learn to use a jackhammer.

Asking students to undertake something they consider unusual can, however, have a pedagogic value. If, to use the same example, Harvard women were asked why they thought learning to use a jackhammer humorous, they would see that it is a violation of traditional sex roles, and, furthermore, that it is an activity relegated to those of a different social rank. But such a strategy was not the intention of the predominantly middle-class City Community College teachers who were unfamiliar with the social-class milieu and, hence, unaware of the sensibilities of their students. The humorous effect, though, was the same: for the male students, being asked to intellectualize was seen as a violation of traditional sex roles and as something people of their station did not do. Harvard women students might learn to use a jackhammer in response to a challenge, but to City Community College students, acquiring conceptual knowledge, truly valuing it, and using it freely was a more serious endeavor, as it also meant modifying their self-images. This undertaking was no game, no pedagogic trick, and the laughter in the classroom was but one expression of the students' tension.

One way in which male students managed this tension was occasionally to berate each other for even the appearance of intellectualism, as when a student would be teased for carrying a briefcase. Peer pressure, however, could be much more direct:

WALT: "All this stuff is new to me. In high school all you did in history was dates and places, but Bailey says he doesn't care that much about it so long as we know roughly when something happened. It's really kind of interesting when he explains why things like World War I happened but it's hard to understand. I know what he means when he says it, but I can't explain it afterward."

HBL: "Why don't you see him at his desk?"

WALT: "I've done that too. You know Simmy? She's really smart. Ugly, but smart. I usually talk to her upstairs where John and those guys won't see me."

HBL: "Because she's so ugly?"

WALT: "That and I'd be talking to her about history." I ask him to explain. Actually, I know what he means, but I want to hear it from him.

WALT: "Just before a test you should see how they butter her up, but otherwise they don't care. I think Bailey's the best teacher I ever had. He really makes it interesting."

HBL: "You can't let John know that?"

WALT: "I can say Bailey's all right, but I can't say 'Oh, wow, this is the best course I ever had!' "

(Conversation in the lounge)

182

Taking this as an important datum, I made it a point to talk alone with John:

> After a few minutes of social talk I ask John what he thinks of Bailey's class.
>
> JOHN: "Bailey's pretty good. I've never heard a vocabulary like his. He speaks six feet over my head sometimes."
>
> HBL: "Ya, I've heard him lecture. Do you like his lectures?"
>
> JOHN: "You have to read the book to know what he's talking about. Even then it's hard; I got an F and a D on the tests. I thought I'd do better because it's interesting and you pick it up faster."
>
> HBL: "I remember I had a teacher like Bailey once. He was one of the best teachers I ever had."
>
> JOHN: "Ya, Bailey is a little weird, but I'd say he's better than any *history* teacher I had in high school."
>
> HBL: "Do you study much for him?"
>
> JOHN: "No, just to get a C. They say with a C you can transfer, that's a good college grade."

Despite the impression John has given Walt, John does admit that he reads the history book and that he finds Bailey interesting. Walt's impression is not entirely incorrect, however, since John is limiting his effort by settling for a C. The vulnerability felt by Walt is not unlike the many anxieties of the *nouveaux riches* or, for that matter, any person whose status changes, for the new status and image produce a variety of problematic situations: old relations are threatened and may have to be broken, new ones must be established and one's personal life reordered as one devotes more time to new activities, such as reading and studying. Students like

Walt and Brian were criticized not as "grade-busters" or "average-raisers" since liberal arts courses were not graded on a curve, but as people who were too quickly shifting from a working-class to a middle-class orientation. One student was quite explicit about this:

> Frank tells me Larry is generally disliked by "the guys" even though he used to be part of their group. He complains Larry now studies too much, that he takes school as if it were the "only thing around."
>
> FRANK: "He's pushy and always browning the teachers."
>
> HBL: "What do you mean, he's pushy?"
>
> FRANK: "He doesn't want to go to U—— [the state university], he wants to go to —— or —— [small private colleges with excellent reputations]. Do you think he can get in there?"
>
> HBL: "I don't know, really."
>
> FRANK: "Well, if he does, bye-bye Larry. Have a good time."
>
> (Conversation in the cafeteria)

Such students were resented by students in all majors because, in effect, they were willing to leave others behind, including their friends. If they were seen as doing *too* well without seeing anything wrong with that, then they were deserters, they had shown how weak their allegiances were. Of course, students who were doing "too well" did see "something wrong with it," as demonstrated by Brian's and Walt's awareness of the double jeopardy in which they had placed themselves. Their dilemma extended not only to their peers but to their families as well. Said one student whose father and brother were longshoremen:

> DON: "They're glad I'm in college. I'm the baby in the family. But things aren't the same anymore at home. You

know, they tease me. They say, 'Do you really want to be a teacher?' Well, I do even if I feel funny about it."

HBL: "What's there to feel funny about?"

DON: "Doing something different. I think I can do it, even if it means taking shit. Maybe they're just jealous, my brothers."

(Conversation in the game room)

There is always a price to be paid for emancipation, and in cases like this those who "make the move" feel ambivalent about their success in school. They have been told of the virtues and dividends of educational achievement, yet they cannot feel completely comfortable with them. Most male students, however, were more circumspect in their level of effort. If a transition was to be made in their lives, it would occur slowly. Having done poorly in high school, it is not surprising that, still in their own city and still with old friends, they would proceed tentatively and cautiously. Like the training students, they were hedging against the possibility of failure, and they were also cushioning themselves from the social-psychological consequences of success, of becoming "middle class."

The Female Liberal Arts Students

The female liberal arts students were more willing to do assigned work and to participate in class discussions. In most instances they were quicker to respond to teachers' questions and to interject their own thoughts. Most teachers, thus, thought them better students, not because they were somehow more intelligent but because they were more willing to intellectualize. Said one teacher:

I suppose I see the female students as somewhat better—as more willing. . . . I think part of it is the girls' social acclimation. They just get used to studying and used to pleasing teachers. And they continue to do that, and teachers like to be pleased, and that means entertaining the ideas we work with.

Although grading standards varied among teachers, school records revealed that among the liberal arts students females as a group earned a higher proportion of A's and B's, the same proportion of C's, and fewer D's, F's and Incompletes.

The females were less unwilling to intellectualize for two reasons. First, they certainly could not be accused of being "fags" as that term was used by the males. They were, however, occasionally accused by their male counterparts of being "brainy":

I saw Jane's term paper, right? She had diagrams with different color pencils and she printed the whole thing. A couple of chicks [in his class] are really cool, but most of them turn me off. It's not just physically, they're too brainy. I wouldn't want to go out with half of them just for that.

(A male student)

And then, female students were less anxious about doing well because they were less anxious about upward mobility. Their allegiance to or sense of honor in their present life styles was not as strong, and they more readily implied that they were after something better:

At one point a social science teacher discusses the great fund of incidental knowledge picked up by city people in the course of their lives (e.g., concerning deviants, ethnic groups). Country people, he states, tend to be very naïve when they visit the city and they don't know what's going on.

A female student interrupts: "Is that so bad? We don't need all this trouble and aggravation. Someone comes in from one of the suburbs and sees a drunk stumbling on the street and says, 'Isn't that disgusting,' while we don't think anything of it. But they're right. It *is* awful."

Two other students state their distaste for life in their part of the city. Both say they want to get out.

(Classroom discussion)

I ask Georgia why she is in the liberal arts program.

GEORGIA: "What would I do, be in law enforcement? Oh, I could see that in South —— [her section of the city] with everyone stealing cars, getting drunk, and popping pills. It was a great place to grow up, but now it's really gone downhill."

(Hallway conversation)

In her studies of women college students, Matina Horner has stated:

Women as well as men in this society are immersed in a culture that rewards and values achievement and that stresses self-reliance, individual freedom, self-realization, and the full development of individual resources, including one's intellectual potential. . . . The experimental data . . . show that despite the removal for women of many legal and educational barriers to achievement, which existed until the twentieth century, there remains a psychological barrier that is considerably more subtle, stubborn, and difficult to overcome. I refer to this barrier as *the motive to avoid success* [emphasis in the original]. This "fear of success" receives its impetus from the expectancy held by women that success in achievement situations will be followed by negative consequences, including social rejection and the sense of losing one's femininity.[4]

Horner's conclusions are based on the results of Thematic Apperception Tests (TAT's) in which male and female students

187

were asked to complete a story line concerning various hypothetical educational achievements of males and females. Reporting the results of a separate questionnaire study she has stated:

> The responses on the questionnaire are consistent with performance data in suggesting that women . . . will not fully explore their intellectual potential when they are in a competitive setting, especially when they are competing against men.[5]

Horner explains her findings as follows:

> The desire to fail comes from some deep psychological conviction that the consequences of failure will be *satisfying*. These girls [I studied] were motivated by the opposite; they were positively anxiety-ridden over the prospect of success. They were not simply eager to fail and have done with it; they seemed to be in a state of anxious conflict over what would happen if they succeeded. It was almost as though this conflict was inhibiting their capacity for achievement.[6]

Horner's subjects were freshmen and sophomores at the University of Michigan, Harvard, and an unidentified "outstanding eastern women's college."[7] At working-class and lower-middle-class City Community College, however, Horner's findings seem to be reversed. Unlike the females she studied, the women of City Community College seemed more concerned over what would happen should they fail. While they may not have explored their "full intellectual potential," intellectualizing was seen as both a means to and a mark of middle-class respectability, whether by acquiring a job or a husband they otherwise would not have. In reference to academic achievement, social class is apparently a more important variable than sexual identity.[8] Unlike the males Horner studied, the men of City Community College, as discussed above, were more anxious than the women over the social penalties of success. In summary, change the social class of the institution and it is the *males* who fear success for the social rejection and loss of masculinity it might bring. Taking fear of success as an ideal-type construct, with its connotations of intellectualizing and mobility firmly in mind, Table I conceptualizes the differences between distinctly working-class and distinctly middle-class institutions:

TABLE I

"Fear of Success" by Sex and Type of College

		Females	Males
"Fear of Success"	Elite Universities	+	−
	City Community College	−	+

Conclusion

Looking beneath the surface activity of education we find the students of City Community College falling out of, searching for, and settling into life courses, positions, and, in a fundamental sense, identities. In a classic essay, "The Cooling Out Function in Higher Education,"[9] Burton Clark claims that the function of community colleges is to facilitate this process by weeding out unpromising students. According to Clark, democratic societies ask individuals "to act as if social mobility were universally possible," the belief being that social status, privilege, and other rewards accrue to those who try. Then, borrowing from Robert Merton, Clark argues that democratic societies also limit and block culturally instilled goals so that mechanisms are needed to deflect the resentment and mollify the disappointment of those to whom opportunity is denied in order to induce them to take less rewarding work. For Clark, a major function of the two-year college is to cool students' aspirations and temper their frustrations through the gradually accumulated evidence (achievement test scores, vocational aptitude tests, course grades, teachers' recommendations, and counselors' advice) that they ought to change to a terminal vocational curriculum rather than transfer to a four-year institution. According to him this "cooling-out function," as he calls it, works rather smoothly, in part because "the students themselves help to keep this function concealed by wishful unawareness" and are motivated "not to admit the cooling-out process to consciousness . . . so they are saved insult to their self-image." Certainly the students described here would like to escape such insult and pain, but what they told me in effect was that such an escape was dreadfully difficult and that the wounds of blocked opportunity fester rather than heal. To say that students repress such unpleasant thoughts is perhaps a bit of wishful unawareness on the part of those who would overlook the frictions built into the workings of the social-class system.*

This leads to a final objection to the implications of the cooling-out function. Clark concludes that "the provision of readily available alternative achievements in itself is an important device for alleviating the stress consequent on failure and so preventing anomic and deviant behavior." To the contrary, stress and anomic and deviant behavior were already evident in the students' resistance to their school work, in their absenteeism, in their "assaults" on teachers, and in their self-criticisms. But the more profound question is, would we indeed want such seemingly "dysfunctional" behavior to disappear? Were we able to create institutional mechanisms which indeed acted to repress this reservoir of discontent, is this not but one more mechanism by which an unjust status quo can be perpetuated by keeping working-class people in line? I am thinking here especially of the vocational students, those who, in the interests of the smooth running of the social system, have been "cooled out" either in the community college or at some earlier

---

* In fairness to Clark, he does not say he approves of the "cooling-out function" in a sociopolitical sense, it is just that he does not acknowledge the difficulties students have in allowing themselves to be "cooled out."

stage. Is not their alienation and recalcitrance a healthy reaction to an unhealthy and unfortunate social situation? If our schools eradicated the tensions and antagonisms described here without concomitant change in the social-class system itself, they would produce automatons, people too willing to become involved in shallow task performance at the expense of their own sense of vitality and integrity. To appropriate a phrase from Erik Erikson, their spirit would be at last mutilated. The value choice here is clear, if implicit: to ask our schools to perform such a function is to opt for a status quo which retards the movement toward true opportunity and social justice.

REFERENCES

1. William Ryan, *Blaming the Victims* (New York: Random House, 1971), p. 4.
2. Erving Goffman, *Asylums: Essays on the Social Situation of Mental Patients and Other Inmates* (Garden City: Doubleday & Company, 1961), pp. 304–305.
3. Richard Sennett and Jonathan Cobb, *The Hidden Injuries of Class* (New York: Random House, 1973), pp. 97–98.
4. Matina S. Horner, "Femininity and Successful Achievement: A Basic Inconsistency," in Judith M. Burbank, *et al., Feminine Personality and Conflict* (Belmont, California: Wadsworth Publishing Co., 1970), pp. 45–47.
5. *Ibid.*, p. 67.
6. Quoted in Vivian Gornick, "Why Women Fear Success," in Judith R. Lanois, *Current Perspectives on Social Problems* (Belmont, California: Wadsworth Publishing Co., 1973), p. 152.
7. Horner, op. cit., p. 63.
8. It may be, as Komarovsky reports, that after these girls transfer to a four-year school, or begin their first job, parental and peer pressures

may dampen achievement motivation in favor of marriage. In light of the findings of this report, these pressures in themselves may not be enough, for the mobility of these females would first have to be assured (even if not yet achieved) or clearly denied before plans were changed. Mirra Komarovsky, "Functional Analysis of Sex Roles," *American Sociological Review*,Vol. XV, August, 1950, pp. 508–516.

9. Burton Clark, "The Cooling-Out Function in Higher Education," *American Journal of Sociology*, Vol. 65, May, 1960, pp. 569–576.

HENRY-LOUIS GATES, JR.

They Think You're an Airplane, but You're Really a Bird: The Education of an Afro-American

Henry-Louis Gates, Jr., a scholar and a lyrical writer, defines the concept of hurdling autobiographically, as the attempt of a young black person to wrestle from a white institution his own turf, losing a part of himself in the confrontation—both he and the enemy ultimately winning and losing but changing in the conflict. The microcosm of Gates's school experience moves us to understand more about the fate of many gifted young blacks desperately entreated by white institutions in a time of accelerated social change. Through Gates's assets and accident he survived and bested Yale. That he has succeeded so well, both in his own mind and by any critical standard set by the outside world, has mitigated the survivor's syndrome seen in so many achieving young people.

B Y D A Y, *Yale is a tangible, mortar and stone manifestation of an Oxonian ideal of Gothic perfection, a structural expression born of a harsh subliminal chiaroscuro, a not-so-gentle admixture of the striving for the intellect to bridle an untrammeled imagination. The borders of this chiaroscuro are brought into relief by the magnificent pages of illuminated monastic scrolls, at times blending, at times not, with the darkest tales and most deeply felt superstitions that Medieval Europe could conjure to cloak its most basic, hideous fears: Merlin's Wand and the alchemists' transubstantiating Stone; the cremation of Witches to ward off the Plague. Of the richly rational spectra that part and impen these, the Oxonian ideal of Gothic perfection is made.*

By night, the mammoth Gothic structures, strangely out of keeping with a dull, gray New Haven, guard their streets with strangely bearded shadows made by the light and the half-light of the lampposts, else by the light of the moon. Shadows conceal bodies other than my own; a would-be ghoul harbors there, waiting, lurking ominously. Often, trudging wearily through the great expanse of these grounds at night, past a deadened Cross Campus, up and through a locked, wrought-iron passage into Calhoun, I feel the echoes of rapid footsteps, softly far away, now louder, nearer. And the dogged footsteps quicken as I quicken. A crescendo of tension takes hold of my imagination, rips asunder all fibers of courage, reduces them to jangling threads. My breath is lost.

But the footsteps I heard were only the echo of my own: false footsteps. And the shadows harbored only the demons of my own encrusted imagination, which haunt me forever, even by day. And I, deep down, all along, was a black man of thought, blue at Yale. And at Yale, battle hymns are Congregational, with delicate changes of key. Welcome to Never-Never Land, Negro; this is your world: the world you've longed for and dreamed of, the world which cements distinctions among men. It is the world of the Shadow and the Green Lantern, of the Phantom and Spider Man. It is the world of Captain Midnight Decoders, and the repository of all those box tops you used to ship off to Kellogg's, in fair exchange for laser guns. And at Yale, Negro, they think you're an airplane, but you're really a bird.

* * *

The irony of writing an autobiography is that we must presume ourselves to be dead. We must assume that that pilgrimage we seek to share has in some, usually large, measure already been made, devoutly. Depending on our own hubris, and on the depth of pain we choose to disclose, we find the self we selectively remember a revenant amid the tombstones, naked among the dead. "Hurdle," in fact, first described in 15th century English history as a rude sledge on which criminals were drawn to the gallows. This meaning does more than lurk in our consciousness; for me, at least, it informs each attempt to wrestle from a white, unblinking institution my small parcel of space. For in the resolved confrontation, and in the very act of "hurdling" itself, we lose a small part of ourselves, of that strange blend of innocence and arrogance which originally propelled us at all costs into the fray. In the act of becoming, we become in part what we beheld. That, we feel with all the energy we can muster, which would keep us from knowing, keep us from ourselves, yields its secrets only slowly, and only some of the time. And a brief basking in our "victory" soon turns upon us. And we realize, wideeyed, that we have fused somehow with our enemy, and that both of us have won. Yet, strangely, both of us have lost. Now I, a doomed survivor, wander extraterritorial, a revenant amid the tombstones, cursed with second sight that allows me to distinguish the quick from the dead.

The graveyard is replete with tombstones, too many to count. The names are readable, in spite of the fog. Epitaphs even in inclement weather beg to be read. Jerry was first, he died while I was in Africa, away from Yale, for a traveling year, on the "Five-Year B.A." Two rumors compete for his epitaph: "overdose," say the nasty; "hemorrhage," reply his friends. Earl and Shelley are divorced now. Lynn lives with a photographer; her first husband is gay. Glenn graduates this spring, five years late. No one knows if minority admissions will be pursued actively after his graduation, or if his dream will turn green with mold, as did Sloane Coffin and "the Panther Years at Yale." Moe and Wily study law in Nashville; Moe drives a Porsche. He's a clerk. Don thinks he's as pretty as ever, and "styles" with the NAACP. Farley can't write any-more, except his briefs. Moe went to "Nam," Roland got married, and Swano changed his name. Malika speaks Arabic, and still shaves her head; I'm told she's reapplied. And the spectre of Eddie, so I understand, haunts new black Yalies with its fearful propor-tions. He "broke down" senior year, in hot pursuit of his blackness. Once a year, or so it goes, he sneaks back to Old Campus and hides behind the shrubbery, mumbling strangely familiar phrases about "May Day, May Day," and "Off-ing the Pigs." These are the most readable names; there are many others. And mine? What of mine? I stand here, too, peering through the fog, looking for a part of myself that flees my glance. I must warn that epiphany is subtle and intensely personal; I have no simple-minded *Six Crises* waiting to leap from my hat. Those few times when knowledge of my self has stood before me, just a pace and a half out of the shadows, seem almost inconsequential now, from here, and provide germane rev-elations only to the discerning. I dally only to say that I cannot claim to have faced my opponents with anything less than fear. As a Black Oracle, I am afraid, I have been rather a failure: sometimes I have lied, sometimes I have been dumb.

My grandfather was colored, my father is Negro, and I am black. Those appellations, of course, do not contain who I am, or even serve to limit who I thought I could be. Yet, each successive generation of black folks living in this country has shared certain peculiar psychic and social concerns that come as regularly as dusk in a society where being black was from the start a social liability, a restrictive covenant one could run from or live with, but from which one could not escape. Each black American I've met in this country, consciously or not chooses a stance, assumes a posture, adopts an air, which permits him to function with a degree of psychic restraint while allowing for the largest measure of personal movement he can perceive. It is how we define this "measure of freedom," this immeasurable segment of space, which on a very basic level allows us, indeed forces us, to become that which we so longingly behold.

My parents, for instance, never once allowed my brother and me to doubt that we could become whatever we selected, from an infinite range of choices. Nor did they let us doubt that our minds were impeccable things, rich and full, to be catered to, or that the world would yield her secrets if only we turned our attention to her. Yet they were never, oddly enough, overbearing. By my first year of school, at the Davis Free School in Piedmont, West Virginia, I understood in some deep part of me that all that was asked was for me to turn my attention; nothing more or less. Turning our gaze was a tool of mastery, a mastery that went beyond the soon-to-come Little Rock or the imminent civil rights struggle. We never once were allowed to doubt that we were special. And only sometimes did we allow ourselves to wonder why.

My father worked two jobs to keep us well-fed and well-clothed, and to pay the premiums on "college insurance policies," a thousand dollars when we reached eighteen. Our first and only set of World Books taught us most of what we knew about the world and allowed us to develop our minds through wonderful memory games my father designed. His memory was photographic; my brother's excellent. Moma's mink coat we were supposed to call "rabbit," or sometimes "fox" in front of people. But that was special; like our educations, it was insured, unlike the rest of our motley furniture. It never occurred to me that we might be poor, until much, much later a sociologist told me so, pinpointing "the Gateses" in a mass of metallic-tasting demographics that left me empty and numb with the neatness of it all.

The fact of race was never made explicit. Oh, sometimes I'd be in my back room, playing with the World Books or with my guns, and Moma would shatter my marvelous silence with cries of "Colored . . . Colored, on Channel 3." And I'd drop whatever and run downstairs, eager and expectant. And I remember the contorted faces of the Little Rock mothers, shouting cuss words and spitting on children. But that was TV and removed. "Two, four, six, eight, we don't want to integrate," was something funny we chanted out loud with Daddy. We'd all laugh and laugh. And

Moma had told me before that Brenda would not stay "in love" with me and that "I'd figure all that out a little later, much as I would figure it all out. White people funny sometimes," she'd say. And that was all she'd say. I can't say with any degree of honesty if the bristling I feel now about that I felt then, or if I learned to feel it, "when I figured out everything." But I kept getting good grades through all those years. What's more, I was a Gates, and that was enough. And the day Mr. McHenry had taken Ken out on the fire escape for a long and threatening "talk," hadn't he pointed to me as a model for him, once Ken had admitted to writing "I love you" on Brenda's valentine? McHenry was wrong, I thought, and so was Brenda. But knowing would change all of that.

Brenda, in some strange way, led me to the lap of James Baldwin, long about the eighth grade. I used to order Dell paperbacks from Red Bowl's grocery store, with money I got from selling bottles. I remember Baldwin saying something about feeling *human* in Europe, and I wondered what he meant. He said something about coming to terms with the fact of his blackness, high in the Alps in Switzerland, listening to Bessie Smith. I hadn't even heard of Bessie Smith, I wouldn't hear her until my sophomore year at Yale. But that was OK; Baldwin played Bessie for me. I remember the book report I did for my class in which I said some sober things about being a doctor first and a Negro second. But more than this, I remember the funny shade of bright crimson that Mrs. Iverson's face blushed when the nurtured crescendo of my oral presentation somehow culminated contortedly on the word "Nigger." And I sat down, to silence, satisfied with a part of me, frightened with another part, but all the time knowing I had passed through some kind of gate. Unlike the bottles I sold to Red, I was nonreturnable.

I won a "Golden Horseshoe" shortly after that. That's the West Virginia history award that mothers dream about for their kids, and of which my brother had been deprived a full six years before because the hotels in the state capital had not yet integrated. (Just before that, those hotels had turned away Elgin Baylor as well. Daddy told Rocky about that. Somehow, that made it better. "Even Elgin Baylor.") I think we got closer, Rocky and I, when I told him I'd won; but I couldn't tell him how I had won it for him, stepping on whomever along the way.

Exeter came round about. Going to Exeter is not even something people in Piedmont know about. Well, they know about it now, I guess, but not like people at Yale "know" about Exeter. It was a place with a big library that taught a lot of courses. And that's, in the main, what it was for me. Herein is a tale:

The Episcopal diocese's church camp is about twenty miles from my house. At the young Father Smith's bidding, I decided to go for a few weeks, to check out Daddy's church. Having been on crutches for the better part of a year while a broken hip mended, I was a bit fed up with good ole Piedmont and wanted to try something new. My Methodism had fallen into disuse, though I could sometimes still hear Miss Sarah moaning out the Sermon of the Dry Bones and singing about "Sweet Jesus, setting us free." My fifteenth summer, that summer of '65, which brought with it Watts and the riots and the Vietnam war, brought me to the camp at Peterkin, where we "lived under grace." About a hundred upper-class private school kids (and me!) living under grace, tucked away from the world in the West Virginia hills. I think I learned to play bridge, to read Nietzsche, that Watts was a place where black folks lived, and that Exeter was a small town in New Hampshire—all in the same day. That's just about what Peterkin was about: a small group of irreverent kids, bright and tough, secure and unstable, daring the world to hide its knowledge, lest we learn the riddle and "peep" the lie.

I can only recall Peterkin whole from here, the kind of undifferentiated experience time has yet to decipher. It is a block of emotion, made up of nostalgia and the sickly-sweet feeling of *déjà vu*. I had been there already, always. I tasted there for the first time the marvelous world of the life of the mind, bolstered and made firm by the economic freedom to go and do as I pleased. Tandy Tully and Peter Roberts, Angie Strader and Marc Ethridge,

John Doyle and Mary Masters—magi, who loved to dance and loved to sing, who taught me the melancholy folk songs that I would come to know so well marching through Washington against Vietnam. They moved through the world's literature with as much ease as Jack Kennedy could give a speech. Alert and practiced, they were all I had not even dreamed I could be. I left Peterkin reluctantly, as we all did, with the certain knowledge of a life beyond the reach of my buddies in Piedmont. Scotch and brandy, Pete Seeger and Leadbelly, skeptical Anglicanism and fruity atheism, Hermann Hesse and Malcolm Boyd, Friedrich Nietzsche and Erich Fromm—the mixture intoxicated, indiscriminately. Bodies and minds, strong and open, to be touched. To be touched in that once-upon-a-hunting lodge, deep in the Allegheny Mountains, just off the placid unpolluted Potomac brought more pleasure to me than I had known one could possibly turn his gaze toward. Wide-eyed, I, too, tasted and touched. I could never again go home.

Daddy just laughed when I told him about it, how they had figured that he was a doctor, a doctor in New York or Chicago somewhere. Popa had tasted all this before and had turned his back to stay with Mom. Through his laugh, I knew he understood.

So, I was off to Exeter the following year. I had not even *heard* of Exeter til Peterkin, when Marc Foster Ethridge the Third entered my life. His was the mind I most wanted to imitate. He went to Exeter; so would I. An interview with the young Jay Rockefeller, an easy entrance exam, and a full scholarship later, I said bye-bye to Piedmont and Brenda, and drove with my uncle to the New Hampshire woods.

As quickly as Exeter came to my life, however, Exeter left. Or rather, I went from Exeter's life. I just "up and decided" one day that it was past time for me to go back home. Dean Kessler checked my records what seemed to be a hundred times—my test scores were perfect, I had straight A's. There was no reason, he said. "Who gave you authority to leave?" That's what decided it for me. I thought the knock on the door was just Joel Motley whose room was next to mine. It was the Dean, red-faced, angry, confused and a bit disappointed. I think he thought if he yelled at me, somehow I would cower my way back to French 1-A. I gave up the ghost while staring blankly into his horribly crimson, pock-marked face. "Think of our people," Joel had said that night. "Think of yourself. Where is Piedmont, anyway?" Almost, Motley; almost. "I'll be back," I told him, and somehow knew I would. That was my first airplane ride. I can't really say why I felt I had to leave; but I did. Looking back (from here again), I think that Piedmont was just too far to fall back into, so I decided not to fall at all. I went home, homesick for Piedmont, soon to be homesick for Exeter.

I grew, quietly, back home in the hills. In the day, I wanted to be just one of the boys and worked hard not to distance myself from what mattered to my friends. At night, though, alone in my room, I let great minds take me where they would, as far as I could fly. On my own, I came to that peculiar love of a skeptical mind that Daddy had deep down longed for me to come to. He never interfered but the rules and the game were his. Moma didn't even know. I was a Gates, and all that that entailed. Never wearing my split existence very well, I sacrificed inwardly the quest to be loved in fair exchange for the quest to know. I placed myself in the world with my name; I was a Gates.

Maude Fortune was the daughter of Mary Ann, a slave. Her father was the young Camden, of Weston (West) Virginia in summers, of New Jersey in the fall. Young Camden summered on the family plantation in Weston, away from Oxford and the Common Law. The child's, Maude's, straight black hair and high cheek bones determined it: she would be raised a Camden, Old Man Camden decreed. She was a "grandchild." Leonine, Maude came to womanhood, fancying herself a writer of sorts.

She rode well, with her family, and showed and placed. At a show in Maryland, she had taken a first. Edward Gates attended the horses each summer; the banker Katz saw to that. The slave Jane had raised him, with all the security the banker would allow.

His clear blue eyes betrayed his secret; all Cumberland knew. None of us would ever know what passed between Maude and Edward that day in 1867, how one told the other that they shared the same secret, that day under the canvas and the banners that welcomed all Cumberland to the County Fair. But the word passed; they would do what they must do. Shortly after, Maude left her family and married Edward in Maryland. They would be colored.

Through the Episcopal Church, somehow interwoven with my family history (my grandfather, his father, and my father were all Episcopalians), I came to my name. How can I share with you just what all this meant to me, the night Daddy first told the story of Maude, and how she had started our family. Doctors and dentists, lawyers and educators—these were among her offspring; I was descended of them, an inseparable part. Coming to my name like this, an eager, naïve boy from Piedmont, West Virginia, gave me a sense of my own mind larger than mere academic performance. While a great-uncle edited *The New York Age*, Maude brought the world to her mixed brood, pillared somewhere between Du-Bois's *Crisis* and her own St. Phillip's Episcopal Church. "You don't," Daddy had said to me over and over, "*have* to be anything. You may be who you like. Just be satisfied, and I'll be satisfied." My metamorphosis was of the imagination: that person I had hid from the day, I openly showed the night.

After a year at a junior college near my home, where "nigger" was hung on me so many times that I thought it was my name, I decided to go back North, to Harvard or to Yale. I picked Yale, almost from a hat. A cousin taught at Princeton, another had long ago studied law at Harvard. I would make my way at Yale. I headed North, armed with a scholarship and with Tony Whitmore's first edition of Strunk and White's *Elements of Style*, the same edition we had used so much the year before.

How can one recreate the sensations of that first day, when the building that just *had* to be the college cathedral turned out to be Sterling Library! Or how to tell what de Chabert meant in my life, or Burrell and Farley, or Eddie and Earl? How to tell of the feeling of belonging that gripped me as de Chabert welcomed the new students as members of the Black Community at Yale? How to explain, with so little distance separating me now from that time so far away when coming to Yale meant coming to Blackness at one and the same time? How to tell this without rhetoric or triteness or sentiment banning the way? There is no telling.

I barely remember that crucial first month, with daily sessions in the Linnonia and Brothers reading room, turning green bolt-upright, smoking Eddie's Cuban cigars. I was not anxious so much as excited. I had convinced myself that at Yale I would be average, a C (maybe C+) was my big goal. Learning to speak out in class, always before my forte, now came slowly and painfully. But it was History 31 that made the difference, in Burrell's discussion group. Never have I put so much work and expectation, fear and care, into the preparation of a five-page paper. Had the returned grade been a Pass, or just a High-Pass, then I am sure that the tenor of my years at Yale would have emerged as gray as does New Haven each winter. But there it was, in unforgettable bright red letters: "Honors. Nice Paper." Fifteen students, eight seniors, four juniors, and a handful of others, and one Honors. I remember deciding that very night to go to Africa the next year as a "Five-Year B.A.," and one day to be a Scholar of the House. The enthusiasm engendered by that one grade insured for me academic success; a success I was not to share with most of my friends.

It soon became apparent, once the anxiety of "making it" was met, and once the sheer joy at being black (with about three hundred other black folks) tempered, that the fundamental, yet subtle, challenge of my years at Yale would be whether or not I could allow "blackness" to rob me of what I wistfully called "my humanity." This is a complex problem beyond, I think, that peculiar brand of "Mau-Mauing" we so avidly practiced during the economically stable yet psychologically fluctuating late 1960s. You see, as long as I identified the central, all-encompassing dilemma of my "being in the world" with discovering and shouting for all to hear just how the white man had made the black man subservient, had refused to see those whom he had made into the mirror image of his nether side, then the matter of being a human being who must live and die, who must hate and be hated, was not a problem at all—except insofar as these "extraneous" matters crowded into the considerations of being black in a country where color is a brand. What I mean to say is this: Once you are sufficiently removed from the sort of racial discrimination where some hulking Bull Connors stands, arms folded, close-minded before the passageway, then one is *made* to confront all those nasty not-to-be-solved-with-civil-rights type matters. It is unsettling. The very horror of peering into the abyss (and it's a different abyss for each man) is so time consuming that you start looking for a Bull Connors to distract your attention, to block the way. Hence, the strange spectacle of us in 1970 at Yale, preoccupying ourselves with the exact examination of the metaphysical nature of the *Pig*. We wanted to dissect his brain, to explicate his soul; we were convoluted Yacub's, determined at all costs to unlink the Great Chain of Being that had enslaved us since 1619. Where better to serve our people, then, than at Mother Yale? "Changing the system by knowing just what the system is"—that was our rationale, a rationale that became so clichéd that the white kids even stopped asking us if ever we felt guilty about just *being* here. That was the sort of question we would not even have answered in private, behind black doors or alone; we certainly would not have been frank with the white boys. It was another tool to mystify them, and another through which to mask our fears.

Not that, in 1970, there were not things that we should have railed against. There were: Bobby Seale in a New Haven prison, tried each day just a half-block from Calhoun; Eldridge Cleaver in Algiers, driven to exile by threats of murder in a Ronald Reagan prison; John Huggins, whose mother would sometimes let our fines slide over at Sterling Library, murdered by cultural nationalists out in L.A.; Cambodia. These were not some mere bugaboos, conjured for the occasion. We deeply believed there were spectres against which only a moral elite of the young could prevail.

Yet, throughout all our strikes and protests and steering committees, I tried to repress a vague sensation that had these things not been "in the world," we would have invented them, if only to deny the inevitable process of the human mind coming to terms with its own finitude. This, it seems from here, was the ultimate protest; we could only delay its coming.

It was always a fact of Negro life that one's membership could be taken for granted, could be assumed in much the same way one could assume that his Saturday sessions at Combie's barbershop would be rife with Combie's *boo-shit* and with good-hearted lies in general. As my understanding grew of just what all the post-1966 Black Power rhetoric meant, just how ideology could come to bear upon personal, everyday relationships, I came to the painful realization that what "da revolution" implied, what the so often mentioned yet never found vanguard was based on, was a privacy of world view, was a membership in a club so exclusive that, as one for whom the warmth of a village was sustenance, I could never begin to satisfy its ideological membership fee. Whereas the litmus test of liberalism during the early Kennedy years was whether or not a glass was half-full or half-empty, our test for purity was a nonsubstantial one, based on rhetoric: half-digested, and necessarily regurgitated rhetoric. So much did I want to be a part of what even the most dense, the most politically conservative amongst us, the least conscious, could see was a mass movement of mind—a movement far more important, perhaps, to those who came after us than even to ourselves—that I sat, hands covering my ears, not even wondering why no light could shine through the molding cataracts I'd hung over my eyes. Reckoning with your own blindness brings a horror, a shriek so profound that silence is its only measure. Jocasta's scream is a silent one: one is aware, one must act.

Then, almost imperceptibly, I entered into the center of a strange dialectic just after Christmas vacation of my sophomore year. I found myself fighting between becoming the individual I so longingly came to Yale to become and wanting with the deepest part of me to feel black and a vital part of the collective. But this was the easier struggle, I suppose, just because the rules and the contest were so new to me. This was a game we had played before when we had baited the white boy, and always before we had won. The essence of the game was a matter of name. As Ralph Ellison describes it, it works this way:

> Tar Baby, that enigmatic figure from Negro folklore, stands for the world. He leans, black and gleaming, against the wall of life utterly noncommital under our scrutiny, our questioning, starkly unmoving before our naïve attempts at intimidation. Then we touch him playfully and before we can say *Sonny Liston!* we find ourselves stuck. Our playful investigations become a labor, a fearful struggle, an *agony*. Slowly we perceive that our task is to learn the proper way of freeing ourselves to develop, in other words, technique.
>
> Sensing this, we give him our sharpest attention, we question him carefully, we struggle with more subtlety; while he, in his silent way, holds on, demanding *that we perceive the necessity of calling him by his true name as the price of our freedom.*[1] [italics mine]

Always in our history we have had to trick the white man into learning that appearances, especially appearances of social relationships so tradition bound as to seem "human" and "universal," were in fact just appearances, not at all substantive. But when we turned the game upon ourselves the rules became much more subtle, for Tar Baby was ourselves. It is sticky business when two Tar Babies demand of each other their names. For the names changed each moment; as we discarded another now in its place.

The joke, the hole card, of course, was that none of us knew our names; we forgot what we called each other when no one else was around. There is something basic to a change of name that is contingent upon illusion, and the very human urge to forget: "negroes" became "Negroes," who in turn became "New Negroes," who much, much later decided to become "Black." Yet, through all this, there lurks that marked continuity of social tradition and that sense of the past that informs the imagination. We long to forget so we try to forget, we change our names. But the pain stays the same, and so does the pleasure. And once "the moral" becomes whatever it is that makes somebody feel good, then not only is there no longer a "moral," but by this time, nobody can feel good. I won this battle, soon after it commenced, when I realized what it was about: one gains his invisibility not so much because others refuse to see him, but by refusing to run the gamut of his own humanity. Ultimately, one has no choice; at least I didn't. And this rather belabored, quasiallegorical manner of presenting the issue, one with which I was preoccupied for quite some time, one which saw the end of numerous friendships and saw others rendered impossible even before the first furtive gropings had begun, is not meant to deprecate its importance. Seeking the refuge of the group after one has overnight been expelled is so much more horrifying and tantalizing than that same attempt would be had we never been members at all. And that black movement of mind, that urge to forget and to start again, afresh, *created* schisms, cemented distinctions among men, far more insidiously than did the increased social mobility of the sixties when white America opened its doors ever-so-slightly, yet only for some. No longer can we be said to be the organic community we were when King had his day at the Lincoln Memorial. Scars heal slowly and only partially.

It was not so much that I had made some sort of lasting peace with those black people who would have me remade, it was just that by the middle of my first year at Yale I was reasonably confident that some computer in the admissions office had not made a mistake, that I would do well at Yale. I felt no urgent need for the self-protective coloration that refuge in the drove would bring. By this time I could function comfortably with the almost unconscious knowledge that whatever I worked at with sustained interest, I could learn, I could possess, I could remake with all those idiosyncrasies that had long ago characterized my thoughts as *mine*. And so, tired and fed up just enough not to fight anymore, I decided to go to Africa, on Yale's money and on a year of my time.

I didn't know my college dean very well. It was his first year at Calhoun, as it was mine. I remember with some unease those first few months in the college when, walking as nonchalantly through the courtyard as I was able, I happened too frequently for accident (and frequently enough so that for years later I avoided that route) to run smack-dab square into our new dean. "How's it going," he'd ask invariably, his off-white brow wrinkling with concern. "Do you find our courses difficult? Are you studying enough?" Until the first time he had asked, perhaps well into the third week of school, I had pretty much forgotten that I was supposed to feel anxious; I had forgotten the sociological consequences of being black from Appalachia and "at Yale." But I'd try to smile and retort coolly the most relaxed "Yeah" I could manage. And yeah I was studying every night, all night long, pulling all-nighters like some damn Labrador dragging a loaded dog sled through the blubber-white snow. And he'd just smile, not having broken stride, and keep on walking. Even now that walkway is not free of those "conversations," at least not quite for me.

I went to the dean's office once, amply nerved for the occasion, and stated my case as consistently as I could. He smiled benignly, because he understood, then told me how impossible the whole thing was. I think I had stopped listening once I had "peeped" his tone; for "yes" and "no" are secondary to tone, at least when you find yourself sitting across the desk from some white man whose wallet you're trying to share. Hope and aspiration are dashed or realized by that tone.

Back in my room I realized my mistake. So I set out to discover how Yale really worked and whether my pilgrimage to Africa was as unworthy as the dean would have me believe. I thought of my brother, that night in my room, and about his presentation of Weldon Johnson's "Creation." He was an eighth grader and I in the third. By this time the public schools had been integrated for three years, yet integrated always, it seemed to my mind. Or rather the matter never occurred to me until Little Rock, since my school had been "integrated" for as long as I had been in school; not too much had been made of the event, one way or the other. There was, however, a sustained attempt to maintain a conscious balance those first, vulnerable years in all the school's public functions. There was, of course, no question with sports, or rather the "question" was of an upper limit. But "Literary" was our biggest event, outside of basketball and the Junior Fair. It was on this stage at "Literary" that my brother found himself assigned the challenge of delivering, "dramatically," Johnson's "Creation."

At "Literary," two teams opposed each other with oral deliveries of well-known poems and debating matters. Each student, at registration to the high school, was assigned to a team for the War of the Roses. Half of us were of the House of York, the other half of the House of Lancaster. My brother was a Yorkist; much later, I would be a Lancastrian.

There were always favorites among the teachers and these included all the brightest and "best," the best being the offspring of the "better" families, though all of this was subtle, of course. My brother had been pitted, my mother later realized, against the child of one of the best. So, other than just a few cursory sessions with an "advisor" who tutored both sides as to what was "literary" and what was not, my brother was largely neglected, left to his own devices. But each night just after supper, after the stench of basketball practice had been showered away, my mom and my brother did that "Creation" over and over until it was right.

When my brother finally did step out onto that stage not even Paul Robeson could have defeated him! And when he told Moma about the whole thing, about how that old teacher had almost fainted when his clear bass voice shattered the silence, and how she had dared ask him, when the smoke finally cleared, just how he had learned to speak that way, all Moma did was smile. "Guess she had to earn the right to learn your name."

So I went to see the dean of deans, and stated my case in much the same way I had done a few days before. I waited for him to speak, for my story to sink in; shattering the silence in such situations often loses the day. It was all I could do to keep from screaming, laughing, and crying all the way to the bank. I didn't even think I heard exactly what he *did* say, but I heard what I wanted just in his tone. I could only stare wide-eyed as I watched him tell my dean that of course all this was possible and noble and worthy and that there was always a resource for this sort of proposal, when the proposer was one of the brightest and best. He had wanted to know my name; and I, a Tar Baby, was an arrogant enough part of Yale by now to treasure secretly the knowledge that my college dean didn't know my name. "Hustler" was his first guess; I'm still "Hustler" to this day.

You see, all the while I was defending myself against those black fellows who had forgotten my name, I found myself struggling even harder to keep white people (even at Yale) from changing my name, taking my name from me. "Black, scholarship boy, remarkable verbal potential for one in his demographic group; mediocre performance. C— student." This sort of naming ritual, a self-fulfilling appellative prophecy, they fit interchangeably onto so many of those bright black kids I loved at Yale, quite unlike a well-cast mold. So many of us who came to New Haven eager to fulfill that part of ourselves long repressed in ghetto schools and communities far too numerous to name, saw our deepest dreams dashed and our deepest fears realized in that sociological naming ritual. If we weren't crushed in a dialectic over what was "black" and what was "blacker," then we were crushed by those bored administrators and uninspired teachers who could not see the longing and the impatience to know buried deep behind the particular mask that each of us chose to wear. Perhaps slipshod, perhaps not so holy, yet these were *our* masks, and the care and the concern and the struggle and joy that went into fashioning and wearing them was all that some of us ever had at Yale and all that some of us have, now, left of Yale.

But, I was fortunate; I loved Yale. I loved the library and the seminars, I loved talking with the professors; I loved "peeping the hole card" in a person's assumptions and turning his logic upon himself. Yet through it all—through distribution requirements and pre-this and pre-that—I came to understand the Nigerian poet's admonition that "those who know their native culture and love it unchauvinistically are never lost when encountering the un-familiar,"[2] be that "unfamiliar" the very world itself. And what is the world? "All," replied Wittgenstein laconically, "that is the case."

Through it all I demanded of every person with whom I chanced to interact that they earn the right to learn my name. More often than not white folks stopped at "Hustler." And I, like Tar Baby, know I have won. Yet, had I been born a hundred years before, I bet I would have been a rainmaker, a traveling snake oil salesman, a nineteenth-century American medicine man, telling the more dubious among the crowd to "Step back, non-believers, or the rain will never fall." I listen for news and watch the mail for word of those I knew here, for news of those I loved and those I despised, of those few I trusted and of those few I feared. Only occasionally do I feel guilty that I was the lucky one, and only sometimes do I ask myself why.

REFERENCES

1. Ralph Ellison, *Shadow and Act* (New York: Random House, 1972), p. 147.
2. Wole Soyinka, Personal Communication, January 10, 1974.

JAMES A. THOMAS

Heavy Traffic on the Purple Brick Road:
The Route to Law School

*James Thomas, a law school dean of admissions and dean of
student affairs, is condemned to live with and then deal
with his selection mistakes during the three-year student
tour through legal studies. Thomas examines the earliest
motivations of law students; he is vexed by the blighting
of educational purpose caused by the competitive race and
the rejection of valued, innovative law school applicants
whose records are uneven. He sees that the consequences of
the admissions process may be destructive not only to the
student as a person but also to the profession, and he wonders "if there are more valuable and important qualities to
be sought after in applicants than intellectual superstardom."*

THE PAGEANTRY of a Yale University commencement is
splendid. Everywhere are lines of students and academics, prome-
nading regally to the strains of William Walton's "Crown Im-
perial March." Had he ever witnessed one of Yale's annual events,
Walton surely would have thought this the precise use for which

his piece is best suited, with apologies to George VI of Great Britain for whose coronation it was composed. Everything is colorful and phantasmagoric, rather like my memory of first viewing the motion picture *The Wizard of Oz*.

As faculty marshal for the school of law my task is to keep more than one hundred law degree candidates, each adorned with the purple tassel of law, in reasonable order. The line of march takes us over the Cross Campus, through the Noah Porter Gateway, across New Haven's Elm Street, and onto the Old Campus for the culmination of more than twenty years of education for the law students. There is, in fact, something about the long line of purple caps and hoods that is vaguely reminiscent of the yellow brick road to Oz. Many of the student travelers on the purple brick road are surely as interesting, and as varied, as Dorothy and her motley companions.

I invite you, therefore, to share with me some of my impressionistic meanderings along the purple brick road. If you are concerned that my experiences have no practical relationship to you, take heart—chances are excellent that your children will, at one time or another, consider a journey along this same purple pathway.

The Setting: Background Material in Black and White

During our admissions season at Yale Law School the telephones ring incessantly, both in my office and at my home. One casual thought repeats itself in brief interludes between calls—what do New Haven's six innocent citizens bearing the Thomas surname think about the inexplicable popularity, signaled by telephone calls from a group of unknown men and women, that recurs for them each year. I ponder my vulnerability, and consider my liability, were it known among them that I am the J. Thomas actually being sought by all those anxious people.

What is it like today to be Dean of Admissions at Yale Law

School? Yale is the toughest law school in this country for an aspiring law student to enter. Though a degree of excitement does occasionally enter the picture, for the most part my working life is routine. Along with my admissions responsibilities I am also the Dean for Student Affairs, sometimes known as the Gripe Dean. In that role I counsel students in their academic and personal lives. A colleague, noting my two roles, wryly pointed out how fitting it was that a dean of admissions be required to live and deal with his mistakes for three whole years.

The Professional-School Mania. When one considers the varieties of crazes that have taken root and flourished within the past decade in our American society, it should come as no surprise that there developed in the late 1960s a professional-school mania. American colleges and universities were aglow with student activism. Issues such as university governance, grading system reform, investment policies involving university resources, and even such sacred cows as tenure, became the active orders of the day for student involvement. Paralleling these issues in the political community was the question of our government's involvement in Southeast Asia. Another major question before the public and the students was how best to preserve our precious natural resources, including water and air. Because so many current issues were law related, a concomitant increased awareness of and interest in law study developed. Add to these concerns the Watergate affair, which kept our entire nation confronted with questions of legality and justice for several emotion-laden years, and you have all the necessary ingredients for law mania. The intense preoccupation with professional schooling was exacerbated by economic recession.

Law school admissions persons have noted the increase over the past five years in the numbers of law school applicants who already have Ph.D. degrees. They come from various backgrounds and disciplines seeking prestige and job security. With jobs becoming simply unavailable, large numbers of trained technicians, artisans, and others saw in the law, whatever might be its drawbacks, a profession in which people seemed to be steadily employed. Like the funeral business, law was viewed by many desperate applicants as capable of sustaining its dependents financially, even if many other forms of human enterprise should fail.

The number of television shows featuring lawyers and doctors during the period 1970 to 1975 was striking. Law was more than just a widespread observable phenomenon. For adolescents it was so constantly on display, so much a critical element in the society before them, that their heightened consciousnesses made them ripe ground for the germination of the idea of legal study.

One of the requirements for application to the Yale Law School (and most other law schools) is the submission of a short essay. Though most commonly the requirement takes the form of "Why I want to study law," the subject matter, for the Yale applicant, is left completely to the individual. Essays over the past six years reveal an interesting panorama. The particular instruction at Yale is stated as follows:

12. Write not more than 250 words about a subject of your interest.

Many enterprising pragmatists view the requirement as an opportunity to say what they feel the law school admissions people want to hear. Most often twelve to fourteen years ago, these statements took the form of expressed interest in governmental efforts to bring about various kinds of social and political reforms. The civil rights movement, then peaking, was a special favorite subject of many who thought of Yale Law School as a place where issues of social policy were paramount. Literally hundreds of essays spoke of commitment to equality of opportunity under law, with many expressing a career interest in the Department of Justice.

In recent years, following the Watergate debacle, government service has been less popular than public interest work in the private sector. The interest in consumer-related issues, the popularity of Ralph Nader, and the development of Public Interest Research

Groups are current manifestations of what applicants see as sure-fire topics of interest to admissions decision-makers.

Let us look at the statistics to get an idea of how many people have decided to walk the road toward law school.

Accredited American Law Schools (ABA)[1]

Year	Total Enrollment	First Year	LSAT Candidates
1963	49,552	20,776	30,528
1964	54,265	22,753	37,598
1965	59,744	24,167	39,406
1966	62,556	24,077	44,905
1967	64,406	24,267	47,110
1968	62,779	23,652	49,756
1969	68,386	29,128	59,050
1970	82,499	34,713	74,092
1971	94,468	36,171	107,479
1972	101,707	35,131	119,694
1973	106,102	37,018	121,262
1974	110,713	38,074	135,397
1975	116,991	39,038	133,546
1976	117,451	39,996	133,320
1977	118,453	*	128,135

* Figure not yet available.

In the past fourteen years the enrollment of law students has more than doubled in the ABA-accredited American law schools. Even these figures do not tell the full story, however, because interest in legal study must also be measured by looking at the phenomenal increase in numbers who have applied for law school over the years. Though there is no readily available repository of information about the numbers of law school applicants to all schools, an approximation may be determined by discounting the number of persons who took the Law School Admission Test (LSAT) in a particular year. Discounting would account for repeaters of the test (28 percent in the 1975 to 1976 processing year) and for those who decided not to apply to law school after having taken the test. The chart above shows the more than fourfold increase in LSAT candidates over the past fourteen years.

Another method of estimating the numbers of law school applicants in recent years is to use the numbers of Law School Data

Assembly Service (LSDAS) applicants. LSDAS is a service operated by the Educational Testing Service (ETS) through which college transcripts are received, processed (usually converted to a common 4.0 scale), duplicated, and submitted to all law schools designated by the applicant. The numbers of LSDAS registrants suggest at a minimum that in recent years there have been more than two applicants for every available place in the first-year class.

Year	LSDAS Candidates
1973	81,913
1974	85,999
1975	83,100
1976	82,243
1977	78,717

At Yale, the size of the law school has remained constant for a number of decades. Each first-year class ranges from 165 to 175. The number of applicants, on the other hand, has doubled on an annual basis since 1963:

Year	Applications	Year	Applications
1963	1557	1970	2740
1964	1767	1971	3300
1965	1942	1972	3035
1966	1789	1973	2840
1967	1754	1974	3200
1968	1839	1975	3143
1969	2360	1976	3503
		1977	3389

The Journey: Switch to Technicolor

Many applicants, judging from their essays, purport to have begun planning for law school at a very tender age, with intense interest in a legal career peaking in the years preceding college. These early preoccupations are often expressed, oddly enough, by students from families in which there are no lawyers.

And lest there be any doubt that some high school students do have fairly well-defined interests in the study of law, each year several high school classes either write to us as a group for information, or try to arrange visits to the law school. The groups are reasonably well informed and attentive and specifically inquire about what steps during college would enhance their chances of getting into a good law school. They already know about the increasing competitiveness of law school admissions. To no avail I offer my strong opinion that it is much too early for many of them to be thinking specifically about a postgraduate career. I characterize their impending college years as an opportunity to sample many different subjects and areas of possible career involvement. But as they look reverently about my office their expressions and comments tell me that my sermon for that week has gone unheeded.

Having made a legal career choice in college, the student questions whether specific courses have to be taken to assure a proper curriculum preparation for law school. The student inquires not just "What courses must I take?" but also "What courses should I take?" to maximize the chance for successful entry into a selected law school. The answer nearly always given to queries about course selection in college is that formulated by the Association of American Law Schools back in 1952. The view expressed then is still accepted current doctrine:

> The Association's responsibility in matter of prelegal education cannot best be met by prescribing certain courses and extracurricular activities for students planning later to study law. Such an endeavor is foreclosed by the wide range of a lawyer's tasks, and the correspondingly wide range for choice of relevant prelaw preparation. . . . But while it considers the prescription of particular courses unwise, the Association can properly call attention to the quality of undergraduate instruction which it believes fundamental to the later attainment of legal competence. That quality of education is concerned with the development in prelaw students of basic skills

218

and insights. It thus involves education for comprehension and expression in words, critical understanding of the human institutions and values with which the law deals, and creative power in thinking. The development of these fundamental capacities is not the monopoly of any one subject matter area, department or division. Rather, their development is the result of a highly individualized process pursued with high purpose and intensive intellectual effort by persons with at least a reasonable degree of native intelligence. Perhaps the most important variable ingredient of a proper climate for this process is the quality of undergraduate instruction. Certainly it is not any particular course or combination of courses. Shortly stated, what the law schools seek in their entering students is not accomplishment in mere memorization but accomplishment in understanding, the capacity to think for themselves and the ability to express their thoughts with clarity and force.[2]

Despite this oft-repeated message, many students become anxious about choosing the proper course of study to assure their qualification for entry to law school. This misplaced concern for taking the proper curricular path then collides head-on for some students with their real interests. The pass-fail courses now encouraged in many universities stir fears that the law schools will not approve the selection of such courses. Even in the freshman year, telephone calls or letters to law school admissions officers attempt to discover if it is inappropriate to take this or that course pass-fail. Five or six times each year an oversolicitous parent will inquire about particular major fields of study and will ask me to indicate a rank order of colleges preferred by our law school.

Enrolled law students confirm that during college much thought and deliberation goes into the student's selection of courses and instructors. Those students who aspire to attend a first-order competitive school must carefully manage their undergraduate curricula not only to avert the disastrous B grades and the fatal C grades, but also to steer a course away from an indulgence in pass-fail offerings. Such overindulgence may mean that much greater weight will fall upon the LSAT and, even if the LSAT score is an exceptional one, at some top schools the volume of high scorers threatens acceptance. At Yale Law School this year we had more than 1400 applicants with scores on the LSAT above 700, which represents score performance above the 97th percentile, demonstrating that this fear is not without foundation.

The amount and intensity of pressure upon college instructors for A grades is higher than it has ever been before. This development may be seen in the number of grade challenges, but also admissions officers are observing an increasing number of grade changes upward as we evaluate the transcripts during the middle of the senior year. In some undergraduate schools this pressure comes not from the students alone, but from various departments which regard their success in placing students into graduate and professional schools as the measure of their teaching effectiveness.

Grade Disputes. From the time some students enter college the apprehension about admission to law school drives them into combat with their professors over disputed grades. Curiously, at the time that battles are being waged over grades these same students, on the other hand, are wooing their teachers to write favorable letters of recommendation. Some of our students indicate that this pattern of alternate fighting and courtship between student and professor results in a bizarre Alice in Wonderland ritual. The learning process becomes subordinated to the all important end product, the course grade. At some institutions a grade of B is regarded as punitive by students and, I fear, some faculty. On the other hand, at schools where grade inflation is less than usual many students will panic, fearing that the law schools will not be aware of their unusual plight.

Letters of Recommendation. Letters of recommendation have become so devoid of meaningful content that rarely can an admissions officer put any faith in them. The pattern reveals an inflation of praise, an overstatement of merit, a conspicuous avoidance of anything negative, and a boiler plate of sanctimony that is reminiscent of Victorian poetry. What was once carefully guarded language with limited use of superlatives has become multilevel hyperbole where one damns with a fairly high amount of ordinary praise. How often the letters begin, "This is the best student that I have had in ten years of teaching!" Unrestrained superlatives without carefully drawn supportive data are often counterproductive.

The Law School Admission Test. For many students the LSAT hovers ominously in the shadows like the Wicked Witch of the West. Few events in students' lives are approached as apprehensively as the fateful Saturday morning when the "law boards" must be taken.

Just as the Scholastic Aptitude Tests (SAT's) were important in determining what college high school seniors could attend, so the LSAT governs the undergraduates' choices of law school, or so they perceive. For students from the Middle West and parts of the South, the American College Testing Program's battery of tests (ACT's) has a similar impact. Moreover, the law schools themselves broadcast the importance of the LSAT in loud, clear, and sometimes devastatingly forthright prose, aided by the use of admissions grids[3] and prompted by the notion that the higher the LSAT median at a law school the better the student body. College juniors and seniors are bedazzled and beguiled by scores of published "how to" manuals and by LSAT prep courses, some of which promise to deliver better test performance for a fee. In a clear response to the proliferation of such courses, the Law School Admission Council[4] in recent years has attempted to provide all students with some general test-taking strategies in the nature of coaching materials.[5] The idea has not been to drive independent entrepreneurs out of business, but rather to try to provide a measure of equality of access to such materials for all applicants regardless of their financial standing or the fortuity of their location. This effort has been sustained despite serious doubt among Council members and among ETS testing experts that the materials have any value beyond the limited exposure benefit and practice effects stemming from coaching studies.

A study recently completed by the ETS reinforces the belief that a strong link exists between LSAT scores, performance in law school, and, ultimately, on the bar examination. The researchers claim that the LSAT scores as predictors of law school grades parallel the empirical relationship between undergraduate and law school grades. Even if high scorers on the LSAT are top performers in law school, however, there are many observers who question the relationship between doing well on the test and achieving success in law practice or any other related endeavor. The ETS is currently collecting information from lawyers who were graduated five, ten, and twenty years ago, to learn if their legal education truly prepared them for their daily work. After an elaborate discussion of these interrelationships, the ETS admits that there is more to "lawyering" than grades and tests can capture![6]

Reliance on objectively measurable criteria—LSAT and GPA (grade point average) measurements—ignores the richness of what we have learned in the past twenty-five years about the developmental patterns of youth and young adults. Those whose formative conflicts intrude into their undergraduate scholarship and who can restitute themselves through growth and/or treatment will be lost to a legal career forever as a result of the fast shuffle given their applications by admissions offices. Where is the space for a medium-risk, high-gain candidate? Is not legal education for the accomplished "straight arrow" often associated with the deferral of resolutions of normal developmental crises which manifest themselves later in unhappy careers, broken marriages, and failures of parenting? Law schools striving for heterogeneous excellence in their student bodies may be rejecting valued, innovative student talent. Perhaps a new minority group should be identified and an affirmative-action program established for it.

Students exhibit a willingness to do whatever they can to maximize their scores on the LSAT. Unfortunately, a number of undergraduates have shown a willingness even to cheat on the test in different ways. Perhaps the most common practice has been for the student to hire someone known to be a good test-taker to substitute for him or her at the examination. Occasionally, an admissions officer will notice one of his or her own law students taking the test for an undergraduate. Normal security measures such as the handwriting check in cases of unusual score gains reveal a scattering of impostors. That the Law School Admission Council has adopted thumbprinting as a standard check in some administrations of the test highlights the recognition of the growing incidence of cheating. There are, in fact, suggestions that cheating has become widespread on many standardized tests.[7]

One need only observe an administration of the LSAT at a center to grasp the extent to which anxieties coalesce and surface on the day of the test. Clothing is mismatched and faces are drawn and worn. Many students appear stunned and dazed, as if they had been on all-night binges. Elementary instructions are botched and a steady stream of nervous people visit the rest-room facilities to seek relief for some of the symptoms of their anxiety.

In the days and weeks that follow the test administration, admissions offices are beleaguered by telephone calls, letters, and visits from those who are convinced that they have done poorly. We are told of physical illness, personal or familial misfortunes, environmental test center problems, and surprise due to variations in subject matter from what was expected on the test. Coupled with various pleas and alibis are narrations concerning the poor testing history of the student contrasted with the student's history of grade achievement. It is known, suspected, or hoped by many students that some admissions programs take into account such variables in assessing academic potential. In the period following the arrival of the test scores this traffic increases to a fever pitch.

Students of minority racial background plead the suspected cultural bias of the test and inquire about affirmative-action efforts of the law school. Older applicants, who were graduated from college years ago, complain of the inapplicability of the test to them and ask that special consideration be given their gainful involvement in nonacademic occupational pursuits. Students with relatively unimpressive academic records and very high test scores appear to persuade law schools that they have heretofore been unchallenged but are now ready to exhibit the discipline necessary for law study.

Many anecdotes kaleidoscopically reflect truth and fantasy, integrity and psychopathy, conscious and unconscious behavioral representations, in fact, the whole range of human experience brought to the fore by the admissions crisis. A young man came in late for his appointment because he had been involved in an automobile accident on the way to my office. He was the eldest of five children in his family. His father had died a few years earlier, at the same time it was discovered that his mother was suffering from a terminal illness. His role as family head was burdened by the recent discovery that one of his adolescent sisters was pregnant. His grades suffered badly because he worked to sustain the family. His girl friend abandoned him. Finally, a few days prior to the taking of the LSAT, he fractured the wrist of his writing hand. My response to the young man was sympathetic, but I could not help thinking as he left just how awful it would be if he became a lawyer and his bad luck followed him.

It is a colorful human parade which underscores the meaning given the test by applicants and law schools. The marchers arouse compassion and empathy in law faculty and administrators and compel serious questions about the problems of our society and the direction and ultimate meaning of selection policies.

With all thus far written as prelude, I wish now to glance briefly at the law student within the law school setting. For reasons of privacy I shall avoid identification of individual students. While my observations are pertinent to what can rightly be called a unique law school student body, they are, nevertheless, eminently applicable to the vast majority of ABA-accredited law schools in the country.

The Land of Oz: The Most Elite

It is often said that the law is a learned profession. Selection of law students at every law school in this country proceeds under the assumption that intelligence is the basic ingredient necessary in an ideal candidate. In today's postgraduate market, law, medicine, and business seem to occupy favorable competitive positions. The highest undergraduate achievers academically are drawn in significant numbers to one or another of these professional areas. However, the rich diet upon which law schools are now feeding was not always their bill of fare.

A few short decades ago my predecessors in admissions at Yale Law School had to scramble annually to get enough live bodies to fill the seats available. The admissions task was simply to determine if an individual applicant possessed the necessary academic credentials to get by. Drumming up enough interest in the law was the problem. Stories are legion about latecomers getting into the law school by appearing at the door at registration time with the requisite fee. One such case was a young man named Byron White. We know him today as an Associate Justice of the United States Supreme Court. Justice White, at an alumni meeting a few years ago, delighted in telling of the casualness with which he was admitted late. Today no such casual late admission could occur.

Since 1963 the yearly number of applicants to Yale Law School has more than doubled. Currently, approximately 3,500 applicants vie for the 165 to 170 seats available in the first-year class. There should be little wonder, then, that a successful candidate for admission experiences a sense of accomplishment and relief. That he or she has managed to win a place bolsters the pride of the student and nourishes the atmosphere of elitism within the community. But not only at Yale and a few comparable competitive law schools does an atmosphere of elitism exist. Because of the sure knowledge that only one law school applicant in every two and one-half who apply will get in anywhere today, many schools are experiencing a developing elitism. This elitism will inevitably become integrated as a characteristic of the legal profession itself.

The overemphasis on elitism as a positive value can result in bizarre human behavior. For example, a young woman who had not been admitted was discovered in our first-year class. The story of this stowaway reveals the desperate nature of the elitist drive in the extreme and the cleverness with which the elite prize can be pursued. It also stands as tragic testimony to the damage that can be done to young people as a consequence of the demands of the present selection system.

About three or four weeks into the 1975 to 1976 fall term I was contacted by a professor who reported to me what he assumed was an administrative error involving the number of persons in his first-term, small-group course in torts. Each new student at Yale is assigned in the first term to one small group of about sixteen to nineteen students. The professor reported that he in fact had seventeen students, although he was listed by the registrar as having only sixteen students. My perusal of his class list revealed one name with which I was unfamiliar, even though as Dean of Admissions I was aware of the names of all new J. D. candidates. Also present in our first-term courses, however, are candidates for the one-year degree of Master of Studies in Law. Upon checking with my colleague who sits on the M.S.L. committee, it was clear that Ms. X was not a visiting scholar. My colleague recalled having met Ms. X at our Orientation Day cocktail party, where she had identified herself to him as a "special student." She was not a "special student." The registrar's office reported that she was not on any official list maintained by the law school. Several of the registrar's secretaries knew of her and maintained that she was a law student. One secretary recalled that Ms. X had worked all summer in the Legal Services Office (LSO). LSO reported that Ms. X indeed had worked rather effectively for them during the summer. She came in early summer, announced herself as an entering law student, and was promptly put to work by that busy office. That job situation enabled Ms. X to become known as an entering student by many persons at the law school. When the fall term started Ms. X cleverly selected a series of professors whose courses corresponded with one of a number of curriculum slottings arranged by the registrar.

I called the young woman into my office. Ms. X confessed that she had not been admitted and told why she had attempted to pass herself off fraudulently as a Yale Law School student. She had graduated in June from a fine college with a good, but not exceptional, academic record. She had taken the LSAT twice and neither time did she score well enough in her mind to be seriously considered by Yale. She had approached admissions officers at her university's law school and at a few other schools and had been told that her case was at best a weak one. Most important of all, she had done considerable volunteer legal-aid work, while an undergraduate, which had stimulated her intense interest in law, and proved her ability to do legal work. Her confidence in herself was not completely misguided. The professor whose report began the investigation indicated that her performance placed her somewhere in the middle of an excellent class of law students.

What did Ms. X hope to accomplish with a scheme that was sure to be discovered? After assuring me that her motives were harmless, that is, that she did not mean to hurt anyone, and that she was willing to pay whatever costs she had incurred, Ms. X unfolded her rationale. She had desperately desired to attend law school. With her grades and board scores it was evident that she would not get into a law school of her choice. She felt qualified to attend such a school and was devoted to making a success of herself in law school. Why not, then, go to the top of her list of choices and prove herself by her actual performance there? She hoped to get far enough along so that she could take the first-term examinations and use the results to make a case for retrospective admission.

Her parents knew about the ruse and condoned it. They had visited the school early in the term and observed several classes, including the small-group course in torts. Neither of her parents had finished high school.

227

This unusual tale illustrates how one intrepid person bucked the competitive system and lost in a struggle to advance her educational goals. In a profession that needs to upgrade the ethical standards of its members, it is paradoxical that the severe stress admissions and selection policies puts upon its prospective members invites and threatens breaches of ethical and moral values established earlier in their lives.

The favorable market for law schools has produced an intellectual arms race in which the major law school powers are proliferating the development of bigger and better intellectual weaponry within their student bodies. Is there not a point of diminishing returns in such a struggle for supremacy? Will the legal profession ultimately benefit more from the contributions of intellectual superstars, or are there other more valuable and socially important qualities to be sought? Since there is no consensus amongst policy-makers as to what particular qualities can be effectively identified and utilized, the arms race continues.

Entering Metropolitan Oz. For the entering Yale student, there is an awesome quality to the achievements of his or her select group of peers. In addition, the reputation of the institution as elitist predates the student crunch of six years ago. The setting itself inspires profound respect.

On paper the characteristics of a first-year student at Yale are enough to impress even the most secure, tenured professor of law. Those same paper credentials can intimidate the struggling, young untenured professor, who must anticipate joining issues of mind with near-contemporaries without the benefit of the teacher's ultimate weapon, proven scholarship. For example, the average first-year student in the class of 1978 has an undergraduate cumulative grade point average of near 3.8 on a scale of 4.0. In terms of testing performance, the average student in that class scored about 723 on the LSAT, or just below the 98th percentile.

Most of these students are unaccustomed to being anywhere but in a position of leadership in any academic undertaking. Some respond to Yale by questioning their own capabilities. Short exposure to fellow students demonstrates that everyone is remarkably gifted. But some students seem to be better integrated, more positively directed than others. Real concern develops over why some other students seem to be better at synthesizing their seemingly unrelated studies. It does not occur to the worried student until later that perhaps there is no need to seek a reason why disjointed subjects should be meaningfully related. It is enough that some students appear to have discovered relationships. That in itself may stimulate the worried student to function less effectively.

The introduction of the so-called Socratic method of instruction can further befuddle the student. Through this technique the professor tries to illuminate an area or subject by use of a dialogue of questions and answers between himself and a selected student. The student is often on call for an extended period of time. Many paths chosen by the instructor turn out to be dead ends. In fairness, some law professors do intentionally aim to disarm the student of many preconceived notions. The idea is to strip away those firmly held beliefs long enough to permit reasoned analysis unhampered by personal dogma. The student sometimes considers the professor's actions to be cruel and pointless.

Complaints have come to my office concerning the Socratic technique from angry young men, distraught by the idea of having been picked out for spiteful attack, and from weeping young women, distressed that they were impugned. For an interesting picture of student responses to this and other law teaching techniques see an article by former Yale law professor Robert B. Stevens[*] in the *Virginia Law Review*, Vol. 59 (1973).

Some Ozian Newcomers. Reactions from among two student subgroups—women and minority students—bear special mention. These two groups have increased their numbers markedly in recent years in law schools.[8]

Women constituted just under 28 percent of the matriculants in the class of 1978 at Yale. Nationally, women represent about 28 percent of the total enrollment of law students. The percentage of

[*] Presently, Provost of Tulane University.

women at most law schools is rising steadily, and at a few schools women now outnumber the men.[9]

I am aware of some of the problems that exist for women law students through my student counseling. Overall for women, the picture is changing rapidly for the better. Pockets of male intransigence and hostility do exist, attitudes for which the woman who enters law school would do well to be prepared. I do not advocate a militant attitude in preparation, nor would I overemphasize collective action as the principal avenue for redress of real or imagined inequities. But each woman must be prepared to meet genteel male hostility stirred by the threat posed by the equal rights movement. She must also be ready to assume some roles traditionally defined as male. The women's movement in gaining statutory relief for women is, however, having a major impact upon faculty employment practices in both the public and private sectors and the expectable increases in women members of undergraduate faculties will have a salutary effect upon women students' views of themselves.

The academic achievement of women at law school has been comparable to the achievements of men (unlike at Yale College, where the women's grade point average has exceeded the men's performance). Women participate fully in the clinical, forensic, and scholarly aspects of law student life.

One observed characteristic, however, seems to have more impact upon women than upon men. The social microcosm of the female law student is more apt to come unglued than is the usually less sophisticated universe about the male student. This perhaps has something to do with differences in the emotional makeup of men and women, and with today's society's still different social expectations for men and women. But whatever the reasons, the breakdown of relationships with friends, particularly with spouses or those affianced, responsibility for the care of children, deaths or serious illness involving loved ones, and financial dependence upon parents are all likely to strike a more telling blow to the female law student than to the male student. The consequent effect upon the student's law studies is sometimes severe enough to bring her, or him, before the academic dean. Obviously, these personal tragedies and special responsibilities are not exclusive to women.

Law schools have remained quite aloof traditionally from the residues of *in loco parentis* roles which have been observable in various undergraduate colleges in the past decade. Increasing the presence of women in law school student bodies has diminished, at least for some deans and individual faculty members, that aloofness. Any minority group introduced into a formerly homogeneous community must necessarily require some additional counseling and support services. Law schools will have to look more closely at themselves in this regard and restructure some institutional features to accommodate the changing student constituency.

At Yale, several new policies reflect awareness of the increasing numbers of women. One such policy makes it possible, under limited circumstances, to extend the time for completion of the degree program. The student may petition the dean if his or her situation arises out of "serious illness, severe economic constraints, or major familial obligations." To date, this new policy is being used by women compared with the use by men at a ratio of two to one. Another policy change makes it easier for a Yale student whose spouse attends another law school to attend the spouse's school for one year and to receive credit toward the Yale degree.

Much has to be done at some law schools to accomplish necessary changes in the physical facilities. Both the increasing pressure of federal regulations and the dictates of local domestic tranquility require correction of myriad details which bear witness that most law schools were built when women were not a significant part of the student body or faculty. Attention is even being given by law professors to the elimination of sexual prejudices in their textbooks and other writings. Lectures may be slightly longer now due to the calculated neutralization of gender-related language. Often the use of "his" is quickly followed by "or her."

Three years ago a gracious female law student came into my office to complain about a survey she had just taken. Although only 15 precent of the administrative personnel on the first-floor corridor were males, the only rest-room facility was labeled "faculty," and was used exclusively by men. The women had to go either upstairs or all the way to the basement for vital necessaries. The situation was intolerable. Now this woman law student, being an industrious second-year advocate, hence worldly-wise in the ways of legal argumentation, did not rest her case with the simple recitation of these facts and arguments. She recounted a little story, which took place in the Divinity School, where a similar rest-room problem had existed. Some female students, trusting, no doubt, to the notion that God helps those who help themselves, marched on the men's room, adorned the urinals with flowers and lace, and changed the sign on the door from "Men" to "Water Closet." This extra bit of reasoning provided by the story quickly led the way to the establishment of a facility for women on the first-floor corridor.

The pattern for women in law school is part of a broader pattern of change which the entire society is experiencing. Because customary or traditional thought and action are related to and reflected by the laws of a society, it is certain that the interest of women in law study will continue to flourish.

Minority students are another group of newcomers to law study. We start with a definitional problem. What is a "minority" student? Hours of discussion have been spent on the question. Is educational disadvantage to be the key and, if so, does it encompass the group categorically or must it be tested for the individual? Is historical discrimination supported by law to be a key and, if so, must it be tested nationally, regionally, or locally? Is economic disadvantage a key and, if so, how must the test be formulated?

At Yale we have decided, for the present, to treat certain few racial minority groups affirmatively by addressing ourselves to their special needs until they enter into the student body under their own power. A resolution of the law faculty, buttressed by general mandates from the Yale Corporation, provides authority for the limited affirmative-action program. Just as with non-minority candidates, we seek within this program the most capable students available, insofar as that potential can be measured.

Apart from the legal issues involved in the implementation of the affirmative-action program is the question of what the impact of the minority student's status will be upon the development of his personal and professional identity. Only long-term social-psychiatric studies can begin to provide us with answers.

The minority student's initial concern is to overcome a substantial degree of apprehension about the university itself. What little prior knowledge the average student had about the university tends to feed any doubts already held about his or her own capabilities. Plunging headlong into a pool of bright, assertive peers is for some minority students downright scary.

In discussions about admissions policy the same questions appear and reappear: How does the faculty regard the minority students admitted to Yale? Does the special admissions program signal a second-class categorical reference?

Any minority program should be sensitive to the psychological needs of its students in addition to their educational program needs. Wherever possible, special admissions program goals should be stated affirmatively rather than simply acknowledged negatively as exceptional. In my experience, much of the heated debate with minority student groups centers on the law school's apparent perception of the worth and value of students admitted under special considerations, not on the usual questions of numbers and backgrounds.

Here I am obliged to reveal a feature of my own background, which revelation is regrettable, though necessary. My parents are a delightful colored couple, who are second- and third-generation Iowans. I describe them as they know themselves to be, without the educational and cultural advantages of their sons, both of whom were long enough exposed to the mid-1960s to become black.

Perhaps now my observations will take on a more colorful, if not more interesting aspect. I have often thought of myself—a

233

black dean caught between militant black law students and a threatened, powerful white faculty—as the perfect example of what it is like to be between a rock and a hard place. During the past six years I have drifted back to my old English literature texts on occasion to bolster my spiritual morale. Through the storms of student discontent I rediscovered the power of the opening lines of a Rudyard Kipling poem, "If you can keep your head when all about / Are losing theirs and blaming it on you . . ." During my lowest moments I cling tenaciously to William Cullen Bryant's poem "Thanatopsis." Bryant was a lawyer, and my suspicion is that he may have had some law deaning experience. (How else could he have written so emphatically to law school deans?) Until this day I carry in my wallet Friedrich Schiller's "Ode to Joy," in full German text, in anticipation of the moment when I relinquish my deanly duties to some other brave soul.

Back in the troubled times, beginning with the academic year 1969 to 1970, there were marches on my office, late-night visits of delegations to my home, memoranda of ultimatum on a regular basis (from students and faculty), a bomb threat now and then, and low-key criticism from my family for spending so much time at the office. All in all, now I am happy to be in the midst of more pacific times.

One especially unpleasant episode occurred five years ago when a black law student allegedly threatened a young law faculty member. The event prompted a disciplinary proceeding, sharply divided students and faculty and caused a deep rift in the student body. The incident reminded me that one must sometimes look beyond the words expressed to receive an intended emotive communication. Law professors, preoccupied with the meaning of words and not affects, may just be the least sensitive receivers of this level of communication in the modern world. The facts of the case were not much in dispute. It was agreed that the student had said that he would "knock the shit" out of the professor. Argument developed over the meaning of the utterance, the student claiming that there was no intention actually to batter the instructor and the instructor taking a more literal view of the expression. The student was represented by another black student in his third year who argued that in the southern ghetto context in which the accused grew up, such forceful language was almost a cultural necessity if you were conveying strong emotion. Contrary to normal expectations in such a matter, the students involved took the entire proceeding to public forum. The formal result of the proceeding was a compromise in which the student was found in technical violation but was given, in essence, a suspended sentence with a period of probation.

The sequelae of the episode were felt by the faculty a short time later at a meeting called by students to which it was invited. There, black students spoke emotionally of the hostility of their surroundings at Yale. The outpouring was as intense as it was unanticipated. What occurred was akin to what I had read in some of the writings of Ralph Ellison. The minority students were pleading for recognition. They cried to be heard, to be seen, and to be acknowledged as human beings. Whether the plea was justified, that is, whether things were really as bad as they were being characterized, is ultimately not important. That it was thought to be justified by the students was enough to make the problem very real and certainly intolerable.

Some years later I was on the defensive hot seat over the question of the types of minority students we were admitting. The student *agent provocateur* was a black graduate from Harvard College who had been admitted under the affirmative-action program, and whose eloquence carried him way beyond the usual bounds. As his argument evolved, he was asserting, in essence, that we had erred in admitting students such as himself. Now an argument of that sort can be made seriously, provided that the advocate does not overwork his sense of righteous indignation to the point of outrage. When he recognized that his argument was not evoking its intended response in me, he stormed away to work on it.

Humorlessness. An ability to laugh at themselves has been most evidently lacking in recent generations of law students, white and black, male and female. It may rightly be countered that my generation had more to laugh at by looking in the mirror. In retrospect, I am now happy that as dean I managed to suppress on occasion the compulsion to chuckle, snicker, or outright fall on the floor and double over with laughter. My stoicism was aided by the seriousness with which some present-day students went about doing very funny things. I recall working my way through a series of encounters between black students and the law school dining hall supervisor some years ago. The issue was the absence of soul food on the law school menu. I recall laughing myself all the way back to my house (then on campus), where my wife had a superb meal of neck bones and red beans simmering on the stove. What was funny to me was not the students' desire for "down home" cooking, but rather the idea that the dining service would be capable of mastering the fine art of preparing a chitterling dinner at the Yale Commons. As a connoisseur, my reluctance to attend such a meal would be understood.

The Wizard Provides. The impression that anything is possible for a great university has had other, perhaps more serious, manifestations in recent years. In a great debate over the question of elitism, one student suggested that Yale's historic pursuit of excellence made for misplaced priorities. Yale should be educating the more marginally intelligent student rather than seeking out the most gifted students who need the least help. This argument has all the trappings of a revelation. It is simple, direct, reasonable, and defensible in the abstract, but it is dead wrong. To presume that Yale has a special competence to deal with the marginal student is to aver that a howitzer could be used successfully to shoot arrows. Yale's greatness lies in what it provides for the capable, if not exceptional student.

Because of their expectations of what Yale can provide, many students experience a letdown during the middle year of law school. For the first time, many will seriously examine their motivation for being there. Most students survive the crisis with the view that though law school may not be all that they expected, nevertheless, it is where they want to be.

Is Oz for Everyone?

Some persons are being encouraged into law school who ought not be there. Those students who read high LSAT results alone as assuring a successful career in law ought to be warned against such foolhardy calculation. Intelligence alone does not assure success. Some very bright students get themselves hopelessly entangled in a neurotic web of their own spinning and are unable to extricate themselves. Bright people get ensnared in the thicket of indecision at the behest of others, or because no less objectionable alternative seems available. There are highly competitive persons who see only the challenge of getting into law school and who need continual prizes to sustain their motivation. Like Sisyphus, these people are subject to eternal frustration.

Some find their way out of the web. Three years ago, I said good-by to a brilliant young man who had studied classics as an undergraduate. He had earned a superb academic record and did exceedingly well on the LSAT. He came to law school primarily to satisfy his parents, who intimidated him with sharp questions about what could be done with a Ph.D. in classics. Midway through the second year, at a time when he was thriving academically, the young man approached me and said bluntly that he had finally come to his senses and that he wanted to go to graduate school.

Others not as courageous may go on down the purple brick road to compromised careers or to the agony of later career changes. Still others suffer silently, displacing their unhappiness onto family, clients, and the world in general.

The majority of travelers, however, like Dorothy, end up safely back in Kansas, or Oregon, or New York, where they manage to find self-fulfillment, career satisfaction, and where they make contributions to the forward movement of our society. Maybe the journey is really worthwhile after all.

REFERENCES

1. Information for chart obtained from James P. White, consultant on legal education for the American Bar Association, Professor of Law, Indiana University, Indianapolis School of Law.

2. Excerpt from *Statement on Prelegal Education*, published by the Association of American Law Schools (Washington, D.C., 1952).

3. Charts with one axis plotting undergraduate grade point average and the other plotting scores on the LSAT. Admissions grids are published annually in the *Prelaw Handbook*, a publication of the Educational Testing Service and the Law School Admission Council.

4. The Law School Admission Council is composed of schools with either American Bar Association or Association of American Law Schools accreditation. The Council is the policy body responsible for the Law School Admission Test and the Law School Data Assembly Service.

5. Each applicant for the Law School Admission Test receives sample questions for the test as well as an entire sample test with key. The materials are provided as a matter of policy of the Law School Admission Council.

6. *The New York Times*, September 29, 1976, p. 59.

7. See article by David Ray Papke, "Cheating the System," *Juris Doctor*, Vol. V, No. 5, May, 1975, pp. 12–13, 15.

8. See article by Millard H. Ruud and James P. White, "Legal Education and Profession Statistics, 1973–74," *Journal of Legal Education*, Vol. 26, No. 3, 1974, p. 342.

9. See article by James P. White, "Legal Education: A Time of Change," *American Bar Association Journal*, Vol. 62 (March 1976), p. 357. Northeastern University, University of California at Davis, and Antioch School of Law all had law student bodies in which women out-numbered men in the fall of 1975.

MORTON LEVITT

That Bouillabaisse: Medical School Admissions

Morton Levitt informs us that there are few hard facts about medical school admission that stand the test of time. From his critical review of admission criteria, he returns to Osler Peterson's almost twenty-five-year-old study which found that "a doctor's interests, motivations, attitudes and responsibilities toward his patients, and society in general," influence considerably the care he renders. In the light of the Peterson report, we view with some skepticism the fact that the new Medical College Admissions Test (MCAT), seeking a better measure of the qualities needed to become a doctor, has dropped the section on general information and has increased the number of questions dealing with gathering, analyzing, and evaluating scientific information. In the words of the President of the Association of American Medical Colleges (AAMC), Dr. John Cooper, "It may not be necessary to know what a Haydn symphony is" to be a good doctor. It seems to us that a medical school applicant familiar with our cultural endowment may grow to be a more humane and compassionate physician than a peer whose interests are remote from the humanities. An undergraduate college dean put it cogently: "Instead of narrowing to science scores their notions of what makes a good doctor, the AAMC should expand them to what makes a good person."

Levitt carefully considers issues of minority student admissions to medical school. His discussion is portentous when viewed in light of the Allan Bakke case, now before the U.S. Supreme Court, which was brought against the Regents of the University of California as a result of Bakke's rejection by the University of California School of Medicine at Davis. The Court's decision will likely rule on the permissibility of preferential university admissions policies and also, perhaps, on the broader issues of voluntary affirmative-action programs in general.

THE ANCIENT GREEKS felt that since doctors and judges were the only members of society who could kill with immunity in peacetime, it behooved all to be concerned with their education. Sigmund Freud once commented that he regarded teaching and healing as two "impossible" professions.[1] A man named Chapman, whose first name eludes me, has said, "If a student is not honest, sympathetic, and well-integrated when he enters medical school, he is unlikely to be any of these things when he leaves." Another man named Paine, whose first name was Thomas, wrote, "The state itself cannot be healthier than its people." From the above bouillabaisse, it is plain to see that society has had a long and justified interest in the training of physicians, and, by implication, in those who are selected for the requisite educational process.

Statistics from the Association of American Medical Colleges (AAMC) show that in 1976 some 41,648 individuals the country over filed over 360,000 applications for the 15,613 places open in American medical schools.* Each of the above applicants likely had completed at least three years of college, most had an honor point

---

* Recent (1977) figures reveal a record total of 60,039 students attending the nation's 120 medical schools, almost double the number in 1960. The freshman class entering in 1977 is reported to be 16,136 students.

240

average of something in the neighborhood of a B+, the vast majority had experience in working either in a hospital, a free clinic, or in some other kind of volunteer health program, and each was determined to find a seat in a medical school somewhere in the country. Most came from the middle class, had been educated in the larger state universities or the prestigious private colleges, had been brought up in the suburbs, and spoke persuasively in either their autobiographies or interviews (both usually required) for careers in the primary-care areas of medicine.

That only a fraction more than one-third can be successful in obtaining admission is easily determined from the figures cited above, and those not admitted will make up almost one-fourth of those who apply in the next year. Very few will succeed upon second application save for a handful who had optimistically tried for entrance after three years of college or an occasional late-bloomer who has managed to disown earlier educational deficits through some undergraduate or postgraduate remediation. A small number will enroll in Ph.D. programs in one of the basic sciences of medicine; of this group, a very few will ultimately achieve admission into medical school at one point or another in their academic careers.

Others who have been rejected will journey to foreign medical schools, learn the language, and devote the better part of a decade to qualifying for the Federation Licensing Examination in the United States. In so doing, this much-beleaguered group may become winners for the first time, for their pass rate on that particular test, not unexpectedly, far outstrips foreign medical graduates who do not speak English as their mother tongue. Schools which cater to Americans who have failed admission to U.S. schools have long made up a kind of medical education underground. Their relative status, provision of language preparation courses, and utilization of English texts and/or lectures have become common knowledge to marginal applicants.

More recently, and largely in a realistic effort to make distinctions between the above group and many poorly educated and non-

English-speaking immigrant doctors, some states have initiated legislation designed to encourage medical schools and hospitals to provide expanded clinical opportunities for expatriate Americans to qualify for licensure. While the facts are as yet not in, preliminary results suggest that performance of this small segment is widely skewed, that is, some operate at a level very close to that of their American-educated colleagues, but many are unable to overcome the deficits, presumed or otherwise, which seem indigenous to being medically educated abroad.

The above caveats do not apply to English medical schools, which rarely take Americans, or even to a handful of the great medical schools in the world wherever they are located, but surely the road back to this country's health system is a difficult one under most circumstances. And the path isn't any easier for those who envision remaining abroad after the completion of their education. In some countries only a highly selective group of students is allowed to complete clinical training and thereafter to practice independently. In other countries laws regarding foreign employment may completely restrict professional opportunities, and the now almost archaic literary term "innocents abroad" becomes sadly operative.

Some disappointed applicants in the medical school pool opt for careers in osteopathy. It was not uncommon a few years back to find a surprisingly large number of young adults who had previously appeared in medical school admissions offices in attendance at osteopathic schools. Recent changes in the attitude of the medical specialty boards now make this alternative choice a reasonable one. Unlike present practices, cross-fertilization was impossible a decade ago, and many who attended osteopathic schools once were forever barred from either conjunctive training or practice opportunities.

Finally, not a few of the unsuccessful applicants find employment opportunities in the paramedical fields, work in pharmaceutical houses, in physical therapy, optometry, or podiatry, as chemists or medical technicians, or in one of the many counseling professions. Still others never recover from their feeling of disappointment at not having had the opportunity for medical training and become virulent critics of the profession which refused them admission.

Some significant theoretical issues differentiate American medical education today from either its earlier national antecedents or its European counterparts. In our country, a careful effort to make realistic appraisals of the ratio between the number of students and the educational support required is *de rigueur*. The effort demands a careful review of such matters as classroom and laboratory space, available faculty, financial support, and sick patients for teaching purposes.

There is also a stringent effort on the part of medical schools to admit only those whose preparation seems to predict the completion of the educational course. The narrowing effect of these considerations upon the choice of successful applicants (and its ultimate impact upon the practicing profession itself) will be discussed later, but the prevailing philosophy in American medical education makes the size and composition of the class relatively predictable.

Neither of these two factors seem to merit the same attention in foreign medical education, where admission criteria are much more casual, and where there exists a corresponding willingness to allow for educational diversity. This is not to argue that foreign schools are more open and democratic, because this is not the case. Only the upper classes in most countries can aspire to advanced education, and it is from this group that medical students are derived. Still, observers of medical education in other countries are impressed by the large numbers (often as many as a thousand are admitted annually to a single class), and the more relaxed attitude toward time (some students take as much as seven or eight years to complete their professional education).

Despite these assertions about the narrowness of opportunity in American medical schools, we still attract applicants from all over the world, and while the chances of a foreigner gaining entry into one of our schools are very slim, American postgraduate programs (generally more hospitable to foreigners) are indisputably appealing to other nationals.

Earlier dire predictions about the impact of the end of the military draft or the decline of the post-World War II baby boom upon medical school admissions have proven erroneous. The number of applicants rose annually from 1970 to 1973; since 1973 there has been a small decline each year in the growth rate of applicants, with an approximate 0.1 percent decrease between 1975 and 1976. This slight decline in applicant growth rate is more than compensated for by an increase in the numbers of applications submitted per applicant. In 1975 there were 8.65 applications per applicant; in 1976 there were 8.83 applications per applicant. There are 4,788 new places and seventeen new medical schools in the United States since 1970 despite the fact that the doctor in the next generation will not enjoy his present-day autonomy and economic rewards.

What are the general characteristics of those admitted to medical school? Of the group accepted for the 14,185 seats in the class which was graduated in 1977, 7.5 percent were twenty years of age or under while only 4.5 percent were over twenty-eight. Very few individuals over thirty are ever accepted into the medical curriculum (probably less than 1 or 2 percent annually), and efforts to alter ethnic composition, especially a few years back, have brought their own particular kinds of problems. Legal suits are actively being mounted as part of the white backlash and have made medical schools cautious about attempts to expand their programs. Women, a very small minority in years past, are now encountered in relatively large numbers within our medical-training institutions, composing, in 1977, 23.7 percent of the total enrollment and 25.6 percent of the first-year class.

The Association of American Medical Colleges (AAMC) attempted to clarify admissions conditions in a summary published in 1976:

Clearly, applicants should recognize that their best chances for admission lie with medical school(s) within their own state and with private medical schools in neighboring states. Selection by a public school in another state is highly improbable unless a nonresident candidate has exceptionally strong credentials. It has been estimated that the typical out-of-state applicant only has about 1 chance in 50 of being admitted to a public school with strong limitations against accepting out-of-state students.[2]

With so many students wanting to enter medical schools for almost twenty years, it might be expected that a great deal is known about the scientific basis for admission. Law schools and schools of veterinary medicine, both recently becoming oversubscribed by applicants, have turned to medical schools for selection data, criteria, and predictions. Indeed, medical schools have intensively studied the admissions process. Two national workshops of the AAMC have been devoted to these efforts, and countless articles have appeared over the years in the *Journal of Medical Education* describing individual and collective efforts. Moreover, at least two sections of the largely expanded AAMC, the Group on Student Affairs and the Group on Research in Medical Education, annually devote the major portion of their programs to problems surrounding admissions. Still, there are few hard facts which stand the test of time.

Admissions Procedures

Almost all medical schools depend upon a similar series of admissions documents which include: (1) undergraduate academic performance; (2) scores on a nationally standardized test, recently revised, known as the Medical College Admission Test (MCAT), which measures knowledge in the areas of biology, chemistry, and physics—the test is designed to evaluate the student's problem-solving ability as well as his scientific knowledge; (3) letters of recommendation, either from college faculty or preferably from a college premedical advisory committee which tries to summarize individual recommendations in a predictive fashion; and (4) a personal interview, either on site by a member of the medical school admissions committee or by a colleague considered well qualified, if the applicant is some distance away. The interview is regarded as the sign of genuine interest, since most medical schools can only meet personally with those under serious consideration, although here political factors (those recommended by legislators, alumni, etc.) or geographical considerations (applicants from within the state or from the same campus as the medical school) may influence this decision.

The admissions committee, made up of a judicious mix of senior and junior faculty and, commonly these days, a sprinkling of students, reviews and evaluates the folders. A numerical grade or letter ranking is assigned each folder and those who have received the highest ranking are offered places in the class in successive order until the required number is achieved.

Since three groups of applicants are readily identified—those most handsomely qualified, those patently unacceptable, and a very large number who fall somewhere in the middle range—selection will proceed along fairly well-established lines. The prime candidates are likely to be sought by most of the schools to which they have applied, so recruiting efforts are most serious and persevering with this contingent. There is a widespread and probably justifiable feeling that the significant academic differences between most medical schools can be drawn from comparisons among the top third of the class, and so superior candidates are high priority admission targets for schools wishing to sustain scholarly quality.

With almost as much speed, poorly qualified candidates are identified and notified that no place exists for them. The academic records of this group are below acceptable standards, their MCAT scores are low, their motivation is diffuse, and often they have been rejected a number of times at all the medical schools to which they have applied.

The extremely large middle group provides the greatest admission challenge since they are often distinguishable from the superior group only in ways which come to seem less valid the more they are studied. Diversity in grading practices from school to school (data now becoming available suggest that some schools give almost no grades below C), differences in quality between colleges (how does an A in chemistry from Winnemucca Community College compare to a C+ in the same course from one of the nation's most demanding institutions?), widespread confusion about admission-test results, when the average margin of error is plus or minus 5 to 15 points (is a score of 595 a significantly different prognostic indicator than 575 under these circumstances?). All of these items confound efforts to make useful intragroup distinctions.

Letters of recommendation, always eagerly sought by applicants and eagerly read by faculty committees, receive mixed reviews since: (1) almost anyone can find somebody on the faculty willing to help out, and (2) standards of judgment on the part of the supporter are so ambiguous. Such communications have now become even more opaque. Federal legislation against confidentiality has brought about the expected "warm porridge" effect. Few faculty members are brave enough to risk the threat of legal actions from disappointed applicants looking for a ready scapegoat.

The personal interview, the last stratagem available to admissions committees, has similarly encountered threatening weather. All of us, whether we're scientists, humanists, or just ordinary folk, believe that eyeball confrontation yields much that is valuable. The interview, unfortunately, correlates with very little, save the prejudices of the person conducting it. All studies, within and without medical schools, which seek to link subsequent performance with interview rating yield a harvest of locusts. The introduction of a new class of raters, medical students who are only a year or two older than the applicant, has only served to further confound interview evaluations.

Perhaps we tend to like people whose standards and values are much like our own, and the difference between the skilled interviewer and the less experienced one may well be that the former has over the years been forced in painful fashion to admit to his fallibility and hopefully has built in a "shit detector." Ernest Hemingway felt each creative artist needed such a device to protect himself from those who sought to exploit him.

Even interviews by psychiatrists have not been notably more successful in making predictions since psychiatrists are mainly experienced in differentiating the normal from the pathological, or gradations thereof. There are two consolations, however, pertinent to the admission process, and they relate to the matter of selection for professional success.

The first has to do with the admittedly ambiguous relation between admission criteria and academic success. Here the research does provide some helpful data. The most reliable prediction of medical student achievement is a sophisticated equation combining the applicant's undergraduate academic performance and his MCAT record.

An interview can be used as an additional item of evidence rather than as a central consideration. It can evaluate verbal facility, general appearance, and likely qualities like sociability and worldliness. It cannot really serve to predict more subtle nuances like intelligence or, more importantly, emotional stability.

The foregoing is important because an admissions committee is compelled to choose the bulk of its accepted students from several hundred applicants who resemble each other very closely, and with techniques which are sometimes either whimsical or impressionistic or both. Human nature being what it is, those responsible for selection tend to look for ways to winnow down the long list, and with the selection cake so bountiful and standards so evanescent, it is small wonder that many worthwhile candidates are repeatedly passed over.

Thus, a single bad year, a poor mark in a required course, or a lukewarm letter of recommendation can occasionally turn the tide against an otherwise qualified applicant. In this last regard, I well recall a thirty minute discussion at an admissions committee meeting about one recommendation: "I would expect that George will become a good, if not excellent, clinician." A split committee debated the seemingly imponderable question: Was this a good recommendation or a bad one, that is, was George a "bumbler" from whom distinction could never be expected, or was his professor suggesting that an inspiring educational atmosphere might well yield an exceptional person? A phone call to the professor in question brought only the news that he was in England on sabbatical leave. Finally, someone on the admissions committee recalled that "everyone" in the Northwest knew that this particular educator set exacting standards, and that the suspicious phrase was in effect a strong endorsement.

While the comedic and tragic possibilities seem almost evenly balanced in the scenario sketched above, it is hardly offered as a typical example of the daily work of admissions offices in medical schools. It exemplifies, however, some of the dilemmas which must be confronted in making selection decisions from a pool of hundreds of well-qualified applicants when only a few can be admitted to professional training. The possibility admittedly exists that anyone who remains unselected at half a dozen schools has either had a fair review overall or has unfortunately applied to a set of schools with the same preconceived biases.

The second consolation concerns the connection between standards of performance in medical school and those ill-defined qualities associated with success in the medical profession. There is no general agreement about those personal qualities and/or merit badges which identify the outstanding physician. What seems irrefutable is that we really must know what we are seeking when we try to be judicious in selecting the raw material. Cynics in the computer industry have a vulgar way of expressing a similar thought in explaining to the uninitiated what a computer can or cannot do: "Garbage in, garbage out," that is, poor programming leads to uncertain results. The most significant contribution to the measurement of physician success came in 1953 from Osler Peterson and his colleagues at the University of North Carolina. Peterson attempted to obtain information about the problems of the general practitioner in the hope that the relationship between his "education, training, and continuing professional needs would become clearer."[3]

The study was based upon an evaluation of the physician's skill in making a diagnosis. Physicians classified as "low-level performers" were characterized as having a less comprehensive grasp of clinical skills which reflected inadequate clinical training. Physicians performing at a high level of professional competence were characterized as having been better medical students and having better training in internal medicine.

Peterson offered the generalization that better medical students (defined as those in the upper one-third or upper one-half of their class) appeared to acquire necessary clinical skills quickly, while less adept students needed relatively longer periods of time for the acquisition of these skills. The utilization of internal medicine as the core training area seems supportable since this area surely is at the heart of medical practice.

At the time of the study, however, there were relatively few facts available nationally about undergraduate records or performance on the Medical College Admission Test. This precluded Peterson from making meaningful comments about the admission process, but he did instead recommend that the quality of medical care could be improved by increasing "the length of training to that point at which a given physician, regardless of academic standing, achieves clinical competence."

Factors negatively related to physician performance were attendance of postgraduate courses and hospital and medical society meetings, and the *reading* of medical journals. Factors that did appear to have some positive association with physician performance—good laboratory facilities, provisions for patient comfort and convenience, the number of journals *purchased,* and the employment of trained technicians—were felt to reflect the physician's interest in his work rather than being determinants of his level of work. Peterson concluded that some combination of medical school performance and personality was the overriding consideration in predicting the level of later professional competence.

Thus, Peterson was drawn to some admission-related phenomena, namely the consideration of the physician as an individual. Here he argued that the doctor's interests, motivations, attitudes, and responsibilities toward his profession, his patients, and society in general, exerted a considerable influence on the level of medical care that he rendered. Peterson's conclusion was inevitable: "Identification of the attributes and characteristics of the individual who will make a successful student and practitioner of medicine presents a formidable problem but is of such importance that an attempt in this direction is justified."

A longitudinal study of a group who entered medical school in 1956 has been in progress for twenty years under the sponsorship of the AAMC. It is addressed to the broad question of the levels of ability and personal and social characteristics and the relationship of these characteristics to the type of career chosen and to later performance in that career. Some twenty-eight medical schools are participating and they include a representative sample of tax-supported and private institutions, geographic regions, and student ability levels.

This research will provide both pre- and post-dictive elements which may well yield the most comprehensive evaluation of the relationship between physician nature and nurture to date.

Almost a decade ago, Daniel Funkenstein of Harvard tried to identify institutional characteristics, and then sought to match those with the personal characteristics of applicants. He postulated that schools had specific and readily identifiable goals; some were known for the production of medical scientists, others for high-level clinicians, and even a few for family practitioners. Funkenstein contended that experienced admissions committees could factor out of applicants' records those qualities that made for a good marriage with institutional goals and that both medical students and schools would profit from this complementarity.

Apart from an elitist notion which undergirds this idea, he failed to recognize that young people change drastically during their educational experiences and that some medical school graduates finally decide on their careers as late as their internship year. This was clearly demonstrated in a study by Richard Saunders in the early 1960s which discovered that better than one-third of those surveyed at the beginning and end of their first postgraduate year had changed their professional "minds" about where they were going in medicine.[4]

Still, this was not all that was wrong with this effort to find a good match between students and medical schools. Cross-fertilization has much to offer both parties in any venture—educational or marital. Ivy League schools have traditionally enriched the lives of students from rural areas and the opposite is also patently true. There is much less cant these days in admission selection, and we have all come to believe that any student can find a fruitful climate for his educational ambition in almost any of the 120 approved medical schools in the United States.

There are, in addition, factors in operation which skew the admission pool. Surveys have indicated that rising tuition and severe cutbacks in student financial aid may well cause a dramatic change in the nation's medical school classes. To illustrate this point, the *American Medical Association News*, in its February 16, 1976, issue, contended that "those students who do get in and stay in come from wealthier families every year and graduate with larger debts than ever before." Student financial aid, long the responsibility of the federal establishment, has come upon hard times, and Washington appears to be antagonistic about continuing to provide scholarships and loans for students in the health sciences. National capitation programs which have supplied medical schools with money on a registered-student basis may well end, and there is little enthusiasm to be found in the statehouses for their resumption under local authority.

With the present political givens, medical education will become even more the province of the upper middle class. Each medical school class is wealthier than the one before. The median family income of the 1975 entering class was $21,333, which was more than 9 percent higher than the median family income of the class which entered in 1972.

Medical schools which have come, over the years, to rely on federal grants are facing a rapidly changing financial picture. With state governments showing considerable resentment over rising educational costs, it is likely that tuition fees will increase rapidly over the next few years. A confidential survey made in December of 1975 by the Congressional Budget Office has revealed that medical schools contemplated tuition increases over the next three years ranging from 36 percent to 159 percent from levels which average $3,660 per year for private schools and $1,195 per year for resident tuition in state schools.

In the nation's capital, Georgetown University School of Medicine increased its tuition to $6,800 for the entering class in 1976, and was compelled to move to $12,500 for the entering class in 1977 because the federal government withheld special funding for professional schools in the District of Columbia area. Albany Medical College charged $8,600 for tuition, books, room and board for the 1977 freshman class. To dramatize its plight, the Albany Medical College has conducted negotiations with state-supported schools to accept transfer students from Albany who are unable to pay the elevated tuition costs. In order to place soaring medical education costs in context, note that tuition, room and board in the 1977 to 1978 academic year in the Ivy League undergraduate schools cost in the neighborhood of $7,000.

When Northwestern University Medical School raised its 1977 to 1978 tuition by 57.6 percent to $6,855, a group of 264 second- and third-year medical students filed suit in the Illinois Circuit Court to hold the increase to 10 percent. The school claimed that the tuition increment was necessary to avoid dependence upon federal funding.* Students filed a similar suit against the New Jersey College of Medicine and Dentistry in February, 1977, but it has not yet been adjudicated.

Prime losers will, of course, be the ethnic minority students whose lack of financial resources render them highly vulnerable in a falling market. Economic trends notwithstanding, the message will certainly be heard throughout the country. Christopher Edley, Executive Director of the United Negro College Fund, has felt the cold wind, and his comment is trenchant:

> For 25 years we have struggled to motivate blacks to attend college. Now just when it seems we have had a breakthrough, the rules are being changed. A decrease in financial aid to low-income students . . . say[s] that the education of the poor and disadvantaged is a low priority and that in an economic crunch they will be the first to go and the last admitted.[5]

Affirmative-action programs which began in the universities in the late 1960s have had a major impact upon admission policies among schools of medicine. Surveys by the National Medical Association in the mid-1960s revealed that there were very few black

* Congress passed the Health Professions Educational Assistance Act of 1976, linking grants to medical schools to the schools' willingness to accept as many American citizens as possible as third-year transfer students from foreign medical schools. The medical schools protested that the government had no right to dictate admissions criteria or tell them whom to admit. Twelve schools stated that they would rather forfeit $11 million in federal aid than comply. Many schools began to increase their tuitions so they could be in a position to turn down government aid. Congress amended the 1976 Act in December 1977 to require the schools to expand their third-year classes by five percent for one year only, allowing the schools to apply their own admissions standards to applicants from abroad. If the schools do not increase their enrollments, they will face the loss of millions of dollars for the academic years 1978 and 1979.

medical students anywhere except at Howard and Meharry, the two predominantly black schools. Although Chicanos or American Indians were not studied, one can assume that their status was not vastly different.

Women were always present in small numbers in American medical schools at that time. The admissions community was pre-occupied with the amount of time women devoted to medical practice after graduation, which precluded their admission on an equal basis with male applicants. Admissions personnel averred that women physicians practiced one-third less time than their mascu-line classmates after graduation. This damning assertion prevented all but the most superior female applicants from being admitted to medical schools and created a challenging, hostile ambiance during interviews when a woman applied. We were suspicious of women who spoke of combining marriage, children, and medical practice, and conversely, came to select those who openly or implicitly denounced their biological rights and opted for typical masculine careers. Although no one ever said so directly, attractive women were usually regarded with suspicion since "we" all knew that they likely would be married either while still in medical school or im-mediately thereafter.

These biases contributed to a double standard in admissions. Women were discouraged from applying to medical schools by premedical advisors and, consequently, those who did apply had very strong academic credentials. Once admitted, they often per-formed superbly in medical school. My impression, based upon a quarter of a century of observation, is that women students were often found at or very near the top of their graduating classes.

Currently, while women are not admitted to medical school in accordance with their numbers in society itself, they constitute al-most a quarter of the total enrollment. This is a consequence of fed-eral emphasis upon affirmative-action standards as well as a deepen-ing concern in society about the rights of women.

With few exceptions, the larger group of women now admitted seems to perform almost as well as those few did before, and the diminution of restrictions in postgraduate education allows women to be trained in many medical specialties formerly closed to them. In the past, women had been accepted primarily in pediatrics, psychiatry, or general practice and were later not infrequently found in college health services or equally protected environments.

Today many barriers have been broken, and while one rarely finds females training in the surgical subspecialties (perhaps the last bastions of masculinity), they are often encountered in internal medicine and in general surgery. Changes in women's social roles suggest that the earlier surveys on the amounts of time women devote to practice might well be obsolete. Should these studies be redone, we might find very little significant difference between the sexes during this decade.

Other minority groups have fared less well. William Cadbury, a respected college dean at Haverford, made the first effort in the mid-sixties to open places for blacks in predominately white American medical schools. Aided by the Josiah Macy and Rockefeller Foundations, Cadbury selected a group of black students who had either failed of admission to medical school or who were not accepted in a medical school of their choice. Each of the handful selected was given an intensive summer's experience at Haverford in communication skills. Those who survived were then placed at some of the country's strongest liberal arts colleges for a year-long premedical science program. Cadbury's skill in remedying previous educational deficits came to be recognized, and those students recommended from his program were not only readily accepted into medical schools but were able to compete on an equal basis with their classmates.

By the beginning of this decade the same influences of increased social awareness and federal legislation brought forth some dramatic remedial measures. Minority applicants were eagerly recruited in strategy contests which retrospectively appear not too far removed from the playing field. They were offered substantial scholarship awards and loans to attend medical schools. While some were well qualified and would have been admitted under any circumstance, the larger number were students who had either been tried and found academically wanting, or who arrived with backgrounds that predicted mediocrity or failure in the rigorous medical school curriculum.

"Patch" programs became the order of the day, and typically those medical schools that accepted the largest number of minority students would devote the summer prior to entrance to remedial work. Most schools put together an intensive corrective session prior to the onset of the fall semester, trying in a few weeks to compensate for long-standing educational deprivation. The facts were simply these: most of those admitted in the minority programs would not have otherwise been accepted in medical school, for their records were recognizably inferior to those of students from majority backgrounds applying concurrently. This disparity was acceptable on the basis of economic disadvantage—a persuasive argument.

Still, minority students were older, wearier, most likely married and with children, and often heavily in debt. They had attended many schools of diverse quality in many locations, and not a few were educated while in military service. For a significant number, their personal situations and educational deficits were not remediable, and more often than not they could be found at the very bottom of their respective classes. For a number of years now it has seemed both unfair and unrealistic to judge them on the same basis as other medical students. It has been charged that their borderline performance coupled with our reluctance to remove them from the rolls for academic failure have constructed an artificial "bottom of the class" which enables other students to remain in medical school who might similarly have been dismissed in the past. Thus, fairness to minority students comes to require leniency for majority students, and in the final analysis, perhaps the public will be the potential loser.

Considerations like this brought Bernard Davis of the Harvard faculty to write an editorial which appeared in *The New England Journal of Medicine* on May 13, 1976. Davis's concerns were stated in a straightforward fashion:

> Many faculty members have wondered whether the stretching of standards in their schools in recent years has not exceeded what is reasonable. The problem is illustrated by a distinguished school that recently waived its National Board requirement and awarded a diploma to a student who had been unable to pass Part I in five tries. The award of this degree was virtually inevitable, after five years of investment by the school and the student. But we must look at the erosion of internal standards, and the postponement of decision, that allowed this situation to develop.

The results were cataclysmic. Davis's statement (easily identified as being based upon events in his own medical school) led to strong denials by the faculty, the dean, and the president of the university. Even the New England Medical Society, which publishes the prestigious *Journal,* criticized the editorial board for printing the article.

Cynics in the field of medical education have speculated that the "intemperate" response evoked by Dr. Davis's plaint was closely connected to the fact that the individual described was a minority student. This same group contends that the convulsive response which the article elicited would never have developed had Davis been writing an article which did not touch this admittedly sensitive nerve in American education. The supporters of the move to censure him contend that Davis's efforts created the impression that students admitted to the Harvard Medical School have diminished in quality in recent years. They also argue that the individual involved had indeed met all requirements for graduation save for the single one cited by Davis—the passing of National Board, Part

I—and that this technicality should not impede the graduation of someone otherwise qualified.

Pro and con articles continued to appear in the *Journal* and in other medical education publications as well. It is hard to separate truth from fiction in a controversy that has such a complicated base; still, the fire and smoke give evidence of the strong feelings involved in issues relating to the admission and graduation of students from diverse backgrounds.

Another assay of minority performance has recently been made at the University of California at San Diego Medical School.[6] The results of this survey seem more promising, but no one will really be able to make a final judgment on such matters until we know how minority applicants fare on National Board Examinations, on State Licensing Examinations, and on Specialty Board Examinations. Meanwhile, the whole issue of minority admissions has come under litigation with reverse discrimination usually the complaint. One suit—Bakke versus the Regents of the University of California*—brought by a white man who had failed to be admitted to medical school, was decided ambiguously by a judge in Yolo County, California, and has moved through the state and federal courts on appeal.

Certain minority students, dismissed for failure to meet academic standards, have recently begun to enter into litigation with universities. Four former students of the University of Illinois are reportedly suing for readmission to medical school claiming that their dismissal for failing to pass final comprehensive examina-

---

* In 1976, the California Supreme Court in the Bakke case invalidated as unconstitutional under the Fourteenth Amendment the special admissions program at the University of California School of Medicine at Davis. The U.S. Supreme Court on February 22, 1977, agreed to decide on the constitutionality of state university admissions programs which give special preferences to minority group members, often to the disadvantage of better qualified white applicants. Verbal arguments were heard by the Court on October 12, 1977, and unless the case is referred back to the lower courts, a decision is expected to be issued in June or July, 1978. Despite the expectation that the Supreme Court will rule on narrow grounds, the case has assumed large proportions, with broad political and social ramifications far beyond the admission of Allan Bakke to the University of California School of Medicine at Davis.

tions was unfair. A press conference organized in their behalf featured the militant support of Reverend Jesse Jackson. Another facet of this legal development has been seen in the University of California at Davis, where a minority student forced by the medical school faculty to repeat the basic science courses has instituted proceedings requesting general damages which "would probably be a sum commensurate with the plaintiff's earnings for two years of practice as an M.D." The courts have shown an increased willingness to entertain such suits, but there is as yet no visible trend in judicial decisions.

The matter of the courts reviewing faculty judgments about student performance may portend serious consequences to our tradition of academic freedom and invade historically determined and tested faculty prerogatives. The judiciary seems ready to undertake the review of the question of student competence, perhaps an extension of its usual functions in assessing competence in malpractice suits brought against graduate physicians. In my own opinion, I think that David Riesman of Harvard spoke best for the country's social conscience when he wrote:

> In the case of the law, liberty and property may be at stake, but rarely life; in the case of physicians where life is at stake, it seems to me bad medical students become iatrogenic physicians and should not be graduated, and that there is a solution, which is to keep both the moral standards and the technical standards high.[7]

These problems in both their practical and philosophical aspects are being directly confronted by the AAMC and its affiliated institutions. Recent studies[8] focusing upon the three interrelated areas (recruitment, selection, and programs after admission for women and minority students) have attracted wide attention. Relative to selection, it has been suggested that optimal prediction of academic success may depend upon different combinations of tests or measures which relate to the race or sex group involved. Apparently, standard scholastic aptitude tests and grades are consistently poor predictors of academic success for black applicants.

To implement these concerns, the Office of Minority Affairs of the AAMC has developed a Simulated Minority Admissions Exercise[9] which emphasizes the use of nontraditional predictors of student success. High on the list are such items as positive self-concept, realistic goals, understanding of and ability to deal with racism, a preference for long-range goals, and the availability of a strong support person.

Finally, the current studies emphasize a need for the institutions to "provide more flexible programs for students from different backgrounds with different learning styles and different understandings of what medical school is all about." There recommendations are seminal in that few of us previously had seriously thought through the complex problems associated with the admission and integration of this group of minority students into the traditional medical school.

In our eagerness to redress past grievances, we may have surrendered to the siren call of numbers without paying attention to the vital issue of qualification. Today, most of us are prepared to argue that those minorities admitted with subpar credentials must give some evidence of compensatory characteristics, that is, there must be elements in their records which convince us that their past deficits are remediable in existing or prospective programs. This overview requires honest answers to searching questions: "What is it that X can become, and in what time interval, and what can X ultimately bring to the profession of medicine?"

Two other admission areas have attracted concern in the last decade. The first concerns health requirements for applicants. A dozen years or so ago, it was commonplace to see otherwise-qualified applicants denied admission because of longstanding physical disabilities which were thought to impair, seriously, performance as a physician. Prime among such "silent" illnesses were epilepsy, poliomyelitis, diabetes, and sensory disorders including loss of sight or hearing. Apart from cosmetic considerations ("Shouldn't a physician look healthy?"), many argued persuasively that the undeniably stressful demands of a medical career would be excessive for applicants with serious infirmities.

For reasons not entirely clear to me, admissions restraints for the physically impaired have been relaxed. Perhaps it came about because admissions committees were becoming more reflective and realistic about assessing the effects of a disability upon performance in the varied medical specialties. Competent students with physical disabilities are now being readily admitted in a comparatively straightforward fashion when it has been demonstrated that their deficit has not undermined their capacity to cope with the exigencies of daily living. An eastern medical school recently graduated one man who had been blind from birth and whose passage through life was made in the company of a seeing-eye dog.

The second area attracting attention in the last decade pertains to the admission of applicants who have suffered with emotional problems. Two studies[10, 11] that Ben Rubenstein and I did in the 1950s and 1960s sought to evaluate admissions committee responses to students who "admitted to having been in psychiatric treatment prior to admission." Both studies supported the hypothesis that an applicant who stated that he had been in treatment was not as likely to be accepted as another applicant, if all other qualifications were equal.

Each survey attempted to deal with the following three questions:

1. Does the training for life and death responsibility of the physician rule out admission to or continuance in medical school of students who have suffered emotional illnesses?

2. Are such persons *ipso facto* constitutionally inferior and therefore incapable of meeting the requirements of medical training?

3. Does this not suggest or encourage an outlook on the part

of faculty and student that the acceptable hallmark of adjustment is the ability to keep all aberrations out of sight?

Underlying these questions was the basic assumption that the student's ability to adjust to the rigors of medical education must be considered the first step in achieving success in the medical profession. A student who survives medical school is, all things being equal, a better bet than one who has broken down; while one who suffers an upset so manifest that all or most of the institutional personnel become aware of it should probably be carefully evaluated before being allowed to continue. On the other hand, the authors argued that a student who is emotionally ill but adapts well enough to keep his upset under cover, whether or not he is in therapy, represents the better investment.

Although the questions cited above were directed at events transpiring within the medical school community itself, we felt that the proposition was equally applicable to premedical education. Today, most applicants to medical school make use of a standardized admission application known as AMCAS (American Medical College Application Service). The form contains two pertinent questions: "Do you have or have you had any chronic or recurrent illnesses, emotional problems, or bodily defects?" and "Has your schooling or employment ever been interrupted because of the health problems referred to above?" The inquiry, seemingly uncomplicated at first glance, includes two relatively new notions. The first idea is that "chronic" or "recurrent" illnesses can be contrasted to transient states, and the second is a welcome concern with severity to be seen in the matter of "interruption" of routinely-expected functioning.

Although no new formal data is available, the impression exists once again that admissions committees are currently somewhat more receptive than before to the admission of students who acknowledge having been in psychotherapy. Earlier definitions of emotional illness have now been subjected to considerable refining, that is, untold thousands of young people do consult psychiatrists, psychologists, and social workers in college mental health clinics or elsewhere episodically or for extended periods of time.

Earlier practices seemed to make little discrimination between certain kinds of consultative experiences which are usually defined in psychiatric diagnostic statistical manuals (DSM) as "reactive disorders," and those more serious conditions which interfere with the functional capacity of an individual to survive in an academic environment. In reviewing these complicated issues in 1958 and 1967, we suggested that "correlative methods must be devised for the evaluations of applicants and that medical schools do have additional assessment tools at hand."

Conceding the fact that young people often are in conflict with themselves or with the external world, we felt, nonetheless, that there were areas of life where the individual must manage competently and where functioning could be accepted as a measure of that individual's ability to master his or her conflicts. These areas include the following:

1. A person's objective overall performance as compared to potential (the usual combination of HPA [honor-point average] and MCAT or CEEB [College Entrance Examination Board] scores).

2. The ability to conduct oneself with a sense of ethical responsibility.

3. Demonstration of internal discipline, that is, the ability to live generally within the rules of the institution or society.

Borrowing liberally from physiology, we called this the "functional capacity" of an individual and argued that these three areas should be managed without undue organic or functional upset and with some degree of enthusiasm and humor. We felt then and still feel today that selection and assessment programs that focus on such dimensions of functioning seem to have the best chance for success.

How this information can be readily elicited is another question. Obviously, a candidate for professional school admission has already lived one-quarter to one-third the human expected life span and has had a bulk of experiences which, when viewed reflectively, make up a life style. It is necessary that admissions officers spend enough time with the student and with the student's record to grasp something of this style and to decide whether preferences and potentials are consistent with the institution's overall goals. The intent here is not to imply that there should be one particular kind of applicant; it is hoped rather that the functional assessment will prove to be the most meaningful component in faculty evaluation of students.

At the same time, the problems of implementing this proposal are recognizable. Admissions committees cannot be expected to make decisions concerning the applicant's suitability for professional training in a few minutes; they must be prepared to spend as much time as is necessary for such assessment. In rethinking the problem, the following questions must be considered: Is the time ripe for recommending that medical schools *not* solicit information about emotional illness or psychotherapy? Will this procedure free admissions committees to devote their attention to a careful assessment of the multidimensional performance criteria previously listed? If such information is not solicited on application blanks, it will not be recorded. If it is not solicited, won't those form letters of recommendation tend more to be based upon the broadest possible description of student performance? Most experienced observers of the medical school admission scene would answer all these questions in the affirmative.

Federal legislation regarding confidentiality (Family Educational Rights and Privacy Act of 1974) sets limits to the kind and amount of information that can be routinely furnished either a prospective employer or an institution of higher education. No one can deny that there are some inherent risks in such a proposal, for it seems to ensure that at least a few seriously disturbed individuals will be accepted in those professional schools that demand personal stability and psychological integrity.

One such incident recently occurred on the West Coast where a student with superior undergraduate credentials and recommendations from the arts college on the same campus was admitted to the medical school. He suffered an acute schizophrenic episode as he entered the clinical portion of his training. When he was hospitalized at the university infirmary, the medical school learned that he had a long history of psychological infirmity, information which could have been made available if the medical school had sought a routine clearance from the health service for each student admitted from its parent campus.

Apart from the basic inequity of the proposal to a particular group of applicants (no other campuses were volunteering similar services), there are serious ethical issues involved in such "tagging." We can agree that this student should have been denied admission. Yet, there is a clear and evident danger to numerous other students who were in psychiatric treatment, but who survived handily the stress of medical school. The greatest good for the greatest number still seems to be the most convincing argument.

I have tried in the preceding pages to speak forthrightly about a number of problems that are encountered intramurally and extramurally on the road to admission to medical schools. There is little doubt that someone's favorite ox has been gored in the effort, but I am (and always have been) sentimentally drawn to Robert Hutchins's definition of a university as "bodies of men pursuing the truth, discussing it with one another, and criticizing the environment with utmost freedom." This is, of course, not the way things really are in any educational institution, or anywhere else for that matter, but it is the way things ought to be.

Changes in medical education, and there have been many in recent years, impact directly upon both the practicing profession and those who wish to join it. It is impossible to believe that social changes and the educational changes that inevitably follow will fail to influence the characteristics sought in those who ultimately bear life and death responsibility for their fellowman. Still, no one can predict at what point and in what form these alterations will come about, and one is reminded of Robert Glaser's provocative recollection in *Daedalus*[12] of the current-day Chinese historian's answer to a question seeking his assessment of the significance of the French Revolution: "It is too soon to tell."

REFERENCES

1. August Aichorn, *Wayward Youth* (New York: Viking Press, 1925), p. v.

2. Association of American Medical Colleges, *Medical School Admissions Requirements 1976–1977* (Washington, D.C.), p. 13.

3. Osler L. Peterson, "An Analytical Study of North Carolina General Practice," *The Journal of Medical Education*, Vol. 31, no. 12 (December 1956), pp. 1–165.

4. Richard H. Saunders, Jr., "The University Hospital Internship in 1960: A Study of the Programs of Twenty-Seven Major Teaching Hospitals," *The Journal of Medical Education*, Vol. 36, no. 6 (June 1961), pp. 561–676.

5. The New York Times, January 31, 1976, p. C25.

6. Harold J. Simon and James W. Covell, "Performances of Medical Students Admitted via Regular and Admissions-Variance Routes," *The Journal of Medical Education*, Vol. 50, no. 3 (March 1975), pp. 237–241.

7. David Riesman, Personal Communication, December 29, 1975.

8. Davis E. Johnson and James W. Covell, "Retention by Sex and Race of 1968–1972 U.S. Medical School Entrants," *The Journal of Medical Education*, Vol. 50, no. 10 (October 1975), pp. 931–932.

9. *Ibid.*, p. 932.

10. Morton Levitt and Ben Rubenstein, Presentation to the Panel on Medical Education at the Annual Meeting of the American Orthopsychiatric Association (Chicago, Ill.: 1959).

11. Morton Levitt and Ben Rubenstein, "Medical School Faculty Attitudes Toward Applicants and Students with Emotional Problems," *The Journal of Medical Education*, Vol. 42, no. 8 (August 1967), pp. 742–751.

12. Robert J. Glaser, "A Note on the 'University Troubles' and Their Impact on the Medical Schools," *American Higher Education: Toward an Uncertain Future II*. S. R. Graubard, ed., *Daedalus, Journal of American Academy of Arts and Sciences*, Winter, 1975, p. 258.

ERIC K. GOODMAN

Medical School, Law School, and Beyond

Eric Goodman was an uncommon student who might today be in either medical school or law school but who opted instead for a creative writing fellowship at Stanford. Politically active, sensitive to social inequity, with a reservoir of life-sustaining energy, Goodman underwent a career crisis that inspired him to sort out his ties to his family and gave him new insights into himself. He now moves forward eagerly, an author and editor, trying to resolve issues delayed by a system which has elliptically shaped his considerable resources and motivations.

IT WAS ASSUMED I would become a doctor. I don't know who made the assumption, how or when, but somehow, it existed. There was little conversation to the contrary, not even much thought. I was an A student throughout high school, working summers in hospital and research laboratories, secure in the knowledge that somewhere, sometime in the benevolent future, I would earn my M.D. degree. That result was probable, even likely. All that stood between me and medical school were four years at Yale. But in the end, I never made it.

Freshman year at Yale was a time of changes. No one was worried about the recession or a future career. Long hair still prevailed on campus, students were heavily into drugs. In April, 1970, the U.S. mined Haiphong harbor, and Yale was closed by a student strike. Academic concerns were an adjunct to, not the center of my existence; personal growth, realization of potential mattered more. I met one virulent premedical student early in the fall who was worried about exams after the first two weeks of the term, and dismissed him as perverse. I'd grubbed for grades throughout high school in order to reach Yale. Enough of that, I thought; just don't get any C's.

I enrolled in Yale's highest-level freshman chemistry course as well as the prerequisite for the English major. One afternoon a week, I volunteered as an aide in a mental hospital. Another freshman and I worked on a biochemistry research project that he later wrote about for the *Yale Scientific*. I fasted five days to protest the resumed bombing of North Vietnam. And late in the spring I decided I was going to major in English.

A minimum of one-third of the courses taken by students bound for med school are required by the medical school admission committee. The extreme pressure to perform well in these science courses results in an atmosphere of controlled mass hysteria that is at its most dense and deadly in the lecture hall set aside for organic chemistry.

I took "Orgo" as a sophomore, the year during which I first became involved in Yale's undergraduate writing community. I was the fiction editor, then general editor of the *Yale Daily News Magazine*, a publication sponsored by the undergraduate newspaper. Slowly, my self-perception changed. I was no longer premed, but a writer who happened to be preparing for medical school—an identification that allowed me to detach myself from the horde trooping off to organic chemistry three times weekly. It became "me" against "them," an antagonistic stance that made it easier to write and edit, but that in the end was destructive to my plans for med school.

269

I look a leave of absence from Yale in the spring of my junior year to start a novel. I lived in New Haven, still edited the *Yale Daily News Magazine*, and, under the informal aegis of John Hersey, produced seven mediocre chapters, most of which I later discarded. In May, before leaving the country for Mexico, I completed an American Medical College Application Service (AMCAS) application, arranging with my parents to have it submitted on the first possible date. AMCAS is an organization that coordinates a standardized application procedure used by most U.S. medical schools. Students submit one application to AMCAS, which forwards a copy to all participating schools indicated by the applicant. Upon receipt of the AMCAS package, medical school admission committees ask a certain percentage of applicants for additional information—professor recommendations and a dean's office summary. By submitting my AMCAS application early, I was ahead of the game.

The ten weeks in Mexico were different from anything I'd known. It was as if I were vacationing from my life; the achievement-oriented value structure I was accustomed to no longer mattered. In Cuernavaca I lived with a Mexican family that hadn't heard of Yale. Letters from journalism friends who were pushing to publish in newsstand magazines didn't make any sense. Yale, my novel, were distant concerns; medical school, a vague annoyance somewhere out there, easily dealt with later.

That sense of serenity was shattered by the pile of requests for additional information on my desk when I arrived home. The world, my life-as-it-really-was, snapped out at me—time to give serious thought to what I was doing. Did I really want to be in medical school?

The previous spring, between writing the novel and preparing for the trip, I'd dodged the issue. Completing the AMCAS application was simpler than discarding it, since the latter would have required a decision to *not* fill it out. Acts of negation are extraordinarily difficult for me. Everyone wants to hear you say "Yes," and by nature, I'm a crowd-pleaser. Now the summer was ending, I had only ten days with my girl friend before we were to be separated by the beginning of another year of school. It wasn't a time propitious for difficult decisions, and I followed the line of least resistance, called in additional information requests to the Yale Career Advisory Service and began applying to schools that were not part of the AMCAS system (primarily high prestige institutions: the Ivies, Stanford, and others that proclaim their special status by requiring separate applications and fees).

My academic record was certain to induce at least a few medical schools to invite me for an interview. Normally, pre-medical students regard interview offers as cause for celebration. They are the next-to-last step in the application ritual and indicate that one's undergraduate record has met with considerable approval.

Actually, interviews mean a good deal more than that, because the average pre-med student has invested so much of his time and psychic energy in preparing for medical school, he puts his self-esteem on the line. Rejection at any stage is a blow to one's self-regard, whereas a large number of interview offers and subsequent acceptances justify the heavy personal investment in preprofessional preparation.

But interviews presented a problem for me; remembering why I wanted to attend medical school was becoming difficult. I couldn't visualize myself there. Without a clear rationale for attending any medical school, finding convincing reasons for selecting one school in particular would have been a fabrication.

Part of my bond with Barbara, my girl friend, had been a common desire to become a doctor. She was a pre-medical student, and in a big way, at Johns Hopkins University, a school where everyone seemed to be pre-med. There is the unspoken assumption among high school seniors that because Hopkins Medical School is part of the larger university (a) it will be easier to gain admission to the medical school if one is a student at the university and (b) its mystique will rub off on the unsuspecting undergraduate by his mere presence in Baltimore. Neither is substantially true.

I disliked Johns Hopkins the entire time Barbara was there.

271

There exists on that campus a feeling of jangled nerves, an over-weening concern with what *they* (medical school admission offices) want. For most students on the Hopkins campus, the undergraduate years are a corridor to be passed through as quickly as possible en route to medical school. There appears to be no academic excitement or emphasis upon intellectual growth. Rather there is provision for the garnering of as many brownie points through research projects and advanced science courses, that is, biochemistry, genetics, and so on, which students think *they* require. The Hopkins administration encourages this attitude by granting college credits for high school work, thereby allowing students to finish a B.A. in two and one-half or three years. I feel that this cheapens an undergraduate degree, reducing it to a task to be completed as quickly and as painlessly as possible.

Barbara was as disenchanted with Yale as I was with Johns Hopkins, but for different reasons. Whatever changes had occurred in me, she attributed to my tenure in New Haven. Our relationship was essentially backward looking, setting up our senior years in high school as the norm and ideal against which all other times were to be measured. In high school I was already interested in literature but I was primarily committed to science and an M.D. degree. My growing interest in fiction and journalism were changes Barbara distrusted. Not only were they Yale-wrought; they punched holes in memories of a unified past and lessened the prospects of a unified future. Barbara assumed we would eventually marry; I enjoyed the intimacy of the relationship but marriage was not one of my primary considerations.

Shortly after my return to Yale for the fall semester, I met Sue, a Yale senior, and became seriously involved with her. Despite regular dating during our years apart, neither Barbara nor I had ever committed ourselves to anyone else. But I had been seeing Sue for only two weeks when I knew from the intensity with which the relationship developed that it might replace my long-standing bond with Barbara. My aspirations in medicine and my affection for Barbara were fused, and I realize now that my love for Sue represented a move away from medicine.

After a month at Yale I visited Barbara in Baltimore. We passed the hospital where she had worked the previous summer as a research assistant. As she began to describe the lab, what she had done, whom she had known, I felt myself choking. Stay out, a voice screamed. Don't let them get their hands on you or they'll destroy you.

In retrospect that premonition was a strange one for someone who was acquainted with the workings of hospitals and their laboratories. I'd worked five of my first six semesters at Yale as a hospital volunteer (including three as an emergency-room aide), and the tasks were always rewarding. But as Barbara talked, the hospital's bulk loomed gray and squat as a mausoleum. I was sick to my stomach just thinking about spending any time there.

That ended it. Saturday I told Barbara that medical school and I would never be joined. To my surprise, she was very understanding. One of my objections to becoming a physician was that, in my limited experience, medicine did not appear to be sufficiently creative or intellectual. Another possibility I'd explored earlier in the fall, still within the context of a medical school application, was enrolling in Duke University's special program which would train me as both a lawyer and a doctor. I enjoyed a fantasy of challenging the social inequities of the medical system; administrating, making things happen, was something I'd enjoyed doing as a magazine editor. So we talked grandiosely about my running the show somewhere, perhaps going to law school, or capitalizing on my experience and interest in journalism, becoming a communications czar.

Before proceeding, I would like to make explicit certain of my idiosyncrasies, so that my impulsiveness might be better understood:

1. I am ambitious and seek recognition. This predisposition has led me to distinguish between public and private careers. Al-

though lawyers and doctors constantly work with people, they are engaged in private professions. Financial security and regard by the community-at-large are available to them, but true appreciation of their work is limited to a professional peer group. Writers, on the other hand, work alone but practice a very public profession. Success is measured ultimately in terms of public recognition and influence. A successful writer is admired by the general public.

2. I am overly influenced by the expectations of others. "I will not" is infinitely harder for me to pronounce than its converse, "I will." No matter what course one decides upon, there is often a respected someone, be it lover, friend, or parent, who will counsel the exact opposite. My parents, concerned with my future well-being, had indoctrinated me early with the idea that to be successful meant being a "professional." My friends at Yale, most of whom were writers, couldn't understand why I would want to waste time earning a professional degree when what I really wanted to do was write.

3. Many things make me happy.

4. I tend toward fatalism, abandoning to serendipity decisions I should really make myself.

I returned from Baltimore flushed with the decision not to enter medical school. However, I took no action other than to cut my physics lecture with great regularity.

Yale offers a variety of first-year physics courses that fulfil medical school requirements and range in scientific rigor from transparent to intense. I was enrolled in the Physics for Poets course (transparent rigor), and anticipated no difficulties other than finding sufficient motivation to attend classes.

I floated for several weeks. During this time there were two important developments. My love for Sue preoccupied me, and interview offers began to arrive from medical schools. In response to these developments, I broke the silence Barbara and I had established during our four-year union and told her about Sue. The announcement abruptly ended our relationship.

In my struggle with vocational drive, I had ended my relationship with one woman for another. There was no vacuum or dead space, no loneliness or uncertainty. It was a decision motivated only by what I could touch and feel.

My ambivalence about medical education grew with the arrival of interview offers and the rupture of my relationship with Barbara. How was I to deal with my hopes for myself and the expectations of a gallery of my parents, relatives, mentors, and friends?

A problem. Nonetheless, I had either to attend those interviews or to utter the egregious "No." Performing well at those interviews would require method acting. The receipt of three interview offers by mid-October signaled the prospect of being admitted to one of the better medical schools. I could envisage myself enjoying a successful medical career with a faculty position at a vaunted medical school, and still having my evenings free to write novels.

I withdrew my applications shortly after receiving an interview offer from Tufts University, my first choice. Ignoring the advice of several concerned advisors, I then dropped Physics for Poets, making subsequent application to medical school impossible without a return to college to make up the missing credits.

The sudden release was exhilarating. Years rushed by at a gallop. The blood-rush of expanded horizons pounded at me. Precharted paths fell away, no longer in synch with what I'd become. I picked up a "miscellaneous" button at Yale's Career Advisory Service to symbolize my break with the past, wore it proudly for a few days, then hung it on my bulletin board. Freedom.

It didn't last long. I'd bagged medical school primarily because of my interest in writing. It didn't make sense to spend seven years preparing for a career that would only serve as an adjunct to my true desire to write fiction. It would get in the way, jeopardize my writing, ultimately compromise my existence.

Certainly, well reasoned. But I needed another career, another line to advance on. I'd set up fiction writing as my ultimate goal, but wasn't confident or honest enough to risk everything for it. How was I going to support myself? What if I couldn't make it as a writer?

So I suffered—but I wasn't alone. Nation-wide unemployment stood at 8.9 percent in the spring of 1975, and many seniors were alarmed. After spending $25,000 for a Yale degree, being graduated into the worst job market of the entire post-war period was nobody's idea of a good time.

Modus operandi varied. Some friends refused to deal directly with the situation, preferring to spend their last six months partying, enjoying to the fullest the little time they had left together.

The majority of Yale's 1,235 seniors, however, were furiously filling out applications for one sort of graduate school or another. Many others were participating in a series of job interviews administered by the Career Advisory Service, Yale's on-campus employment agency.

The catch phrase at Career Advisory is "Keep Your Options Open." Students are encouraged to apply to any program, to interview for any job in which they think they might *conceivably* be interested. For many students, I suppose, this rationale is the most practical: procure the widest choice of options and don't make a decision until you're forced to.

It's a position, however, which I find difficult to live with. My preference is to decide whatever it is that I'm going to do and rush headlong into it, aware that I'm liable to run into a brick wall, bounce off and have to start again, somehow aware that the second and third dash may also produce brick-cranium collisions.

As long as those medical school applications were pending, I didn't feel free to consider other options.

Freedom, as I said before; freedom. Then worry, soul-searching, hedging bets, finally keeping my options open: I applied to law schools.

Many people apply to law school. It's faddish. Not because it's *the* thing to do. Rather, it's an *easy* thing to do. Compared to premeds, students applying to law school have a ridiculously easy time

276

of it. There are no required courses—anyone can apply, regardless of major. There is no expensive and anxiety-laden interview procedure; with few exceptions law schools do not interview applicants. Even the application is simple—factual questions and a short essay.

As a result, the application process exacts a relatively small psychological investment. You're just a number, a few figures and a check to cover administrative costs. Most undergraduates I knew would have been surprised if law school admission committees considered anything else. Career Advisory's graphs were treated as gospel. (Career Advisory has compiled a color-coded graph for each law school in the country, plotting the grade point averages [GPA's] of previous Yale applicants against their marks on the law boards. Intersections marked by little blue dots were admitted. The reds didn't make it.)

Using just these two variables, very accurate predictions can be made about a student's chance at any law school: I was admitted to all schools in whose "blue" area I fell, put on hold and later rejected by the two—Harvard and Stanford—where my marks fell in the "blue-red" border, and as the graph predicted, rejected at once by Yale.

It was damn scary. Withdrawing my medical school applications and dropping out of physics was the first real break-out of my entire life. Leaving school the spring of my junior year had been an important decision, but involved little risk. I could stroll on the high wire of creativity knowing full well that a return to Yale for senior year waited like a soft, nylon net. No problems; write, experiment, live.

But by November of senior year, the view from the high wire was more frightening than exhilarating. The real world was down there. Not unlike many Yale undergraduates, the real world was a place I knew little about. I'd worked summers and part-time during the school year, but at student-type jobs. The only thing at which I was truly proficient was studying.

There were other problems. As I've said, I'm ambitious. I want material comfort, but that's secondary. What my heart hungers for in its most candid, blurting moments is public recognition.

My background is socially-mobile, middle-class Jewish, replete with preformed expectations, a work ethic, and a tendency toward overachievement. My father is a successful insurance salesman, my mother an administrator in a metropolitan-area secondary school. My other brothers were both married by the age of twenty-two; I was the only child in the house by the time I was twelve. Ten years later they are still married to their first wives; each has a boy and a girl. Although we're friendly, until recently the age difference was too great for real closeness. They were more like youngish uncles than older brothers.

The social and financial circumstances under which my brothers grew up were very different from those I knew, and the differences were significant enough to shape the pattern of my development and the way in which I make decisions. My brothers and I shared a bedroom during their adolescence; I had that room to myself when they moved out. My parents' real income more than doubled in the years immediately following my brothers' marriages, and with only one child to support, their life style changed. They began to vacation out of the country, often taking me along. Whereas my brothers' adolescent summers were spent working, the summer after my junior year in high school, my parents paid my expenses to Strasbourg, France, where I worked for $120 a month as a lab technician. Finally, and perhaps most significantly, my brothers attended the City College of New York, now part of CUNY, and lived at home until they married, while at eighteen I went off to Yale.

Because I'd been given more, because I'd matured in a different decade, because I'd always been a better student, because of details too numerous and too individually difficult to assess, my expectations and what was expected from me were very different from those of my brothers. As I understand their generation (or at least their group of friends), their primary goal was "getting ahead." If an individual setting out into the world can be assumed to have to answer a maximum of three vocation-related questions—*what* you want, *why* you want it, and *how* you get it—my brothers and their friends had only to deal with the last. *What* they wanted—economic success—was such a given that the *why* never became a consideration, at least in my perception of them. All that remained was *how*, and each was single-minded and achieved according to his ability. My brothers attended law school, and as quickly as they could, established their own practice. They are now partners in a four-man law firm that owns portions of several businesses, they earn sizable salaries, and except for the fact that they'd like those salaries to increase, they are very happy.

Money never mattered that much to me. Without giving the subject too much thought, I'd always assumed I could be secure if that was what I wanted. My exposure to Yale and the students it attracts confirmed that opinion. So many kids were wealthy that it couldn't be too special. Moreover, "rich kids" didn't appear to be any happier than anyone else, just richer. Add to that the emphasis of the 1960s on personal fulfillment, and my brothers' primary goal lost most of its appeal for me.

Certain, however, parentally instilled ideals are shared despite all other value-system differences. My parents are children of the Depression and place a high premium on security. This idea coalesces for them in the concept of a profession. From my earliest adolescence the indisputable value of becoming a "professional man" (a doctor or a lawyer) was impressed upon me. I was made to understand (I recall my mother saying so on a number of occasions) that in today's job market, no matter what someone intends ultimately to do with his or her life, education beyond a B.A. is a requirement. Thus, even if I never practiced medicine, going through medical school was important because it would help me later.

This explains why, despite having withdrawn medical school applications in order to devote myself to writing, I eventually applied to law school. At a pre-logical level I couldn't conceive of *not* becoming a professional. The parental rationale "You Never

279

Know That You Won't Need It Later, and Besides It Can't Hurt"
is hard to resist, especially when the phrase has been repeated so
often that it's difficult to distinguish between what you've been
told and what you've come to believe.

Reasoning of this sort results in providing for a future without
planning what it's going to be, a horizontal movement that produces material comforts without bringing the individual any closer
to self-awareness. My brothers' objection to my abandoning the
idea of medical school was that it was a sure way to be comfortable; if after ten years I didn't like it, I would be secure enough to
live well until I found what it was I did want to do.

There are several other explanations for why I drifted into the
role of a law school applicant. Sue was applying—it was con-
venient. We wanted to be in the same city after graduation, and
attending the same school was the easiest way to manage that. Job
hunting, with contingency plans for the four or five cities containing the law schools to which Sue was applying, was more of a labor
than I was willing to undertake. In fact, simply looking for a job,
in light of all the media coverage of the recession, was enough to
send stronger souls than mine into Career Advisory in search of
information about law schools. Job-hunting is odious, especially if
you're a college senior and haven't worked long enough at anything to form an idea of what a good job is. Finally, if you're a
writer halfway through your first novel, and have come to divide
waking hours into writing and not writing, with the latter classifi-
cation meaning that portion of the day in which your psychic
energy is not heavily involved, then a good job doesn't really exist.
You don't want to be working in the first place.

The problem dichotomizes on two major issues: Do you look
for work that is intrinsically interesting or a drudge job that
doesn't drain your creativity? Do you pursue a high-paying career
that will allow you to live well while your writing is developing
but that involves the risk of trapping you through its comfort, or
do you opt for a low-paying occupation that supplies just the

necessities? What about the fact that novelists don't generally publish until their late twenties, and studies of creativity have shown that as a group, novelists don't reach their creative apex until their early forties. . . .

For those who have reached a closure about career choice, painful considerations of this order aren't a problem. For me, however, it was a question of finding the strength and courage to say who I was and what I really wanted, of determining a goal and finding the surest way to reach it.

That, as I view it, is at the heart of the concept of hurdles. The acceptance of limitations, the recognition that in passing from one stage of development to another, certain valued baggage must be left behind. The realization that in return for a special dream, one must relinquish others.

"Giving up to get" is a process that continues throughout life, unconsciously at first, then with maturity more consciously. Marriage, choice of career, having children—each involves a delimitation which is a mélange of conscious and unconscious factors. Intellectually, I prefer to make a conscious choice. In practice, however, I'd allowed a mix of unconscious motivation and fortuitous circumstance to decide for me.

And why not? I'd been successful at almost everything I'd done, sort of your representative Yalie; reasonably talented at most things, with a negligible number of "opportunity's doors" closed to me in advance. Whatever decisions I'd faced in the past (e.g. choice of college—I was admitted to both Swarthmore and Yale, my first choices) I could leave to serendipity, or, as I preferred to regard it, a charmed and benevolent fate, and not suffer either way.

Because I'd gotten almost whatever I wanted, I wanted almost everything. And at Yale, where the pattern is to apply to graduate school, where a substantial number of people you do not respect intellectually are guaranteeing themselves security, it's difficult to say "No" for a dream. My dream was the pursuit of a crystalline image in language, the slimmest chance that something I'd created would someday matter to someone besides myself—that I was going to be read, appreciated, even loved.

Turning your back on the sure bets for the wildest, craziest one of all is hard. I've always competed and overcompeted with everyone and everything in a game with set rules, and usually I've won. Giving up the promise of a secure career such as the ones my brothers pursue turned out to be more than I could do.

In effect, I failed. Not because I applied to law schools, not even because I enrolled at Columbia Law School as a first-year student. Simply because for myself, in my own value system, I acted for the wrong reasons; I caved in.

I dutifully mailed in my law school application. Although I'd made sure to tell everyone who knew that I'd applied to medical schools that I'd changed my mind, I didn't tell many people about law school. If my explanation was accepted too readily, I silently found fault with my listener. If I was challenged and forced to explain myself, both listener and explainer felt uncomfortable.

There was another problem. One of the more distasteful aspects of the entire application procedure is the tedium generated by the river of anxiety which threatens to drown those caught up in it. There's nothing more disheartening than listening to people talk about who's applied where with what marks and law boards, what so-and-so's chances are, and who has "pull." For no matter how hostile your response, some people will deliver their prepared professional school spiel. One friend of mine was rejected by Harvard Law School but called its admissions office to announce that an error had been made. He was subsequently placed on the "hold" list, retook the law boards, and spent the entire spring discussing the admission process and wondering aloud what his chances were of getting into Harvard. Three weeks before he was to start at Columbia Law School, Harvard did, in fact, admit him. He's there now.

Another friend, who'd been extremely reasonable and thoughtful during the six years we'd known each other, went mildly berserk senior year, discussing nothing except law school whenever we were together. I began to avoid him. An acquaintance began each of our conversations by asking if I'd been admitted anywhere else since we'd last spoken. After a time, I wanted to cut off the whole law school world. Blissfully, acceptance letters began to arrive, and the resolution was in the offing.

Sue was accepted by every law school to which she applied, including Yale, Columbia, Stanford, and Harvard. Neither of us wanted to be at Harvard, reputedly the most competitive law school in the country. My outright rejection by Yale was a problem; that was where Sue most wanted to be. Columbia was a possibility, the best school to which we were both admitted. But my ambivalence toward the law prevented me from asking Sue to attend Columbia instead of Yale. Preconsciously, I'd retained the option of leaving law school if I decided being there was a mistake. I didn't want the responsibility of changing Sue's plans if I wasn't sure of my own.

We worked out a compromise. Sue sent deposits to both Yale and Stanford. I told Columbia to hold a place for me, then waited for Stanford's final decision (I was on their "hold" list). It arrived in early June: No. Sue withdrew from Stanford, firming up plans to be at Yale. I forgot about the tentative acceptance I had given Columbia and resumed work on the novel.

It was an intense, joyous summer. Sue and I were both in New Haven, worked full-time day jobs, and wrote each evening and weekend. We didn't see very much of anyone else, edited each other's writing (Sue was busy with freelance articles) and tried not to think about our impending separation.

I finished the first draft of the novel in July, spent the remainder of the summer preparing a clean, typed version. Notices kept arriving from Columbia, asking for a definition of my status: "yes," "no," or "maybe." I was a "maybe" into August, when, accepting the inevitable, I told them I was coming. Sue and I hurriedly found apartments in New York and New Haven, and for a long time our lives as law students were established.

I liked Columbia Law School, despite leaving after five weeks. In fact, I was happier than many people who stayed. One of my apartment mates, also a first-year student, was ferociously depressed for the first few weeks of the semester. He'd told Columbia he was coming the year before, then had an allergic reaction to the idea, similar to what I'd experienced in Baltimore. He withdrew several days before the semester, worked for a large national magazine, and was now back at Columbia for a second try. Like myself, he considered himself a writer, the law being something that he was doing for a time.

Columbia's students come from what might be referred to as "elitist" backgrounds. Not that everyone is wealthy or on anyone's Social Register. But the undergraduate joke about having "prepped together" carries over nicely to Ivy League law schools. Ten percent of my first-year class at Columbia were undergraduates at Yale. The other Ivies accounted for another 45 percent. If the Seven Sisters (Vassar, Smith, etc.) and schools such as Williams and Amherst are included, the percentage of students from prestigious eastern institutions inches toward two-thirds. Which is to say that Columbia Law School is sort of a club to which my four years at Yale had gained me entrance.

To my dismay and pleasure, I seemed to be a promising law student. I enjoyed the legalistic reasoning I'd studiously avoided as an undergraduate. It came easily; I could feel myself understanding more quickly and completely than most students around me. Law school teaches professional skills, primary of which is how to think like a lawyer. Journalists and lawyers possess similar organizational skills—the ability to extract a cohesive account from a fact situation that may be convoluted, vague, or in some other way, rendered obscure.

Because I have that ability, law school was a source of constant positive reinforcement. Stratification sets up quickly in law schools, people tend to be ranked. It seemed to me that I was well thought of. I was asked to be in a study group composed of other people who held a high rank. All that was needed was to study hard, keep my nose to the legal grindstone, and I'd succeed.

Didn't I want to be a novelist? Since it was important to me that the answer be "Yes," I tried to write on a regular basis. I started several short stories. I researched nonfiction articles. "Thinking like a lawyer" is extremely effective, but it is not the most attractive way to think by any means. Facts and only facts matter. Legal writing is not writing at all, at least only rarely so in a creative sense. Facts are compiled and presented in an orderly fashion. Research—getting the facts out—is the most important part of a lawyer's job. How they are presented doesn't seem to matter that much. After three years in law school, would I still be able to write fiction that wouldn't sound like a memorandum or a brief? Weren't the two mutually exclusive? I was determined that law school was not going to dominate me; I was going to stay in control of the experience.

My attitude, I think, was fairly unique at Columbia, certainly among the students I knew. Most had resigned themselves to a three-year grind, assuming that to get through law school and do well they were going to have to suffer. For many students who were in law school because they didn't know what else to do, the anticipated grind was particularly oppressive. Sacrificing for something you believe in or want badly is not so much a sacrifice as an investment. Deferring pleasures from one's existence for a course of study arrived at by default, however, is an agony, although not necessarily ill-advised. People become what they're doing, even if they hate it initially. In the first few weeks at Columbia I met a number of people who looked as if they were trapped and had long since given up dreams of escape. Projections, perhaps, but there were many grim faces.

Despite my obsessiveness, I was enjoying myself. I was relaxed, intrigued by the course work, and keeping what I thought was a reasonable perspective on the entire experience. My only difficult moments came when I tried to explain to someone why I was in law school; explanations of myself invariably sounded as if I wanted to be a writer. Why, the interrogation went, if you want to be a writer, are you in law school?

Why indeed? Don't you know (I would ask myself) that if you go through law school you're going to be a lawyer? Don't you realize that being just a lawyer, although you would probably enjoy it, will never satisfy you, and certainly won't if you haven't at least tried to make it as a writer?

Yes, I'd answer, but . . . And for five weeks, the "buts" had it. Sue was of the opinion that I should leave law school, at least for a year. She charged me with not being as committed to becoming a lawyer as I was to writing novels, and that, therefore, I didn't respect individuals for whom law was the primary goal. I feared that I was once again merging my career struggles with my commitment to a woman.

Circumstance intervened. A series of articles Sue published in a newspaper produced an unexpectedly pyrotechnical reaction. There was some evidence that she was in physical danger, and for a week, she stayed with me in New York.

I didn't attend many classes while Sue was there. Then we decided that it would be safe for her to return to New Haven— she'd been considering dropping out of Yale or spending the year at another law school. I was reluctant, however, to let her return by herself. But what to do about my classes? Missing another week would seriously jeopardize my semester at Columbia.

Discussion began to center on my situation: I could leave Columbia for at least a year. Initial response to my novel recommended that considerable revision was needed, especially in the closing chapters. Where was I going to find the time while still in law school? Wouldn't continuing at Columbia compromise my efforts as both a writer and a law student, resulting in mediocre performances in both areas?

By the end of that week, I asked Columbia for a leave of absence. Missing a week of classes had made the decision easier—I realized that I didn't have to be there. Paradoxically, having enjoyed my time there also facilitated the decision. The law was something I now knew I could do and do well, a career to return to if I was ready to devote myself to it on a full-time basis.

The Columbia Law School Dean's Office granted my leave of absence immediately, assuring me that barring unforeseen developments, there would be no difficulty in being readmitted. The date was September 26, one year after the trip to Baltimore when I'd decided not to attend medical school. Though the route had been circuitous, I'd arrived at the same place I would have if as a college freshman, I'd decided to be a writer. But I would like to believe that the journey itself, laden with conflict and crisis, has provided me with painfully acquired insights.

A folk-rock musical for which I wrote the book and lyrics after leaving law school has been produced in New Haven. I supported myself in the interim through a combination of odd jobs and freelance writing assignments, eating less than I'd like to, and though I miss the security of law school, it will be there if I want to return.

Unfortunately, the basic question of what I'm going to do with my life, exactly how to handle the transition from student to tax-paying adult, is one I still haven't answered. I still feel as if I need a career, that more than most people I need the awards offered by a profession, yet most of my friends are in school somewhere, while I'm out chasing down a dream. At times what I'm doing doesn't quite seem real, as if again I'm vacationing from my life. Nothing in my experience as an overachiever prepared me for leaving law school, yet I wake up in the morning and realize it happened.

I recently spent a year on a creative writing fellowship at Stanford and the novel that grew out of that experience is making the rounds of the publishers. Further down the road in my career experimentation, I am now a magazine editor. While I have clearly abandoned the notion of a medical education, the option to return to Columbia Law School is still present but so much dimmer. I am still so unfinished; next year is a hurdle I'll take when I come to it.

ETTA S. ONAT with Angela S. Moger

Gladly Would She Learn and Gladly Teach: The Female Graduate Student

With muted passion Etta S. Onat and Angela S. Moger document the toll taken by gender discrimination. Not only is the admissions procedure for women arduous and often demeaning, but from the start their presence elicits a welter of biased commentary from senior male faculty, the same educated men who would react with disdain should colleagues express views tainted by racial, religious, or ethnic prejudice. The combined problems of gender prejudice and the need to prove their excellence heighten the ambivalence of women about their roles. In contrast to the quasi-political arguments put forth by a literature that claims to summarize the broad concerns of women in academe, the authors persuasively detail the microscopic anatomy of the conflict, underscoring the deplorable personal and professional costs to the women who survive, to academe and, ultimately, to society.

The Female Graduate Student

"Ceux qui s'appliquent trop aux petites choses deviennent incapables des grandes."—Pascal

WHETHER ONE is a man or a woman, it is not easy to be a graduate student. It is, however, much harder for a woman. The difficulties, frustrations—real or imagined—most often perceived by males can be intensified for females. The female student, moreover, experiences pressures and problems because of her sex which make the graduate career more painful.

Some of these problems are due or related to various forms of sexual discrimination—sometimes conscious and direct, more often habitual and subtle—frequently encountered by women in what is still largely a man's world. Some stem from woman's own uncertainties about her place, from psychological stresses resulting from inner conflicts between, on the one hand, the traditional roles long thrust upon her (and assumed by her), and, on the other hand, her awakening desire for individual expression and achievement. From St. Jerome to Milton, through Swift to Norman Mailer, woman has been held to be inherently inferior to man (if not his temptress and curse), and allowed lesser, limiting roles. Like Milton's "First Parents" in *Paradise Lost*

> Not equal, as their sex not equal seemed:
> For contemplation he and valor formed,
> For softness she and sweet attractive grace,
> He for God only, she for God in him.

There has always been a feeling among scholars that scholarship is not woman's work and, furthermore, that women get in the way of men working (some of these scholars are, indeed, currently advocating the higher education of woman, while honestly doubting that it can be of highest value).

As long as women accepted uncritically their lower place in the hierarchical scheme of academe as in the universe, accepted unquestioningly the corollary myths and assumptions about woman's place, her strengths and weaknesses, the sex-related pressures and conflicts were not so great, if they existed at all. Certainly such was my experience as a graduate student in the early 1950s, and I think also that of contemporaries at my graduate school and elsewhere.* We did not feel discriminated against as women, nor do I recollect that we experienced the often intense psychological stresses of today's graduate and professional women. When I was told that I "had the mind of a man," I took it merely as a compliment; men, after all, were possessed of a keener, more critical intelligence. When as a teaching assistant I was assigned an all-girls section of freshman composition (one of the last vestiges of such separation of the sexes in Brown's undergraduate colleges), I took it merely as the "luck of the draw," even though there was no separate faculty for female students. It is only in retrospect that I question why a teacher whom I greatly admired both for the quality of his mind and for his prose style (and who had delighted me by his praise of my work) encouraged me to apply for an editorial position at his beloved Phi Beta Kappa: Did he fear that I would not get serious consideration as a teacher and scholar? It is only now that I get angry at the fact that my then department chairman, when grudgingly informing me of my promotion to assistant professor, warned me not to expect further promotion (and tenure) because "the boys in the college have had enough of women teachers in high school," although all classes were by this time entirely coeducational.

I think the reason I, and students like me, were not conscious of sexual discrimination is not so much that conditions were better for women then as that our perceptions, and, accordingly, our expectations, were different. We played the academic game according to all the accepted (male) rules. Like our male fellow-students, we single-mindedly pursued our graduate careers in the male-dominated institution according to the established (male) pattern and with "male" determination. We were not troubled by the scarcity of women in the graduate student body or on the faculty

* The "I" throughout is the voice of E. S. Onat.

(there were none in the English Department at the time). Our role models, if we thought of such matters at all, were the male professors we most admired. Our problems were the commonplaces of graduate students of both sexes: the pressure of papers, the lack of money, the uncertainties of placement. "Thinking male," we pretty much accepted without question or agony all the prevailing assumptions about woman's nature and woman's place and all the attitudes about woman, as student and as scholar, so depressingly familiar to us now.

But in recent years more and more women are, like our "General Mother" in *Paradise Lost* on her first awakening, "much wondering where/And what I [am]." Conflicts inevitably result. Constantly under pressure to prove their commitment and their excellence, women graduate students find themselves victims not only of prejudices and stereotypical attitudes but also of their own ambivalence about their roles. For if the feminist movement has freed the modern woman from the yoke of gross discrimination and opened up for her avenues hitherto reserved for males, it has in turn often shackled her with new burdens in the form of a moral imperative to professional achievement.

The past decade, to be sure, has brought improvement in the regard which women in academe are accorded by their male colleagues. Because of the women's movement on the one hand, and federal legislation on the other, it is no longer either comfortable or legal for administrators, faculty, and students to indulge in the grossly and overtly discriminatory behavior often encountered by female students in the past. It is doubtful that any university president would today openly voice the same reaction Nathan Pusey did when he realized the draft would reduce the number of men applying to Harvard's Graduate School, that "We shall be left with the blind, the lame, and the women."[1] Nor is it likely that many directors of graduate studies at Yale would now say directly, as one is reported to have said some twenty years ago to a former student seeking readmission and fellowship aid a few years after her marriage to a recent Ph.D. from the same department whom she had followed to an appointment elsewhere, that "the department cannot waste money on a married woman"; or another, more recently, "You are such a nice little mother, why do you want the Ph.D. anyway?" Surely a male student possessed of any awareness of the law, if not of sensitivity and tact, would consider carefully before stating an opinion on the admission of women like the following expressed ten years ago by one (self-serving) young man:

> There is no way to avoid the fact that they are chicks coming to a male institution. Any responsible faculty member sitting on an admissions committee must weigh the chance that a particular slot filled by a female body will not suddenly become vacant due to marriage, pregnancy or both just as the sweet thing is about to do something really exciting in an academic sense. I've heard full professors complain of this—I can't blame them. The X Department seems to have a plethora of females—perhaps to the disadvantage of the males?[2]

There are, of course, still those who think of the female graduate student as a bad risk, uncertain in her commitment to scholarship, malingering on her way to the degree, in constant danger of dropping out altogether. The climate of today's campus, however, is less tolerant of such openly expressed disparagement or of such an unflattering stereotype of the female graduate student than it was some years ago.

Increasingly, women are present in graduate schools in greater numbers and, by and large, as more equal members of the university community. The stacks at Harvard's Widener Library have been open to women graduate students for some time now; and we have come a long way, I trust, from the time when Yale's female graduate students had their needs as human beings thought of largely in terms of "properly equipped . . . living quarters [with] ample provision for social amenities."[3] By all accounts, few women enrolled in the Graduate School at Yale sense discrimination in admissions policies or unfairness in the award of financial aid, believing that they have equal access to all university facilities. But even those women who are fortunate enough to be in exceedingly open departments and who feel that graduate study is freer from sex discrimination than other areas of academic life—a feeling which may, indeed, foster a false sense of security in women students—acknowledge that there are subtle differences in the treatment of male and female students; subtle manifestations of discrimination which are more a matter of attitude than of policy, and hence are extremely difficult to "regulate." Nor are expectations easily "legislated" away. It is the rare woman who has not experienced any sex-related problems and pressures.

Women have been present as graduate students at Yale* since 1892, when the establishment of the Graduate School of Arts and Sciences as it is presently structured provided for the admission of women "in full standing"—with what debate and consternation one can well imagine. Half a century later they still were not fully accepted. Dean Furniss complains in his *Brief History* in a footnote that his suggestion in 1942 for a simple commemoration by Yale of her half century of higher education for women was "rejected with scorn by the Secretary of the University" whose attitude, he goes on to say, "was typical of the older Yale College graduates in the faculty and administration. They appeared to be embarrassed by the presence of women in the student body and would have no part in calling attention to Yale's lapse in this matter."**

Now, almost a century later, in many departments women

* Perhaps here is the time to say that although I make reference in these remarks primarily to the Yale Graduate School, I do not mean to imply in any way that the problems here discussed are unique to, or more prevalent among, the female students at Yale. The problems, as all too readily evidenced by the accounts in the many self-analyses prompted in 1970 and 1971 by the call to affirmative action in Executive Order 11246, as amended, are widespread (see reports produced by the University of California at Berkeley, Harvard University, the University of Chicago, and Stanford University, to cite but a few). What is true is that my tenure in the Yale Graduate School administration has coincided with both the general tide of the women's movement and my own awareness of the female condition; and it is during these years that I have become increasingly concerned about the problems faced by female graduate students.

** And yet, it is interesting to note, in 176 pages of text there are only two references to women students.

293

graduate students are frequently made to feel that their presence continues to be an embarrassment; that, like Margaret Mead's female graduate student of years past, they ought to be listening through "the crack in the closet door," or, as reported by an illustrious Yale alumna of her experience as a rare female "reader" in the early 1950s, from a chair in the corridor "lest [she] distract the students whose papers [she] would grade." At best, they feel they are tolerated rather than fully accepted: " 'Nice' to have around, great to have one 'grace' every class, but not really part of the academic establishment," seems to them to be the pervasive attitude toward women at Yale. Women complain that during orientation sessions for entering students of both sexes some department chairmen and directors of graduate studies address their comments as if to males only: "When a man enters our department, he usually takes one or two years of course work"; "A man will begin his exams . . ."; "The dissertation is the most important part of a man's academic career." Some printed materials, they point out, appear to be addressed only, or primarily, to men.* The problem is perhaps more one of awareness and tact than of prejudice; but it is annoying to many women to find themselves regularly and routinely addressed as if they were invisible. The problem, however trivial, is another reminder, as one student put it, of the "image of the Yale man which operated in the hearts and minds of almost every Yale professor that makes it very difficult for women to find acceptance as academic colleagues on the graduate level."

A much more disturbing phenomenon is that some faculty (and by no means just the older, more traditional among them) still subscribe, albeit unwittingly, to long-ingrained, habitual assumptions about woman's role, her strengths and weaknesses, assumptions which affect their regard for and treatment of female students. Curiously enough, this is true even of males who are

---

* Federal legislation threatening punitive measures for noncompliance finally accomplished what six years of persistent prodding by women's groups on campus could not: with the current printing, the Yale University catalogues no longer use the masculine pronoun exclusively.

otherwise honestly sympathetic to and supportive of the academic woman's struggle for equal opportunities. Persistent attitudes are not easily modified either by institutional fiat or by federal law. The prevailing opinion of many males still is that women are poorer risks than men as potential teachers and scholars:

That they are less committed and therefore less likely to complete their training,* or to contribute to their professions should they earn the degree. As one chairman explained in assessing the situation in his department:

> Every year we are confronted with large numbers of female applicants with outstanding credentials (all A's, high GRE's, and superlative recommendations) and we let them in with eager anticipation. But later on more of them drop out than their male peers. Even more of them disappear from view, professionally speaking, after earning their degrees.[4]

That, if not less gifted intellectually, women often are lacking in motivation and perseverance, and do not have the drive associated with men students:

> While inherent talent does not seem to have a sexual bias, motivation and a willingness to attempt an obviously difficult problem apparently do. Women students require more encouragement and more direction than men students of equivalent talent and training and as a conse-

* The assumption that women usually drop out along the way to marry and have children was, of course, for a long time the standard—and almost universally accepted—justification for discriminatory policies in admission and award of financial aid. It was not at all unusual for male (and female) professors, in their recommendation of the occasional "brilliant girl," to stress that "not to worry, there is little danger that she will marry." Knowledge of the law may have driven such remarks underground, but it is not clear that the sentiments they express have disappeared from the minds of men (and some women, for that matter).

Cultural patterns (e.g., it is women who must preside over the rearing of children; one moves for the husband's job, not the wife's) which create obstacles to success for professional women and their effects on the morale of women students are discussed later.

295

quence, their theses tend to be at a somewhat lower level than those of their male counterparts.

That, although often better than men in courses, "women generally do not enjoy laboratory work" or are not suited for it, and that "in almost all cases they are less proficient in the laboratory."

That a married woman, whether graduate student or faculty, is a transient appendage to her husband's career:

> . . . in all too many examples, girls who are part way through their graduate training program end up marrying a man who has just finished his—or who has been in the profession for a year or two—and in consequence as the husband obtains attractive employment in some location other than that at which the girl is pursuing graduate training she moves with him and her training career is terminated. This unhappily has been the case for four very excellent girl graduate students whom I have had working with me for periods of up to two and a half years. . . .*
>
> Intrinsically, I most certainly do *not* feel that women are poorer risks than men as potential teachers and scholars. However, I believe that this societal tradition that the woman's responsibility is that of uprooting her career wherever it may be, to move wherever her husband may find it advantageous to settle himself, is one which works in the strongest possible way against deep professional involvement on the part of many women.

That academic endeavor, whether on the way to the Ph.D. or up the ladder to tenure, demands full-time attention and full-time commitment, and women cannot, or do not want to, give the ex-

* The assumption that all women follow the same path, that they are considered to be guilty until proven innocent, is a source of great irritation to women graduate students.

tended total devotion to scholarship and research required to succeed in the profession:

> Part-time scholars are inferior to and therefore less desirable than full-time scholars, because scholarship requires total dedication and cannot tolerate frequent distractions and interruptions. Women are forced to be part-time employees more often than men, because our society expects them to tend their own children; therefore women are often poor risks as students or as faculty members, because of their circumstances. . . .

and:

> I suspect that fewer women than men find personal fulfillment and satisfaction in research; . . . It seems likely —whether we approve or not—that there are good reasons why women will continue to dominate faculties of kindergartens and men will continue to dominate the faculties of graduate schools, despite concerted efforts to achieve a better (and perhaps healthier) balance in both.

And so goes the litany. The list could have been longer, but surely the sampling cited above is already sufficient to support the perception that the psychological orientation of the men among whom she must work contributes in varying degrees to the problems and pressures of the female graduate student.

In the face of such assumptions it is no wonder women conclude that the atmosphere is inevitably more hospitable to the male student than to the female, even in the absence of outright hostility toward the female. As one woman explained in describing the attitudes she observed in her department, "The male graduate students were at least in part future material for faculty status. The women, by definition and without exception, were not. Therefore male graduate students were 'cultivated' to an extent that women were not. The faculty sought personal and professional relationships

with the men of a cordiality which it did not extend to women."*
It is not surprising that they should feel that professional commitment among women is little encouraged and little expected:
"When I told a professor, privately, in my last year of graduate school that I planned to be married the following summer, he asked me in his first amazement whether I intended not to take the degree." Often noted is the absence of a climate of encouragement of and support for professional growth and development:

> From the first day's arrival there is a definite pressure not to achieve, only occasionally overt. There is a lot of resentment from one's male classmates merely to our female presences—which seems to stem from the belief that women "don't really belong" [in science], that the only reason we're there is to pass time until marriage, that we aren't "serious" students. It becomes difficult to compete in such an atmosphere.

From a Ph.D. in a nonscience field:

> There is a general feeling amongst university faculties that it is not as important for a woman to achieve a high rank as it is for a man. . . . Even if women are not ac-

---

* As a member of the Greene Committee I was privileged to read the responses to our questionnaire from women graduate students, former and current, a questionnaire designed to elicit their perceptions of their positions in their departments and in their later careers. The intensity of the recurring theme of disheartenment, as well as the frequent testimonies to discrimination, hidden or overt, conscious or unconscious, was startling and dismaying even to a female.

Many of the quotations in this essay are from these letters. Others are from responses to a subsequent questionnaire directed to alumnae in the attempt to learn about their experiences as students and professionals.

I have since then talked to many thoughtful graduate women, at Yale and elsewhere. One advantage of being in the administration, as I am, is that some students feel freer to speak their minds to someone they do not regard as being in a position to affect their present and future careers. From their remarks, I get the impression that although there have been some "atmospheric" improvements (the feeling of isolation and alienation, for example, is not so great now that there are more women in almost all graduate programs, and women in the undergraduate college), in general the current crop of female students, and especially married ones, do not yet perceive women to be accepted as full contenders in the academic arena.

tively discriminated against, they are obliquely discouraged from trying to achieve—not just a full professorship, but anything with status in the "male world." This was my experience at Yale as a graduate student, and I doubt that those same professors would have treated me very much differently if I were an up-and-coming assistant professor.

In such an atmosphere, women students can hardly be encouraged to develop an image of themselves as scholars. They sense that some of their professors have different expectations of their performances than of those of male graduate students—expectations based not on ability as individuals but on the fact that they are women.

Further complicating all this is that women also have preconditioned attitudes and expectations, often no less stereotyped. Women students are generally agreed that they are as gifted as their male counterparts. Frequently, however, they are more insecure about their gifts and about their place in the profession.

> I do not think there is any difference in the quality of the work produced by male and female students in my classes, although my impression is that the men tend to talk more in the discussion sections. From my own experience I would say that even at this level of education women are still somewhat inhibited by the stereotype which operated so powerfully in my Mid-Western high school—a smart girl should not disagree with men, be they teachers or fellow students. My own tendency is to speak up only when I can add a fundamentally supportive point to the professor's analysis. I try to counter this tendency, since I really believe it stems from a long "conditioning." Other graduate women I have talked to also acknowledge, and often deplore, what can only be described as a subtle but powerful pressure to manifest their intelligence in the more "feminine" mode of "agreeing."

So wrote a second-year student in the early 1970s (who went on to write a distinguished dissertation and to accept a place on Yale's faculty) about a problem often acknowledged by women—their own tendency to be "feminine" in socially conditioned but professionally undesirable ways.

For women do recognize that, whether from long conditioning or from lack of encouragement, they sometimes have less expectation of themselves or uncertain commitments: "The kind of expectations—the self-image—I had grown up with," wrote one alumna, "made it extremely difficult for me to take myself seriously as having professional potential, so that I lost a lot of time . . . taking courses or jobs that seemed more appropriate—even though I hated them. Parental pressure that I do something practical—have a skill or training to fall back on—has some bearing here." Another, more recent alumna wrote, "The worst problem I had to overcome was within myself, for example, the feeling that I needn't be serious about graduate school and a career because I was going to get married and be supported by my husband. Almost every female academic I know has faced or is facing this problem in some guise."

The debate about the "feminine nature" and the "feminine role" has gone on for centuries, and it is not my intention to prolong it here. The point I want to make is that, in my opinion, in a graduate school where the pressures on students of both sexes are already considerable, a source of additional stress for many women is their own (often hidden) ambivalence about their role as women and their role as professionals.

What I do want to explore further, however, is the source of that ambivalence: Is it fundamental to women, or is it a function of the double standard applied to them from without? Let me restate, from another angle, then, some of the points on which I have touched briefly. In the academic community, no less than in society at large, the traditional stereotypes about "feminine" and "masculine" behavior still prevail to a large extent. To be efficient, aggressive,* hard-working is somehow thought not feminine by many people, and women demonstrating these qualities are usually thought to have problems; whereas enterprise, initiative, and ambition are considered not only necessary but desirable characteristics in men seeking academic success. Men's achievements enhance rather than detract from their sexuality. Academic excellence in women is held to be somehow incompatible with femininity. This notion endures and is not limited to men. Three or four years ago, one graduate woman reported that her roommate came home and cried because her major professor had told her she was a brilliant student, which she assumed to mean that she was not attractive or feminine. Just recently, I heard a panel discussion by women students and junior faculty on "Must We Sell Out To Succeed?" in which it was clear that to them success was equated with loss of the conventional feminine role.

In other words, it is not only true that faculties do not often take the initiative in cultivating and supporting a female graduate student, it is also true that the student herself is often reluctant to make the necessary overtures to engage the interest and support of her teachers. In an atmosphere in which the graduate student must be aggressive in seeking guidance and supervision, the female who finds the implied loss of femininity difficult to cope with can be at a serious disadvantage. According to many students (of both sexes) the help and concern of a "mentor" can make "all the difference in the world"; a supportive and involved dissertation supervisor is often the difference between an unpleasant and a tolerable thesis experience. However, they hold, the availability of guidance and supervision depends very much on the student's own initiative and the teacher's being impressed enough to single out a student for attention. The need to attract the attention of a professor who will guide one through graduate school and into a job often leads stu-

---

* I use this word in its favorable sense of "a bold and energetic pursuit of one's ends," and not in the derogatory sense of, at best, "pushiness" and, at worst, "ruthless desire to dominate."

dents into competitive acrobatics and insecurity. In such situations the relatively passive female graduate student or the woman who herself feels, perhaps unwittingly, so committed to traditional stereotypes about woman's role in society that she must fight endless internal battles is obviously at a distinct disadvantage.

Furthermore, a woman may find it difficult to be taken under a senior professor's wing as his protégée. At institutions where women represent a reasonable proportion of the faculty and student body, men have learned to accept female "aggressiveness" as they do their own, and women can work with less inhibition and self-consciousness, and are consequently under less tension. In departments where there are no women faculty and only a few graduate women, however, professors (and male students) may not be comfortable with women who challenge them, and women's talents may not be fostered as much as men's. It is not unusual for the graduate women in science departments to complain that female students are often slighted in terms of an advisor's time and/or interest until they can "prove" themselves by bringing out good data on their own; that few professors write papers with women students, preferring the safer alternative of publishing with male students; and that women are often not encouraged as much to prepare papers for presentation at meetings or for publication.

Moreover, in a predominantly male institution, it is felt, male professors find it difficult to advise female graduate students even when they want to be helpful. The teacher who is impressed enough to single out a woman student for attention runs the risk of having his motives misinterpreted. Thus women are often called by their last names long after everyone else in class is on a first-name basis, with a correlative distance in the accessibility of the teacher as a natural result.

Sexual tension plays an important role in professor-student relations, recognized or not. Some professors can't deal with me because I'm not "one of the boys." I think they are defensive-hostile towards women; this makes it harder for me to deal with my hang-ups. One advisor has always seemed particularly ill at ease with me, and I think it has to do with his stereotypical ideas about women. To think of us as intelligent, he must consider us like men.

Alternatively, other professors treat their women students with "a difficult to define 'courtliness' " which ultimately reveals a far from flattering bias and which increases a woman's inhibitions. One student stated the issue clearly and succinctly:

> Certainly I do not subscribe to the more radical bitterness of some women liberationists who have concluded that no woman can ever be truly herself when in the presence of men, but although I admit that the difference in sex almost always creates certain tensions, undercurrents of sexuality, I feel that certain professors play with these potential tensions in a way which could be avoided to the benefit of their women students. I think that Yale professors should be more aware of the difficulties created for their women students when they, however innocently, encourage an atmosphere of gentle flirtation in the classroom or the conference.

Consequently, an additional problem (which derives from either the unease or the courtliness) is that women students find it difficult to talk to male professors about their personal difficulties as graduate students, especially since they think few are cognizant of the special problems faced by women in such an environment. In departments where there are no senior and few junior female faculty (and this is true of many Yale departments and of many graduate departments throughout the country), a woman who cannot surmount the difficulties of establishing a close advisory relationship with a man must work alone or drop out. It is perhaps not surprising that the few women in ladder faculty positions in many departments were as graduate students more often than not, protégées of the few well-known women professors in their discipline. But as one woman faculty member suggested from her own experience, a woman who makes it successfully through graduate school may be less likely than the average man to have engaged in the sharp battle to attain notice and top ranking, less likely to have fit into the father-son patterning of the mentor-student relationship, and more likely to have pursued an independently creative path requiring perhaps greater dedication, intelligence, and self-direction than conventional paths which yield recognition and recommendation as one of the department's "two top students."

Not given the specific encouragement men are given, women students find it harder to develop close relationships not only with faculty, but also with male students—the kind of easy-going intellectual communication essential to a happy and productive academic experience. I recall very well the observations made by an attractive and intelligent woman student, a recent graduate of a prestigious women's college, that her male fellow-students often made her feel as if they did not take her seriously as an intellectual equal. "I walk up to a table of men students who are engaged in what seems to be a serious conversation, and the minute they notice me talk turns to trivialities. It's as if they feel that any woman with a pretty face does not have the mind to follow a conversation of any depth." It was only with the women students, she went on to say, that she could engage in serious conversation of any kind, and "as you know there are not all that many of these around."

And so problems considered by students to be endemic to graduate study in general and to "high-powered and intensely competitive" programs in particular can be aggravated for the female student. Thus, the lack of any real intellectual community among graduate students themselves may in male-oriented programs ("exclusive male clubs") be heightened for the female into a feeling of isolation, if not alienation. In situations where men, students and faculty, feel uncomfortable with women scholars, or find enormous difficulty in working with them, the result is a relationship that is uneasy at best. Such an atmosphere is hardly conducive, in women, to an even-tempered yet determined pursuit of their intellectual goals.

In fact, the pursuit of intellectual goals may be made more frustrating for the female because of the Catch-22 situation in which she frequently finds herself. On the one hand, as we have seen, she is taken less seriously, and less is demanded of her than of the male student—he is "the professional, the lifer," she is "along for the ride." On the other hand, to be taken seriously she must perform not only as well as her male counterpart but better, must "simply be twice—or even more—as good as a man to be taken equally seriously." I have had several talks recently with a promising young assistant professor about her experiences as neophyte teacher and scholar. She confessed her anger at both herself and her teachers: Anger with the male professors who, with a kind of reverse discrimination, had been less demanding of women students (especially the prettier ones) than they had been of the males, so that the first year's teaching experience was more difficult than necessary. Anger with herself because she still felt that she had to be so much better than her male peers, believed she had to be a superstar in order to compete. An older, more established female scholar has stated that, "I have taken it as an assumption that I had to be about 1.33 times as bright/able [as her male peers]. I *am working* on being assertive enough to match my capability."

As I've said previously, some of the anxiety and alienation suffered by the women student results from her own ambivalence, but it is exacerbated by the knowledge that she is not always taken seriously as a future teacher and scholar. Women in male-dominated fields depend so much on recognition by their male colleagues that when they are barely tolerated as women they become increasingly doubtful about their own merits and professional competence. Perhaps, indeed, the most debilitating effect of sex discrimination is the blow to one's self-confidence as a woman and as a professional. Consider the case of a graduate woman I shall call Jane Doe.

A graduate of an excellent college for women and the holder of a master's degree in her chosen area of specialization, Jane Doe had by age thirty-two earned for herself a considerable career as an executive, having earlier proven herself an effective teacher of undergraduates. She found her position interesting and challenging, requiring her to make many decisions and meet new crises every day. Happily married, the mother of two young children, well thought of by her associates, she appeared the epitome of the liberated woman who had made it in her chosen profession.

Nevertheless, Jane decided that this existence, although reasonably rich and varied, was somehow not enough; that she wanted more time for the purely intellectual side of her life; that she wanted to train her mind further, to, indeed, return to teaching as a full-time career. She decided to pursue her graduate studies, and applied to the Yale Graduate School. In the admissions evaluations, she was ranked the top applicant by the departmental admissions committee.

To the casual observer Jane's first year as a Ph.D. student went exceedingly well. Her outstanding grades earned her a special prize awarded annually to the best first-year students in a few selected departments. She fulfilled various requirements not only on time but earlier than usual; and she was granted advanced standing for her previous graduate work. Vivacious and warmly sympathetic, she was sought out by other, younger students in the department for companionship and advice.

As I came to know her better, however, it became apparent that none of her successes could dispel entirely Jane's deep-seated insecurity. She was constantly fearful of not being taken seriously as a professional by her teachers. Puzzled by the disparity between her self-image and self-esteem on the one hand, and the reality of her achievements on the other, I had several talks with her. The details hitherto unknown to me of her application to and early months in the graduate school furnished a context which made all too clear how her confidence had come to be so undermined.

To begin with, the interview she had had before she was ever admitted to the graduate school was so discouraging that she seriously considered not applying at all. The man who interviewed her seemed disturbed that she wished to be a half-time student. He gave her to understand that part-time study was frowned on and, if permitted, would compromise her status in the department. He told her, furthermore, that it was too bad she had waited so long to return to graduate school (she was thirty-one at the time of this interview) and that he was concerned about the agility of her mind "at this point" and wondered if she would have trouble keeping up with the other students, given what he described as the quickness and intellectual range of younger students. Finally, he observed that the one thing that enabled him to recommend her to his colleagues over the younger student was the fact that, in view of her domestic situation, she would probably adjust better to the blow of being dismissed "than the kids do" if, at the end of the first year, she was found to be academically unacceptable. Jane Doe was devastated by this last remark and wondered if the teacher was telling her indirectly that she was unlikely to make it into or through the program.

After a few days in her own productive environment, however, she recovered sufficiently from her crisis of confidence to file the application. When she was admitted a few months later, she renewed the question of part-time status with the department's general advisor to graduate students. She was assured by him that if she came part-time she would never be regarded by the faculty as a serious student or be recommended for awards and positions. Jane Doe's strongest motivation in wishing to be part-time was a professional one: she had been offered a fine position in her field and the institution was willing to make it a half-time appointment to permit her to pursue her degree simultaneously. Nevertheless, her desire to be a half-time student was not less frowned upon, and she gave up the job opportunity in order to be a full-time student, not wishing to incur the prompt disapproval that had been promised.

At the end of her first term, a member of Jane Doe's department commented on her outstanding grades: "You've done very

well . . . for a married woman; we don't usually take them."
When, at the end of the first year, Jane was informed that she had
been selected for the departmental prize, she was genuinely surprised and even wondered momentarily if there had been a mistake.
By the time her performance had earned the confidence of her
teachers, Jane had so internalized both the earlier hesitations about
her ability and commitment and the surprise that first greeted her
success that her confidence in herself had been shaken. She was
fearful of failing the oral examinations due to inadequate preparation, in spite of the department's confident encouragement that she
take the examinations a year earlier than the students with whom
she had entered.

Jane did well in her exams, and her teachers found her panic
of the months before foolish or disingenuous. Her own words
describe the subsequent set of problems:

> By now, especially in view of my successful early
> completion of requirements, I have earned myself the
> reputation in my department of being self-doubting and
> neurotic; even when I articulate reasonable doubts and
> legitimate concerns, I am admonished for my lack of self-
> confidence and patronized for my intellectual tentative-
> ness (even where that tentativeness is the surest sign of
> my perspicacity). I have projected in the past enough
> unreasonable self-doubt that I am not really heard when I
> express intelligent reservations. In my opinion, the im-
> portant issue is the source of that earlier self-doubt. Was
> my low self-esteem the cause of my problems in con-
> fronting the orals and in asserting myself intellectually
> with my teachers—as I think several people would claim?
> Or was it the effect of the treatment I received initially
> (the expectations and attitudes of others which I finally
> internalized)?
>
> It is ironic that, having proven myself an able and
> serious student, I am now reproached for ever doubting

myself, even on occasions when, as I have indicated, doubt or hesitations arise from dispassionate lucidity and not from pathological self-denigration. I am the prisoner of a view of me engendered by the very people who would now argue its accuracy. It is the extent to which I have ever seemed to subscribe to the definition of me imposed from without that I am considered to have an inaccurate self-image.

Furthermore, all the ways in which I have departed from the usual path and profile of a graduate student—for example, my past career (which has made me the "older" student) and present prospects (the job offers which have come my way while a student)—would have been interpreted differently if I were a man. (A man is always considered justified in interrupting his work if he has to earn money—my need to earn money to finance my education was not considered serious. A woman who interrupts study to earn money or to accept a position which advances her professional career is simply labeled as uncommitted.) Given the substantial record of my past achievements, why were several members of my department unable to take me seriously from the outset and recognize that my difference was a positive, not a negative quality, a strength, not a weakness? But the much more troubling question is why was *I* unable to do so?

Perhaps Jane Doe's hypersensitivity was not unwarranted. When a woman interrupts graduate study, whether to marry, to bear children, or to take a position, she is often thought to be lacking in motivation and commitment; whereas for a man, professional success and social success are judged by standards that do not conflict with each other. The woman professional, judged by one set of standards as a woman and another set of standards as a professional, must cope with the competing claims of her profession and society's expectations of her. But even those women who have reconciled the two roles often find themselves hounded by disapprobation—presumably because they are not at home scrubbing floors and taking care of their babies. In the opinion of one alumna who has climbed the ladder to full professor and tenure, what are traditionally considered to be the problems of women (marriage vs. career, etc.) are not the "real problems faced by women like myself who are struggling to be accepted on an equal basis in the academic world. My problems are not children but hostile colleagues with a deep distrust of females and an equally deep conviction that there must be something wrong with a woman who does not devote herself to changing diapers and concocting stews—particularly if she is in the least bit attractive and/ or married."

I have devoted so much space to the subtle manifestations of discrimination that are more a matter of attitude than of policy because there may well be a direct correspondence between the psychological orientation of male professors and the bureaucratic implementation of some of these attitudes.

The attitude, for example, that a woman student displays a "lack of academic seriousness" if she wants to get married and raise children as well as pursue a scholarly career is still widely held in academic circles, and appears to influence policy toward married women who want to return to graduate work after an interval of several years. Two women, both over thirty and with children, testify to a general attitude of mistrust of their "seriousness" when they applied to Yale, to the same department as it turned out. They were given the status of "probationary" students for their first year; they have since proved themselves very able students (one already having completed her degree and the other about to receive it), but the stress they experienced must have been great during the time when, as one of them jokingly put it, "we both together equaled one 'real' student." What disturbs many women students most is the belief held by administrators and professors that for a woman marriage and children must detract significantly from her value as a scholar. None of their male friends, they point out, has ever been asked at an interview if he planned to "give up" his career for marriage. They realize that the problem is compounded by the tendency of many women themselves (though perhaps in ever-decreasing numbers) to see the problem as an either-or matter: to pursue the conventional female role they must, in Congreve's phrase, "dwindle into a wife"; to succeed in the profession (or so they think) they must be stripped of the role of wife and mother.

Throughout my discussion I speak of the dual role of woman and of some of the complications which result therefrom. I wish to make it clear that I have written about female dualism and the frequency of resultant conflictedness because it is the current social reality that "hearth and home" are the province (and responsibility) of women. I do not regard as ineluctable the ambivalence of women, since many, of course, would have no dividedness to suffer or, I might add, to "live down" if our cultural pattern had not imposed on them as inalienable the management of the home and the nurturing of children. There is nothing in a woman's very nature which more properly fits her to these functions or more inevitably produces in her the aforementioned conflicts. Were men to take over the domestic burden which custom has assigned to women, I have no doubt that I would be here attributing to them the problems and tensions I have ascribed to women. If my comments seem to accept as a given the hurtful (to themselves) vacillation between personal and professional as the state of mind of many women, it is not because I deem that ambivalence or the state of affairs which produces it to be sex-oriented, just, or unalterable. Many of the prejudices (and the impediments they constitute) of which women are the victims would have no support if, first, women were not confined to the home and, then, secondly, not assumed to be guilty or guilt-ridden if they were not there—especially since many women would choose the "dual role" in any case, seeing it as a rich way to live and not a mode of existence arising out of ambivalence and charged with guilt.

Be that as it may, the anxiety and tension resulting from the perceived conflict between the wife-mother role and the profes-sional-woman role constitute an important problem unique to women students, single or married. This stress, largely one of morale, accounts for more dropouts, I venture to suggest, than the accepted myth that women are less intellectually motivated and less gifted than men. The reasons why graduate students drop out are complex; they are not motivated solely by academic difficulties, although certain academic problems undoubtedly do result from acceptance on the part of many women of the cultural assumption that the two roles are mutually exclusive. After a year or two in graduate school they come to feel that somehow by continuing their studies they would be, in effect, opting against marriage and family, and for a less socially acceptable role, that of the "lady professor." Given the fact that most women in our society marry in their twenties, and life as a graduate student means a somewhat curtailed social life, their line of reasoning is something to consider sympathetically. Furthermore, at least on an unconscious level, it is still widely believed that men do not generally marry women who are better educated than they. By earning a Ph.D., then, the woman may be lessening her chances for marriage. This is a prob-lem (whether real or imagined) that the male graduate student does not face.

Again, many women are seriously concerned about the diffi-culties they expect to confront in combining a career with taking care of a family, but see little effort on the part of the university to encourage women to study and teach even though married. Given such encouragement, they maintain, women themselves would be much more likely to work out viable modes of leading the kind of "double life" that most men find fulfilling, one including both career and family. The problem was eloquently summed up by a mother of three who studied full-time and now teaches full-time:

> The woman who undergoes the most agonizing conflicts
> is *not* the one who, despite husband, children, and home,
> is determined to forge for herself a brilliant career at all

costs. Rather, she is the one who loves *both* her careers, as professional and as homemaker, and is forced either to take a subordinate position as the first or to neglect the second. Perhaps I am only dreaming, but it seems that equal opportunities in part-time study and employment could provide the temporary (children, after all, grow up) easing that such women so much need.

The rigidity of the academic structure patterned to the life style of the male is indeed seen as a major obstacle. The part-time study and teaching which are required to accomplish the double life style with a minimum of stress, far from being actively encouraged, are still only grudgingly allowed. It seems very sad to students that a woman who wants to work part-time during the years between her early twenties and thirties, when she is most biologically suited, and feels the greatest desire to bear and raise children, often finds herself fatally out of step with the rigid academic system when she tries to return as a full-time participant. A great problem for women, then, is the timing of higher education and the steps toward professional advancement. Those years in which a man is devoting himself to activities which will advance his career are the very years in which a woman wants (or is expected) to marry and have children.

Even those women who feel that the problem of harmonizing family with career, though complex, need not be insurmountable, are very much aware of the fact that most successful women scholars are unmarried and/or childless or divorced. Such a state of affairs is naturally discouraging not only to young women who look to these rare "successes" for models, but also to those older women who are considering trying to return to an academic career.

This question of "models of success" points to the circular quality of the whole problem of women in academia. The male student has little trouble imagining himself at thirty-five or forty, his "role models" are his tenured professors, adult males training

313

him to be a successful teacher-scholar like themselves. But what of the woman student? More often than not, what she has seen and continues to see causes her to view her future career with pessimism.

Many a talented, highly motivated woman comes to the Yale Graduate School hoping to find herself and her vocation in the academic community. Unless she comes from a women's college (an increasingly endangered species) where her experiences may have taught her that women may be fine teachers and scholars, she has few models to help her as she tries to work out her self-definition. Often, indeed, she comes with an attitude toward her future opportunities which is preconditioned by the less-than-satisfying experiences of her mother or some other female close to her. Thus we learn of the woman, now a grandmother, who almost didn't get her Ph.D. (the first one in history at the University of Illinois) because she envisioned herself turning into one of the brittle spinster types she had seen too much of in her undergraduate college; of the mother who, because of nepotism rules at the institution where her husband taught, commuted forty miles a day to a small, poorly-endowed institution where she carried an eighteen-hour teaching load and was paid less than most high school teachers; of yet another mother who received her doctorate after fifteen years of part-time teaching, and whose subsequent difficulties in finding a rewarding job (her major problem was that her subject was also her husband's) has served as a constant, and discouraging, reminder to her daughter of the problems of being a woman in academe.

Nor is she as a graduate student more encouraged when she sees how many bright, well-educated faculty wives are unhappily unemployed, or are teaching at inferior colleges in the New Haven area, or relegated to an off-the-ladder position at Yale which, on a short-term basis, may be a good alternative, but which, in the long term, turns out to be frustrating. When she considers that more and more graduate students marry their fellow-students, her prospects for a successful career may seem bleak indeed. For she is painfully aware that most frequently it is the wife who ends up at a lesser institution in a job that allows no time for research and scholarly growth and which dulls one's teaching interest and enthusiasm.

So, for the female student (and younger faculty as well), the scarcity of women in the senior ranks of the faculty is a source of great anxiety. A student in one large department that, at the time of her comment, numbered only one woman—an assistant professor—among its faculty, and now four—an associate and three assistant professors—points out the paradox that

> the same department that accuses women of failure has caused their failure by denying jobs to women. . . . My department is not providing jobs (at Yale and elsewhere) for their women graduates, and, if this department is typical of other departments, the women being trained as equals with the men do not get an equal chance to use their skills. It is hypocritical to train people for jobs that do not exist because of prejudice, and it is reasonable to ask why the department bothers to train women at all.

As one dean of a women's college said recently, many institutions believe in educating women but do not believe in the educated woman.

The problem is exacerbated for women studying in disciplines which have trained many capable women Ph.D.'s, but which have few women among their faculties. With only five women professors on the senior level and not all that many even at the lower levels, a graduate student who sees that almost half of her fellow students in the humanities are female may well view her future career with some pessimism:

> Seeing so few examples of women who have made it and realizing that the majority of them have elected to remain unmarried, or if married, without children, the graduate woman understandably feels quite hopeless if

315

she hopes to be anything other than a totally dedicated scholar. She almost expects to fail in the pursuit of her academic career; her sense of failure is complicated by the implicit attitude of many of her teachers and advisors that somehow she is failing to be fully a woman in her very desire to pursue that career in the first place.

It should be clear that there is a "self-fulfilling prophecy" dimension to the situation of the female graduate student. The climate in which she is expected to live can hardly nourish her ambition, her self-esteem, or her mind, for that matter. At worst, she begins to internalize the doubts others have about her, until she is sufficiently debilitated to act in confirmation of the worst prejudices concerning her commitment and ability. At best, she finds a way to thrive as a loner in the absence of a patron, of significant encouragement or of praise, and of intellectual companionship. The fact that she is so often without models and without the means or example which would offer reasonable approaches for accommodating her dualism leaves many such students without hope. It is difficult to thrive in an ambiance where one is considered guilty until proven innocent. Indeed, it may be the surest sign of their mental health that many women have not been able to tolerate such conditions and have chosen to remove themselves from an environment that demands a certain kind of schizophrenia. And those who are very strong, strong enough to survive and persevere in spite of the concrete and the psychological obstacles to their success, often pay a great price for that survival, not the least of which is the attribution to them, on the part of male colleagues, of an overweening careerism or of a lack of femininity. Also, there must be occasional women who develop real personality disorders in their efforts to withstand the tensions pulling them in several directions simultaneously. Witness the following quotation from a recent alumna: "[I experienced] no obstacles because I was competitive enough in graduate school to make it as the 'exceptional woman.' But in retrospect I see the emotional/psychological cost of this."

That such women are often cited as the rule rather than the exception by critical colleagues is an indication of the closed circle of the female graduate student's predicament.

Imagine how the confusion of the female student is enhanced by the fact that the message she gets is not even unilateral or consistent. Institutions and individuals seem to be saying "Yes" to her, while she is sure she feels "No." The very teacher who offers her the worst image of herself and her prospects may do so with such cordiality and even good (if erroneous) intentions that she has to wonder if she is at fault for feeling resentment. Endemic to being the second-class citizen that woman has been historically is the readiness to accept, when anything goes wrong, that she herself must be responsible. Finally, regardless of the posture a female student adopts to deal with all of these complications—it is rather like learning to walk through a mine field (and many decide not to take the risk)—it is clear that she must at least expend valuable energies on problems other than the intellectual ones she and her male counterparts came to graduate school to address.

REFERENCES

1. Ann S. Harris, "The Second Sex in Academe," *AAUP Bulletin* 56 (September 1970), p. 283.

2. From a survey conducted in 1966 to review policies and practices of the Yale Graduate School with regard to the status of women.

3. Edgar S. Furniss, *The Graduate School of Yale: A Brief History* (New Haven: 1965), p. 73. Furniss was Dean of the Graduate School from 1930 to 1950.

4. Quotations in this section are from responses by departmental chairmen to a questionnaire sent by the Committee on the Status of Professional Women at Yale (The Greene Committee), which functioned during the academic year 1970–71.

JOSEPH KATZ

Epilogue: The Admissions Process—Society's Stake and the Individual's Interest

In summing up, Joseph Katz tells us that our present social structure has ordained the admissions race and that for the qualified there is no freedom of choice. Despite the Sturm und Drang of the admissions crisis, however, Katz ironically reminds us that our selection criteria for different levels of higher education do not predict success or effectiveness on the job, and that instruction often bears only a tangential relationship to skills required after institutional attendance. He sees the testing system as an important instrument in the democratization of society, an imperfect device to facilitate social and intellectual mobility. But Katz asks for a more judicious redefinition and expansion of the criteria used for acceptance and rejection, with the ensuing modification of institutional structures to enable different kinds of students to flourish. For those panicked by the admissions hurdles, he suggests that acceptance can be part of failure, with a continuation of old ties and old postures; and that rejection may well be a small event when compared to the possibility that the direction of one's life may be effectively altered by the lessons of the struggle. The admissions process, with all of it weaknesses and imprecision, may still be an avenue to heightened self-awareness. He cautions all participants about the dangers of the irrelevant judgments of impersonal institutions. And he closes the book by drawing up a series of workable recommendations reflecting a mix of his own thinking and the condensed views of the other contributors.

THE READER who has come thus far in the book may well ask whether going to college or to graduate or professional school is worth it. The reader has heard not only about the intense anxiety that often attends the undergraduate admissions process but also about the continuing anxiety in having to leap over a series of hurdles during the college years and once again when one applies to graduate or professional school. The procedures of being evaluated and proving oneself over and over again bear little relationship to the presumed purposes of higher education: the satisfaction of curiosity, joining a community of scholars, increasing capacities for rational thinking, awakening and cultivating aesthetic and emotional sensitivities.

If this picture inspires a somewhat somber mood, the mood may become even more so when one considers that freedom of choice for the student is only apparent. Most people who are now in college hardly had a choice. Whatever the anxieties or the blows to students' self-esteem, college is a necessary stepping stone for even middling social and occupational status.

The Problem of Numbers

In the fall of 1976 there were over eleven million people enrolled in institutions of higher education, a staggering increase from the million and a half who were there in 1940, although the number of people in the United States did not even double in that same period. The magnitude of the increase is puzzling when matched against the availability of suitable jobs. Census data show that the number of higher-level jobs has not kept pace with the increase in the numbers of students. True, during the period of rapid educational expansion in the late 1950s and 1960s there appeared to be an almost unlimited need for well-prepared people to perform the increasingly sophisticated tasks of our society in government, commerce, engineering, computer processing, health care, and other rapidly-growing industries. But by the early 1970s the picture shifted to a concern about mounting professional unemployment and underemployment.[1]

Strictly economic considerations might never by themselves have led to the spectacular rise in enrollments, but when the Truman Commission in 1947 enunciated the ideal of universal higher education,[2] a strong motivation was provided by the egalitarian ideal that had been the linchpin of American ideology ever since the founding of the Republic and was now buttressed by the self-confidence engendered by victory in World War II, the need to recompense the GI's, an expanding economy, and an overly optimistic expectation of what education can do for society even in the short run. The G.I. Bill of Rights made higher education accessible to people previously excluded from it.

In recent decades, the burden of ever larger numbers of people pressing to enter college has exacerbated the problem of whom to admit to what kind of school. Entering students differ widely in regard to aptitude—whatever measure of aptitude one might use—in the degree and quality of their preparation, in their willingness to work, their motivation and energy.

Universities and colleges in this country differ widely in the levels of performance they expect of their students as well as in the quality of professors and of instruction. Schools constitute a hierarchy of quality and prestige.[3] Such ranking may be stereotypically oversimplified, and a school's degree of prestige is not necessarily an indicator of the quality of education a student may get there. Nevertheless each school, buttressed by its reputation, tries to attract the "best" students it can get. Each needs some scheme to sort out who is to be admitted and who not; and it needs to do so in a reasonably economical and impartial way.

The need for "objective" entrance measures wherever the supply of places in desirable institutions is outstripped by demand is indicated by the recent experience of Germany.[4] Traditionally graduation from a secondary school in Germany assured students access to any field of academic or professional preparation. But with the increasing numbers of young people graduating from secondary schools and the looming overcrowding of professions, German universities, too, felt compelled to resort to some measure of restriction. They recently have used the grade point average in the comprehensive senior-year examinations of secondary school as a selection device. (Not surprisingly, the highest grade point average is required for admission to medical training.) And now there is active consideration of the idea of introducing tests similar to the American SAT or ACT.

The advantages of using prior grades and the Scholastic Aptitude Test (SAT) or the American College Test (ACT) or the Graduate Record Examination (GRE) are that they allow institutions to process hundreds of thousands of applicants while giving each individual the chance to be considered in the light of the impersonality of the test, regardless of social class, ethnic and racial origins, personal appearance or the prestige of the school she or he is graduating from. The tests by themselves do not, of course, allow for the deficits that derive from one's background and upbringing. They are impartial not in regard to the past, but only in regard to the present. But at least one's present test scores have an influence independent of social class and ethnicity; students, in fact, have found their scores an entering wedge to institutions that might otherwise have been closed to them.

The anonymity of the tests has been one factor in the democratization of opportunity in the United States. Before World War II, students (and teachers) from other than middle and upper class

Protestant origins tended to be poorly represented in the most selective undergraduate institutions. The percentages of students from other ethnic and class origins have risen markedly since then. The tests, of course, do not by themselves alone account for the change. They, for a long time, coexisted with marked discrimination. A recent study of the history of selective admission in the United States shows that social attitudes and social policy exert a deep influence on admissions.[5] But since the end of World War II democratic ideology, conscience, a flourishing economy, and an expanding system of higher education were important stimuli to opening the doors more widely. The high test scores of people who previously might have been excluded were a prod to conscience and provided a convincing rationale for admission. Admitting these new people has resulted in much greater participation by previously excluded social groups in the leadership, science, and research of the society.

The acquisition of influence, eminence, and power by members of groups previously excluded has been one of the unheralded changes in our society. The educational system in the United States has shown itself to some extent adaptable enough to avoid through the selection process what otherwise might have been a source of political disruption or, alternatively, societal stagnation. A well-functioning society needs the constant infusion of fresh talent and social "recirculation." It is worth pointing out in this context that placing the decision for entry into higher education at about age 18 allows for a rather late selection hurdle. This contrasts with other Western countries where traditionally entrance to secondary school at age 10 or 11 has also determined eligibility for future university admission, thus prematurely foreclosing the possibility of higher education for many students and favoring those of higher socio-economic status. In recent years, however, many European countries have begun to move in the direction of the American system. They have broadened their secondary school programs to enlarge educational opportunities for many more students and so to pave the way for their entry into universities.[6]

Those Who Are Half Left Out

A democratic society will tend toward the ideal of universal education, including universal higher education, but no existing democratic society has developed the means for true equal educational (or economic) opportunity. In the words of one researcher: "A major problem of democratic society is inconsistency between encouragement to achieve and the realities of limited opportunity."[7] Hence there is an incentive for giving the *appearance* of universality of opportunity. For instance, the rapid growth of junior or community colleges in the post-war period has produced college enrollments in some states for about three-quarters of the high school graduates. But community colleges, as has been pointed out, also serve a "cooling out" function.[8] They gradually wean the student to accept a lesser status in life, for example, to become an engineering aide instead of an engineer. They smooth the transition by allowing students time to discover occupational alternatives.

The great diversity of institutions reflects the class system. Attendance at high-cost private institutions and at a few public universities solidifies middle- or upper-class status. This reaffirmation of the class system is shown, for instance, in the fact that considerably higher proportions of students whose family income is above $25,000 are found in the highly selective private institutions than are found in the less selective ones. There are 30 percent more men students from that income bracket in highly selective private universities than there are in the least selective universities.[9]

Recent experiences in Western Europe have been parallel to the United States'. There, too, new institutions of higher education, created after World War II, gave greater promise of higher status jobs than they could fulfill.[10] A dual system of institutions developed. In France, for instance, acceptance by the *grandes ecoles* (great schools) continued to assure access to prestigious and high-paying positions. But students attending other types of institutions began to realize that their occupational hopes were bound to be disappointed. To express their protest, 40,000 university students marched through the streets of Paris in April, 1976, and clashed with police. Nearly two-thirds of the universities were on strike.[11] Yet in Europe and in the United States, graduates of any type of university are still at an advantage. They get jobs in preference to people who had less education. But one of the consequences of more schooling for more people is that graduates are now doing the same work that they once could have done with fewer years in school.

The high rewards of selective admission are seen particularly in countries where the number of university spaces is very limited. Japan graduates 80 percent of its eighteen-year-old population from high school but admits only 20 percent to higher education. Entrance examinations thus become crucial. Some students take one or two years of additional postsecondary school work before sitting for the examinations. Family influence and money do not count in the admissions process, but if a family has money the student can hire the best tutors. The competition for admission is referred to as "exam hell." According to a recent report the following is true of the eight-week period of "exam hell":

> It causes sleepless nights, ulcers and suicides. . . .
>
> To win at least one placement, each student takes a number of exams, sometimes as many as a dozen. The applicants travel all over Japan, sometimes on group flights, to try, for example, for a university in Kyoto, then in Sendai, and Tokyo . . . has single rooms for $52 a night and, for $76, accommodations for a student and his mother.
>
> The price includes two meals "specially designed for easy digestion" . . . graffiti wall boards to relieve tensions. Doctors and dentists are on call. . . .
>
> A typical family will spend more than $1,000 during their 10-day stay in Tokyo."[12]

The Selection and Treatment of Women and Minorities

Undergraduate education has been open to women for a long time, but, once admitted, women have not, traditionally, had the same opportunities as men. And recent research continues to show more or less subtle discriminatory patterns in the treatment of women students by professors.[13] The intensity of feeling that is reported and reflected in Onat and Moger's chapter in this book is shared by many women. It is still hard for many men, particularly men beyond their thirties, to be aware of the humiliation felt by a woman who overhears that "she has a mind as good as a man's." In fact, women students often perform better than men students. For instance, in 1976, a high school grade average of A+ to A— was achieved by 24 percent of the college-bound women and by only 16 percent of the men. (In the highly-selective institutions, 74 percent of the women earned this average as compared to 65 precent of the men.) Though in recent years the proportion of women receiving M.D., LL.B., or similar degrees has increased, in 1975 they still received only 13 percent of all medical, legal, and similar degrees.[14]

Between 1960 and 1973 the proportion of white students in colleges somewhat more than doubled, while the proportion of minority students nearly quadrupled.[15] But equal care has not been taken to keep the promise implied in their admission. Minority students find themselves in settings that are often culturally and socially strange to them, and they may need help with the academic demands of the college. Simply to admit is not enough; admissions must be accompanied by a sustained effort to provide opportunities and supports for academic growth and a commitment to root out prejudicial actions and attitudes which rob these students of a sense of welcome and community.

One symptom of fragile self-esteem is exhibited in the deeply-felt concerns of some minority students admitted to selective institutions who wonder whether their admission was due to their race or to their ability. Even as able a student as Henry-Louis Gates, Jr., at one point wondered if "some computer in the admissions office had not made a mistake," and he describes a fantasy of a patronizing dean's office record containing such phrases as "black, scholarship boy, remarkable verbal potential for one in his demographic group; mediocre performance, C— student." The chapters by Morton Levitt and James Thomas have provided poignant detail about the situation of minority students, as well as women students, in medical and law schools.

First-Generation and Other "New" Students

About half of all entering freshmen in 1976 had fathers who at best had finished high school.[16] They are, thus, pioneers in the new academic environment and often not very well prepared by their families for it. Specific anxieties may be created by fear of alienation from their parents, relatives, and of being uprooted from their social class, religion, or ethnic community.[17] Howard London in his chapter has described the plight of male community-college students torn between the success implied by moving into the white collar world and their fear of social rejection and loss of masculinity if they move out of the blue collar world. Their ambivalence keeps them from responding more fully to their teachers. Their learning and personal development suffer as they cannot find, or are not helped to find, ways of reconciling the expectations of academe with the problems generated by their joining a culture different from the one into which they were born and in which they were reared.

There are other people who do not fit the traditional patterns: people who attend college while having full-time jobs, housewives who have husbands and children at home, people who have to care for relatives suffering from chronic illness, people who are physically or emotionally handicapped, people who have been defined as "dummies" in their previous schooling. These students constitute a vast array of humanity, and yet often little attention is given to their life situations and to providing the sensitive and costly services they need to do well in their student role. Colleges cannot just admit, they must serve. Schools often derive considerable income—whether in fees or legislative appropriations—from the presence of these new students not previously found on college campuses in such numbers. But hypocrisy and neglect reside in admitting them and then acting as if the heavy burdens of their lives do not exist.

The Inadequacy of Tests

Earlier in the chapter, I indicated some of the origins and the rationale of standardized tests in their gatekeeping function. A closer look at the price that is paid for the testing system is now in order. For with all our sophistication in test construction, we still do not possess good enough predictive measures to allow us to select those undergraduate and graduate students whose ultimate performance in life and the professions would most merit their being selected. We do not know to what extent our present instruments and guidelines exclude those who may have more creativity, originality, forcefulness, motivation, and who, perhaps by dint of their independence, refuse to submit to the conformist discipline, the striving for near-perfect performance that now insures admissions to the top colleges, the most competitive graduate school programs and the professional schools. We do know from studies done over many decades[18] that the grades a student earns in college seem to bear no particular relationship to effectiveness and success later on the job. We also know that what a student is asked to do in college and professional school may bear only a partial or even tangential relationship to the skills required on the job.

An astute observer of the testing scene, who himself has made major contributions to psychometrics, has recently written: "Researchers have in fact had great difficulty demonstrating that grades in school are related to any other behaviors of importance—other than doing well on aptitude tests."[19] He goes on to report on a simple check he had made. He took the top eight students (all straight A's) in a class he was teaching at an Ivy League college in the late 1940s and contrasted what they were doing in the early 1960s with what eight really poor students (C— or below) were doing. "To my great surprise, I could not distinguish the two lists of men fifteen to eighteen years later. There were lawyers, doctors, research scientists, and college and high school teachers in both groups. The only difference I noted was that those with better grades got into better law or medical schools, but even with this supposed advantage they did not have notably more successful careers as compared with the poorer students who had had to be satisfied with 'second-rate' law and medical schools at the outset." He concludes that "the testing movement is in grave danger of perpetuating a mythological meritocracy."

There is, further, an inevitable irony about tests that mean to *predict* performance in college. If colleges were truly teaching, that is, enhancing capacities to learn, it would be difficult to predict before the event who would acquire these capacities and to what degree. Some researchers have begun to say that schools are less concerned with raising the performance levels of their students, that is, with educating them, than they are with selecting students who are able to function at the level of expectation of the particular school—so that a "good" school becomes "good" simply by virtue of the students it admits.[20] The problem with the admissions tests is not only that they may favor test-taking skills at the expense of others, but that they help create an educational climate in which selection (and honorific distinction) is given undue weight over improving students.

It may be argued that some people are more intelligent than others, that these people tend to apply and get accepted by the "better" schools, and that they continue to improve there. But regardless of the merits of this argument, the problem remains that the tests help to define "intelligence" in too restricted a way, that they do not identify many people who are able, and that they help establish an academic climate where the exercise of intelligence which leads to high test scores and high grades tends to be given undue weight over the development of a more thorough, more expansive, and more highly motivated intellectual competence.

Beyond Current Aptitude Measures and Grades

One could think of no more massive transformation in our colleges than if they were required to prove that the people who pass through them had been raised to higher levels of cognitive and other functioning than when they entered. This would mean a considerable broadening of focus beyond current aptitude measures or grades. Schools would have to develop diagnostic profiles of students in order to chart their learning capacities. Such profiles would define and distinguish a whole variety of learning and thinking styles: ability for generalization and abstraction, rigorous logical and scientific thinking, mathematical reasoning, capacity for perception, literary and aesthetic sensitivities, imagination, writing proficiency, capacity for listening, practical intelligence as expressed in action. The profile would include, beside intellectual capacities, an inventory of emotional ones; for example, capacity for independence, assertiveness, self-esteem, level of awareness of one's feelings. Learning is profoundly influenced by one's emotional makeup—a fact that schools thus far have made very little use of.

A careful student profile drawn during the freshman year would provide direction for the learning that is to be attempted in college. As things are now, professors do not use the student's prior performance as a base for improvement. In nearly every college course the instructor faces the student with little or no knowledge of his or her previous history. There is little for the teacher to build on, so what the student did not learn in a prior course, he or she may not learn again. One need only think of a skill such as writing to realize that continuous, concerted attention is rarely given, beyond the required freshman composition course, to having a student gradually build up this talent during the four college years.

One of the chief troubles with current aptitude measures as instruments of selection is that they draw attention away from diagnosing the actual skills that are in need of development. Success in school correlates poorly with later proficiency in life because we do not identify the skills and performances that are indicative of personal and occupational achievement. This would be a smaller matter if it were only a question of accuracy of measurement and prediction. It is a much larger matter because it helps to keep us from a much more detailed articulation of educational objectives and procedures. Some advanced psychometricians currently are developing tests that rely not on memory and recognition (of the right answer) in multiple-choice tests, but on the student's actual performance or demonstration of skill. A student's writing ability is not demonstrated through responses to multiple-choice questions. Similarly, a student's reasoning is best shown by having him or her engage actively in that process.

Selection procedures probably could be improved if we recognized a student's demonstrated prior talents at the expense of grades and aptitude measures. One researcher has said: "There is substantial evidence that the way to predict whether a person will manifest a given line of talented attainment later is to determine whether he or she manifests a similar type of attainment earlier."[21] One might thus look for a student's proficiencies in the precollege or pregraduate school years and then devote further schooling to the exercise and development of these talents. Such an approach would also open up the whole question of what are *desirable* aptitudes—something that is long overdue. A few researchers have recently begun to explore learning styles and to draw up fresh maps of cognitive and emotional development.[22]

Selecting the Wrong People

Our present methods of admitting people into the selective institution seems to let some of the "wrong" people in and keep some of the "right" ones out. Many studies of high school students show that little or no relationship exists between demonstrated talent, such as shown in either artistic products or scientific research projects, and intellective ability test scores or academic achievement measures.[23] Creative individuals in particular seem to be among those who are left out. In a major study of creative scientists it turned out that they performed, while in college, at the C+ to B— level even in the fields of their future eminence.[24] Other studies have had similar results.[25] They were made in the days before today's more stringent admission requirements. One wonders whether these creative people might not have been excluded from today's more selective colleges and graduate institutions—and at what loss to society. It is quite possible that people with imagination and a strong bent of mind—conditions necessary for creativity—are not likely to conform to school routine and also are likely to have scholastic records that zigzag on the grade grid; intense concentration on one subject may be accompanied by boredom or disinterest in regard to another.

Other evidence against too exclusive a reliance on academic criteria comes from a study at Harvard that showed a positive correlation between nonacademic qualities of personal strength, as judged by the student's secondary school teachers, and good academic performance in college.[26] The higher grades obtained in college may have been a consequence of the stimulus of college or an accommodation to it. But the prior grades and test scores were not an adequate indication of these students' aptitude. As with the unusually creative people just referred to, the relationship between nonacademic personal qualities and high performance might have been even more pronounced if one had data about these people's lives after graduation. Evidence for this is suggested by a recent

331

study[27] of the graduates of a selective men's college. It found that "increasing scholastic aptitude in adolescence may be related to increasing interpersonal *immaturity* in adulthood." Measures of non-academic psychological characteristics predicted more powerfully than grades and test scores the students' vocational, paternal, and other adult competencies ten to fifteen years after college. For instance, honor students ten years later were "more depressed and less aggressively energetic" than those who had not received honors. (But it must be borne in mind that most of the students studied were in the upper 10 to 20 percent of academic talent nationally.)

Another instance of successful deviation from traditional academic admission criteria is furnished by the State University of New York at Stony Brook. The University has been admitting up to 30 percent of its freshman applicants with a lower grade point average than their peers in consideration of qualities displayed in artistic or other activities outside of the high school classroom. These specially admitted students by the end of their freshman year have no worse an academic record than the rest of their class. My argument is not in favor of an arbitrary openness—there are many C+ students who will never be Einsteins—but for a more judicious redefinition and enlargement of the criteria now used for admission and rejection.

Selling College to Students

Thus far I have emphasized the difficulties of gaining access to higher education and the discriminatory treatment suffered by segments of the student population. But the fact is that the proliferation of colleges and universities in the 1960s has forced most institutions in the 1970s to vie for students. Less prestigious or weaker institutions are in a poor competitive situation; some are close to extinction and others are heavily threatened. Budgetary problems beset even the richest universities. Such situations promote the tendency to think of students as above all customers or clients whose funds—whether the students' own or supplied by the state legislatures—must be coaxed into the institutional coffers. Institutions of higher education in this country have adopted an increasingly commercial outlook.[28] As with department stores the objective is to sell, and interest in the contents of education may, as a result, become secondary. Efforts directed to attracting students have even brought with them the "truth in advertising" problems we are familiar with in commerce. A few colleges have been blatant in false advertising techniques, as, for example, the institution that put a lake on the cover of its brochure—a lake that did not exist on its campus.

For many years the lack of detailed information available to an applicant has been an obstacle to his or her making an intelligent choice. Institutions have always sought a plethora of revealing information from their applicants, but have not shown a reciprocal readiness to reveal themselves in detail.[29] Recently, however, the Fund for the Improvement of Postsecondary Education, a federal agency, has sought to rectify this situation. The Fund has commissioned studies and demonstration programs in which institutions are encouraged to give accurate and detailed descriptions of such areas as costs and financial aid, academic programs, teaching practices, the quality of student life[30]—information vital for applicants who want to choose the environment that will best foster their growth.

If institutions were moved to give better information about themselves, this might have the further benefit of encouraging them to change their ways of educating. By having to search out and document what they do, they would confront some current deficiencies in their academic and nonacademic programs. There are some signs already that actual or threatened enrollment shortages are moving some institutions to consider the student's interest more fully. Private schools in particular are increasingly hard-pressed to justify to parents the great difference in tuition fees between private and public institutions. Recent revivals of general education programs—the attempt to give students a more well-rounded education—have been spurred by the desire to enhance the competitive advantage of a school.

National Portrait of the Entering Student

Who are these students who each year are streaming into colleges and universities? For the past ten years the American Council on Education has collected extensive data* particularly on entering undergraduate students. What follows is the fall 1976 portrait of entering freshmen. The portrait is based on the responses of over 200,000 full-time students and is representative of all first-time freshmen nationwide in all types of institutions.[31]

Most freshmen are young; less than one in ten is more than nineteen years old. As we have already seen, many of them are first-generation college students: about half of their fathers and more than half of their mothers had only a high school education or less. Most of the freshmen come from homes very close to the college they are attending: more than half are not more than fifty miles away from home. Nearly half of them live with parents or other relatives—though many say they would prefer to live elsewhere.

The vast majority of freshmen say that the college they are attending is their first choice. In fact nearly half of them applied to no other school. The most popular intended major is business; one-fifth of the freshmen think they will choose it. Education, engineering, humanities, natural sciences, and social sciences pull about equal proportions of entering students (roughly 9 percent each). Eight percent aim at the Associate in Arts degree (obtained after two years), over a third at the bachelor's, and 29 percent at the

* Philip Rever, in his chapter, has made use of this data source in his description of applicants to the less-selective colleges.

334

master's. A fifth of all entering freshmen aspire to a Ph.D., M.D., LL.B., or similar degrees, but only 17 pecent of the women aspire to these higher degrees as against 24 percent of the men. (It is interesting to note that nearly three-fourths as many people say they are going to college to get a better job as say they go there to learn more.)

As this portrait makes clear, most of the anxieties and aspirations that have appeared prominently in preceding chapters of this book are characteristic of only a minority of students. Nearly half of the students applied to no other school than the one they are attending and few of them presumably experienced anxiety about being accepted. Only a fifth aim at the higher degrees for which entrance into a selective school and the maintenance of a high grade point average are important—and entail anxiety as well. David Tilley, in his chapter, has suggested that for the vast majority of applicants to colleges, acceptance is not seriously in doubt. And Philip Rever documents the admission issues for that vast majority in his chapter on the less-selective colleges.

The attention given in this book to applicants to the highly-selective institutions is nevertheless justified. The number—though not the percentage—of these applicants still is large. The schools they apply to serve as models to others. Moreover, from this group of applicants come many of the people who will exert power, leadership, and influence in our society. It is, therefore, of general social concern that they be selected judiciously and fairly.

The care that applicants to the more-selective institutions exercise in making their choices of schools might well be emulated by other students. As the national portrait of the entering freshmen suggests, many students seem to make their choices by drift. Proximity to home seems to be a strong determinant, and the huge numbers of people who apply to only one or two schools may not have given enough attention to such questions as what school might best serve their needs and promote their growth. Even many applicants to the selective institutions could improve on the information they now have about prospective schools.

Informed Choice

To gain a clearer picture of the possibilities is no easy undertaking. There are about 3,000 colleges in the country, a figure that reduces by about a thousand when one eliminates the two-year colleges. Unfortunately, there are no experts available with a grasp of such a multitude of institutions. Even the best high school counselor could in no way possess the appropriate knowledge of even a fraction of so many institutions—a task made more difficult by their constantly shifting internal nature. But counselors, friends, relatives, formal compendia (such as the College Entrance Examination Board's *The College Handbook*) and informal guides (such as the *Yale Daily News*'s *The Insiders' Guide to the College*) all can help generate a list and enlarge one's sense of the variety of available institutions. (Such enlargement is unfortunately hampered by the mandate of public institutions to charge higher tuitions to out-of-state residents. Higher costs to out-of-state students make it difficult for them to take advantage of what research has identified as a potent source of learning: exposure to people, situations, and environments different from those of one's upbringing.[32]) Once the range of one's possible choices has been narrowed, student newspapers can be a particularly instructive source for knowledge about the institution; they can give a sense of the school's intellectual and social life, its vitality, the degree to which it cares for students. A personal visit to the institution may help to gather impressions and determine the subtleties of fit between institution and individual which go beyond the information that catalogs, counselors, or friends can provide.

After the student has decided where to apply he or she begins what can be a weary process of application writing and various emotion-laden contacts with the admissions office. Students may be made anxious or offended by letters from or interviews with admissions officers. Admissions officers are usually sensitive to these problems, but the process could still be improved. In particular, greater thought could be given to the selection of interviewers and to how such interviews are conducted. But it is important to recognize that admissions officers are themselves often in an ambiguous position. If they are too friendly, they may be misunderstood, raising the hopes of an applicant unrealistically.

The Role of Parents

Intense anxieties about the admissions process may be stirred by the actual or presumed expectations of oneself, one's peers, and one's parents as the chapter by Herbert Sacks has so well shown. Competitiveness and need for recognition are so strong, particularly in adolescence, that the accident of what respected peers prize may distort one's own life plans. Parents in particular, in our upwardly mobile, ambitious, and competitive society, often want children to comply with or live out their own unrealized ambitions. There is a reflected glory cast on the parent by the school his or her child attends.

Sometimes parental ambitions point the other way, and a child's needs may interfere with their own. The funds for a college education may seem better used for a business investment or simply for more affluent living. Still other parents do not plan properly for their child's education so that, at the point when he or she is ready for college, financing poses an overwhelming burden. Still others are not willing to have their children assume greater independence. "If you commute to school, I'll give you a car" is one way of making continued dependence seductive.

In all these situations, separation of parental ambitions and interests from those of their children is no easy task, and Herbert Sacks's chapter might be helpful to parents in showing them how to allow their children a freer choice and to support them in the emotional trials that attend either acceptance or rejection.

Perhaps nothing can be said that will allay the anxieties of parents and their children who are frantically bent on making it

337

into the colleges of their choice and who see their later lives and careers as incomplete and blighted if those colleges do not favor them. But some sobering thoughts might well be considered. The frantic attempt to make it into the college of one's choice may only signal the beginning of many more efforts like it. The next test might be to make it into a fraternity or other prestigious group within the college, to make it into a desirable professional or graduate school, to make it into a high-status law firm or corporation; and from there a repetition of country clubs, honors, and so on. The trauma of the prefreshman applicant can be and is repeated many times; as one seeks to enter graduate school, as one looks for one's first academic position, as one aspires to tenure, as one seeks a national position within one's profession. Life can be a never-ending round wherein one periodically returns to the status of the applicant. This pattern might just as well be broken sooner rather than later. Insight about what is good for one's growth and personal development may overcome the need to gain a sense of worth through acceptance by some organization, club, school, or clique.

The Admissions Process as a Challenge

The admissions process, like any crisis, also offers an opportunity for self-discovery and for learning to be less dependent on circumstances, approval, or flattery external to oneself. One surmises that Peter Wells's dentist, who would rather have been a teacher, missed an opportunity for self-knowledge some time back in the days when he was readying his applications. By contrast, Eric Goodman describes in this book a courageous sequence of facing up to questions about his identity as he moved from contemplated careers in medicine and law to training himself as a writer.

We know from both myth and psychology that every culture provides some equivalent of the ordeal for their young. Adulthood is gained through a struggle in which there is both risk and opportunity for the development of courage. Such experiences help shape individuals who can shed the dependencies of childhood and who, in the affairs and crises of adulthood, have the daring and autonomy without which life can be a craven and sullen affair. Success in the struggle for admission can be one such test and the strength that can flow from it may be an impetus for further exploration and growth. The decisive fact, however, is not acceptance by some college, but the struggle with oneself, the task attempted, the insight gained. Being accepted can in fact be part of a failure, a continuation of the old dependency, of being a good boy or a good girl. Not being accepted may be insignificant in comparison with the accomplishment of taking life more fully into one's own hands and charting a course more in harmony with one's capabilities, utilizing the best there is in the *available* environment.

As a wise psychiatrist once said: "Only fools trust institutions." Even the most benign institutions carry with them much that thwarts, diminishes, even cripples the individual. Universities and colleges are no exceptions. The admissions process may help to condition many for a conformist submission to the institution of the college, to be followed by many more submissions to other institutions: the government, the corporation, the military. "The fat envelope" day too often has become the occasion for false joy and misplaced anguish. Perhaps, this book has in some measure helped to indicate how the admissions process can be an opportunity for learning about oneself, rather than simply an occasion when, as so often in our society, the individual must endure the hurt of being subject to the irrelevant judgment of an impersonal agency.

Recommendations

Having reached the end of the book the reader will have grasped many intricacies and ramifications of the admissions process. This vast process of selection involves a huge array of people, equipment, and paper and stands easy comparison with the Army's induction process. In many ways the admissions process grinds impersonally along serving the purposes of society and institutions and leaving the individual feeling apparently small and powerless. Nevertheless the reader, by surveying and understanding the process, may have gained some insights into how individuals can better cope with the gigantic machinery. The reader has also encountered in this book instances of individuals standing up successfully against the institutional process. Such instances were furnished by Henry-Louis Gates, Jr., when describing his success in acquiring his academic leave after he had already been turned down, and by Eric Goodman when telling us about seeking his own way among the conflicting expectations of schools, parents, girl friends. Some, such as Mark, whom Herbert Sacks described, find freedom in fantasy. Still others, Howard London's community college men, for example, find some sense of self and freedom in the angry ridicule of their teachers.

In this final section my intention is to sum up some of the many implications of this book as they bear upon the improvement of the admission and selection process for society, institutions, and the individual.

I. *Debate about Objectives.* We have seen that there is much implicit confusion about the objectives of higher education. The cultivation of learning is only one objective. Social mobility and economic advancement, also important motives for those seeking higher education in America and elsewhere, are, increasingly, not achieved. Schools may be divided into the most-selective and less-selective institutions. But this division has often been *sub rosa*, and there has been no clear-cut public recognition of the differential benefits that come from attending specific schools.

It is time to engage in a national debate about the objectives of higher education and what can reasonably be expected from it. If, for instance, one faces up to the fact of the differential rewards that accrue from attending an elite institution, then a democratic society needs to ask itself how it can make admission to elite institutions easier for members of social classes and ethnic groups who tend to have limited access.

But the question of more democratic access is only the beginning. Debate is also needed to achieve greater clarity about the purposes of higher education in general. The shadowy distinctions between economic benefits and the intrinsic values of learning often mean that neither objective is realized as well as it might be. Other objectives are often left out of full consideration entirely. One can easily distinguish five different objectives of higher education. They are (1) cultivation of cognitive, affective, and aesthetic capacities, (2) occupational preparation, (3) personal development, (4) preparation for *effective* participation in the political community and the organizational bureaucracies of the society, (5) social mobility and social redistribution, that is, shifting of the social-economic hierarchy. All of these are essential objectives, but they are often slighted in execution. To single out just one, in spite of the splendid scholarship represented in our colleges and universities, only a small number of graduates seem to continue to an appreciable extent the intellectual activities—other than job-related ones—they were required or encouraged to pursue in their courses.

II. Better Tests and Redefinition of Teaching. We have seen that tests are uncertain devices for measuring ability and that they are often inadequate and unjust instruments for controlling access to institutions. Considerably greater effort is needed to replace our current tests with more complete indices of talent and ability. As was suggested, relevant and judiciously selected samples of past performance are preferable to abstract test exercises. The example of art schools, where a student is asked to submit samples of work done over a period time, gives us one clue to the nature of better tests.

We have seen that tests directly affect the kind of clientele that is going to be educated in the more-selective institution and that there is some evidence that the more creative students, or students with special strengths in some areas, may well be kept out.

341

But the greatest havoc played by tests is that they tend implicitly to determine the content of education. Proficiency in tests is mirrored by proficiency in college examinations and the style of learning encouraged by tests is thus implicitly encouraged in college courses. The contents and processes of undergraduate education, therefore, are not challenged as much as they should be. What is needed is a thorough rethinking of the kind of capacities we wish students to acquire and then a reshaping, testing, selection, and teaching in the light of freshly-defined curricular objectives.

Institutions tend to be determined by the kind of students they select, and both research and observation suggest that institutions do not improve student skills nearly as much as they might. (Writing is only one instance of such lack.) Schools tend to be shaped by those whom they select rather than by the education they provide. We need much greater emphasis on educating people than on selecting them.

III. Information and Reform. To allow individuals to make more intelligent choices, schools, as I have suggested, need to provide more detailed information about themselves. That information must be manifold. First there should be spelling out, beyond what is now said in the course catalog, of the academic offerings. Students need a clearer picture of the range of subject matter, the theoretical approaches, the methods of instruction, the availability of teachers, the approximate size of classes. Beyond the classroom, the student needs to know to what extent the school facilitates learning through such services as the library and out-of-class academic clubs, lectures, field trips, and other learning opportunities.

The applicant further needs to know about the social atmosphere, the kind of relationships that students can have with each other, the degree of competition versus cooperation, the potential for isolation, cliquishness, and impersonality. The social atmosphere can help determine in many ways what kind of social being one is to become as an adult. There is every reason why colleges should be places where people learn to be comfortable with themselves, with the people around them, and with their environment. But too many schools are grim places, perceived by some students as almost prison or barracklike in atmosphere, and they, thus, set a poor example for helping young people to create a more human and compassionate society.

Finally, the student needs information about what graduates of the college are doing, at what kind of schools they have continued their education, what kind of jobs they hold, even what kinds of lives they are leading. Though what graduates are doing is always shifting, prospective students can gain a sense of what is in store for them when they see what the school has done for others before them.

Such information will allow students to make more informed choices. But, as I suggested earlier, perhaps an even more important consequence of such information would be that it would lead to reforms. When schools need to describe themselves more accurately, they may be motivated to change those aspects of themselves that do not serve their students well.

*IV. The Non-College-Bound Students and Those Who Defer College Entry.** There are secondary school students whose development and talents will not permit them to fit into the present system at any level—from open enrollment in the public sector to entry into the most-selective undergraduate institutions. Many of these young people require alternative education in the community, upgraded technical schools, internships in business or professional enterprises or just jobs with a future. The expected lowering of the minimum working age from sixteen years will tax the creativity of educational systems, which should develop programmatic options and budgeting proposals in anticipation of that event. For instance, experimental projects which enable students to move into the work force and from there to further education might be considered.

* Sections IV to VI were written by Herbert Sacks.

V. Faculty Role in the Admissions Process. Faculty should consider greater participation in the admissions process in order to help wed educational principle to admissions policy. Their self-interest alone would seem to require a larger role in the process of selecting the students they will teach. Beyond that, faculty talents in sociology, psychology, and political science ought to be employed for thoughtful research by the admissions office which could have far more than local significance.

VI. Pilot Projects to Test New Admissions Models. While many schools in the public sector of higher education have been moving toward almost universal admissions, the more prestigious public and private institutions continue to restrict admissions. There is an acute need for a more judicious definition and enlargement of criteria now used for admission and rejection of applicants to undergraduate and graduate schools. Well-controlled experimental modifications of the present system ought to be tried in a variety of cooperating institutions.

There is, for instance, no space in the entering classes of medical and many law schools for those whose formative conflicts intruded into undergraduate scholarship but who restituted themselves through growth and/or treatment. Such students may be lost to medicine and the law forever as a result of screening of their applications in the admissions offices based upon grade point averages. Special admissions programs with clear criteria ought to be established for this group whose self-awareness and insights into themselves and society may make them a valued national resource.

VII. Rite of Passage. We have seen that for applicants to the highly-selective institution the application process may entail considerable anxiety and even constitute a crisis. Applying to and entering college or graduate school is an important transition point, but society does not provide for it the rituals or recognitions it bestows on other of life's passages where customs and symbols often help the individual to cope with some of the problems and anxieties imposed by the transition. (Rituals surrounding birth, puberty, marriage, death are the most obvious instances of this.)

Selecting a college may be the first "adult" decision that a young woman or man makes. That it is in fact his or her own decision may often be masked by the environmental factors described in this book. Peers with their pressures and parents with their desires and expectations may narrow the space for autonomy. An opportunity may be lost for the individual to begin to learn to make decisions, particularly decisions that show self-regard and that take one's own desires and inclinations sufficiently into account as one charts one's course.

Whatever provides greater understanding of the psychological aspects of the admissions process is helpful—the threats to and opportunities for self-esteem and autonomy, therefore, need particular spelling out. Good counseling and psychotherapy, when available, can have benefits far beyond the admissions crisis by giving the individual a better understanding of his or her aspirations, fantasies, relations with authority and with peers.

Group discussions, if skillful leaders are available, can also be very helpful in increasing awareness about motivation and sorting out pressures and ambitions. (Students should particularly be helped to gain perspective on those "counselors" who impose themselves on their advisees or who tend to dampen the hopes of inchoate minds and hearts, which in their uncertainty may yet have a clearer sense of direction than their mentors.) Perhaps one might also suggest to students that they revive the currently unpracticed art of the diary, to describe what they have done, thought, and felt and to use the "objectification" of the writing process as a (limited) vehicle to enhance awareness.

The admissions process is just one instance of the potential victimization of the individual by surrounding circumstances. It is also an opportunity for learning to make decisions with awareness and regard for self. Beyond that, it invites thinking about one's stance with relation to the external world. Freshmen in their first encounter with higher education can develop some attitudes that will help determine to what extent they will be victims of the world around them or remakers of it.

REFERENCES

1. James O'Toole, "The Reserve Army of the Underemployed," Parts I and II, *Change* (May and June 1975).

2. Truman Commission, *Higher Education for American Democracy* (Washington, D.C.: U.S. Department of Health, Education, and Welfare, Office of Education, 1947).

3. David Riesman, *Constraint and Variety in American Education* (New York: Doubleday Anchor, 1958).

4. Mark Webster, "Open Admissions *Oui ou Non*," *Change*, Vol. 9, no. 3 (March 1977), pp. 16–19.

5. Harold S. Wechsler, *The Qualified Student, A History of Selective College Admission in America* (New York: Wiley, 1977).

6. *The New York Times*, October 12, 1977, p. A12.

7. Burton R. Clark, "The 'Cooling-Out' Function in Higher Education," *American Journal of Sociology*, Vol. 65 (1960) pp. 569–576.

8. Burton R. Clark, *op. cit.*, and *The Open Door College* (New York: McGraw-Hill, 1960).

9. Alexander W. Astin, *et al.*, *The American Freshman: National Norms for Fall 1976* (Los Angeles: Cooperative Institutional Research Program, Graduate School of Education, University of California at Los Angeles, 1976).

10. Henry M. Levin, "Educational Opportunity and Social Inequality in Western Europe," *Social Problems*, Vol. 24 (1976) pp. 148–172.

11. Michelle Patterson, "The Junior Collegization of the French University," *Social Problems*, Vol. 24 (1976) pp. 148–172.

12. *The New York Times*, February 27, 1977, Section 4, p. 9.

13. Nancy E. Adler, "Women Students," in J. Katz and R. T. Hartnett, *Scholars in the Making* (Cambridge, Mass.: Ballinger, 1976) pp. 197–225; Austin Frank, *1975 Seniors at Berkeley* (Berkeley: Office of Student Affairs Research, 1976).

14. Alexander W. Astin, *et al.*, *The American Freshman: National Norms for Fall 1976, loc. cit.*; *The Chronicle of Higher Education*, Vol. 13 (Washington, D.C.: February 7, 1977).

346

15. *Statistical Abstract of the United States,* 1974 (95th Edition), (Washington, D.C., 1974), p. 114.

16. Alexander Astin, *et al., op. cit.*

17. Richard Rodriguez, "On Becoming A Chicano," *Saturday Review,* Vol. 2 (February 8, 1975) pp. 46–48.

18. Donald P. Hoyt, *The Relationship Between College Grades and Adult Achievement, A Review of the Literature,* Iowa Research Report No. 7, American College Testing Program (Iowa City: 1965).

19. David McClelland, "Testing for Competence Rather than for 'Intelligence'," *American Psychologist,* Vol. 28 (1973) p. 2.

20. Alexander W. Astin, "Undergraduate Achievement and Institutional 'Excellence'," *Science,* Vol. 161 (1968) pp. 661–668.

21. Michael A. Wallach, "Psychology of Talent and Graduate Education," in Samuel Messick and Associates, *Individuality in Learning* (San Francisco: Jossey-Bass, 1976), p. 188.

22. William G. Perry, *Forms of Intellectual and Ethical Development in the College Years* (New York: Holt, Rinehart and Winston, 1970); Mildred M. Henry, *The Individual and the Individual's Construction of "Reality,"* Annual Report to the Fund for the Improvement of Postsecondary Education (Washington, D.C.: September 26, 1976).

23. Michael A. Wallach, *op. cit.,* pp. 182–183.

24. Donald W. MacKinnon, "Identifying and Developing Creativity," in *Selection and Educational Differentiation* (Berkeley: Center for the Study of Higher Education, 1959), p. 86.

25. C. Taylor, *et al.,* "The creative and other contributions of one sample of research scientists," in C. Taylor and F. Barron, eds., *Scientific Creativity: Its Recognition and Development* (New York: Wiley, 1963).

26. Dean K. Whitla, "Evaluation of Decision Making: A Study of College Admissions," in Dean K. Whitla, ed., *Handbook of Measurement and Assessment in Behavioral Science* (Reading, Mass.: Addison-Wesley, 1968) pp. 485 ff.

27. Douglas H. Heath, "Academic Predictors of Adult Maturity and Competence," *Journal of Higher Education,* Vol. 48, no. 6, November–December 1977, pp. 613–632.

28. G. I. Maeroff, "Colleges Now Are Recruiting for More than Athletic Reasons," *New York Times,* Sunday, November 28, 1976, Section 4, p. 9.

29. James S. Coleman, *The Principle of Symmetry in College Choice* (New York: Report of the Commission on Tests, College Entrance Examination Board, 1970); *Educational Record,* Vol. 58, No. 2 (Spring 1977), "The Student Consumer Movement" (Articles by Elaine H. El-Khawas, John C. Hoy, Alfred L. Moye).

30. Malcolm G. Scully, "Providing Better Information for Potential Students," *The Chronicle of Higher Education,* April 18, 1977, p. 5.

31. Alexander W. Astin, *et al., op. cit.*

32. Kenneth A. Feldman and Theodore M. Newcomb, *The Impact of College on Students* (San Francisco: Jossey-Bass, 1969) chapter 8.

347

CONTRIBUTORS

HENRY-LOUIS GATES, JR., born in 1950 in Piedmont, West Virginia, is a Lecturer in English and Afro-American Studies and Assistant to the Chairman of the Afro-American Studies Department at Yale College. He is presently a Ph.D. candidate at Cambridge University—Clare College. As a Yale undergraduate, Gates was a Scholar of the House and a Fellow of the Five Year B.A. Program. He is Associate Editor of both *Ch'Indaba* (Nigeria) and the *Yardbird Reader* and has published articles and book reviews on Afro-American subjects including literary criticism. He is working on a book about Wole Soyinke, the eminent Nigerian poet.

ERIC K. GOODMAN, born in 1953 in Brooklyn, New York, was graduated from Yale College in 1975 and is now a magazine editor completing a humorous novel entitled *The Enthusiast.* Upon leaving New Haven he became a Mirrieless Fellow in Creative Writing at Stanford University. He wrote the book and lyrics of *The Good Fortune of Matthew Mann* (1976), a rock musical produced at Yale, and has published an article on the difficulties facing college graduates in the mid-1970s.

HAROLD L. HODGKINSON, Ed.D., born in 1931 in Minneapolis, Minnesota, is the Executive Director of the Professional Institute, American Management Associations, and Adjunct Professor at the University of Michigan. He served as Director, National Institute of Education of the Department of Health, Education and Welfare, 1975 to 1977. He has been Director, School of Education at Simmons College, 1958 to 1961; Dean of Bard College, 1962 to 1968; and Research Educator at the Center for Research and Development in Higher Education, University of California at Berkeley, 1968 to 1975. Among his numerous books are: *Improving and Assessing Performance: Evaluation in Higher Education* (1975), *How Much Change for a Dollar? A Review of the Developing Institutions Program* (1974), and *The Campus Senate: Experiment In Democracy* (1974). He has published articles on a wide range of subjects—university governance, the minority student, faculty evaluation, and research and development in education.

JOSEPH KATZ, Ph.D., born in 1920 in Zwickau, Germany, is currently the Director of the Research Group for Human Development and Educational Policy, and Professor of Human Development at the State University of New York (SUNY) at Stony Brook. He was the Executive Director of the Institute for the Study of Human Problems at Stanford University, 1968 to 1970, and the Director of the William James Center, Wright Institute, in Berkeley, California, 1973 to 1975. He has published articles on curricular planning in higher education, faculty development, male-female relations in college youth, and among his many books are: *Scholars in the Making* (1976), *Service for Students* (1937), and *No Time for Youth* (1968).

MORTON LEVITT, Ph.D., born in 1920 in Detroit, Michigan, is Professor of Psychiatry and Associate Dean for Academic Affairs at the University of California School of Medicine at Davis. He has published numerous books, including *On the Urban Scene* (1972), *Youth and Social Change* (1972), *The Mental Health Field: A Critical Appraisal* (1971), *Freud and Dewey on the Nature of Man* (1960), and articles on psychoanalysis, child development, and medical education.

HOWARD B. LONDON, Ph.D., born in 1947 in Boston, Massachusetts, is Assistant Professor of Sociology at Tulane University in New Orleans, Louisiana. He is writing a book on the culture of the working-class community college.

ANGELA S. MOGER, M.Phil., born in 1941 in Darby, Pennsylvania, is a doctoral candidate in French Literature at Yale University. She was Assistant Dean of the College at Wesleyan University, Middletown,

Connecticut, 1969 to 1971, and Dean of Studies at Sarah Lawrence College, 1971 to 1974. Currently, she is a member of the Advisory Committee on Careers for Women in Business and Administration at Bryn Mawr College and serves on the Yale Council Undergraduate College Curriculum and Life Committee.

ETTA S. ONAT, Ph.D., born in 1920 in Shumsk, Poland, is the Associate Dean of the Graduate School and a Lecturer in English at Yale University. She is on the Board of Directors of the Information and Counseling Service for Women at Yale, and on the Advisory Board of the New England Higher Education Resources Service (HERS) and is the President of the Yale Women's Forum.

PHILIP R. REVER, Ph.D., born in 1941 in Kodiak, Alaska, is Director of the Washington, D.C., office of the American College Testing Program. He is the editor of *Open Admissions and Equal Access* (1971) and the author of *Scientific and Technical Careers: Factors Influencing Development During the Educational Years* (1973). He has written papers on concerned decision theory, student development, and the interpretation of trends in test scores.

HERBERT S. SACKS, M.D., born in 1926 in New York City, is an Associate Clinical Professor of Pediatrics and Psychiatry (Child Study Center) at the Yale University School of Medicine and the Chairman of the Committee on Clinical Practice and Social Policy of the American Academy of Child Psychiatry. He is a member of the Executive Committee of the National Commission on the Confidentiality of the Health Record and the Connecticut Juvenile Justice Commission. He has published articles on the relationship between pediatrics and child psychiatry, the confidentiality of the health record, and student response to social change. He is also a collaborator in the *Professional Standards Review Organization: A Handbook for Child Psychiatrists* (1976).

JAMES A. THOMAS, LL.B., born in 1949 in Des Moines, Iowa, is an Associate Dean of Yale Law School. He is a Trustee and member of the Legal Affairs Committee of the Law School Admission Council and has published articles on law school admissions.

DAVID C. TILLEY, Ph.D., born in 1927 in Philadelphia, Pennsylvania, is Vice-Chancellor for Student Affairs, University of California at Santa Cruz. A former Research Associate at the Research Group for Human

Contributors

Development and Educational Policy at State University of New York (SUNY) at Stony Brook and Dean of Students at SUNY at Stony Brook, 1962 to 1968: he was also the Dean of New Student Affairs and Director of Admissions there from 1968 to 1971. He is the Editor of the *Journal of the National Association of Student Personnel Administrators*, and has published articles on administration of student affairs, college and professional school admissions, and student development needs.

PETER H. WELLS, Ph.D., born in 1941 in Harbor Green, New York, is a teacher of English and the Dean of Students at Hopkins Grammar Day Prospect Hill School in New Haven, Connecticut. He is presently working on a book on the poetry of Jonathan Swift.

Selected Bibliography

Literature of relevance to students, parents, counselors, and administrators is abundant. The following references are but a small sampling of that literature for those who wish to read further. In narrowing our choices we have followed Justice Holmes's caution that "the advice of elders to young men is very apt to be as unread as a list of the hundred best books."

Undergraduate Education

Alexander W. Astin, *Preventing Students from Dropping Out* (San Francisco: Jossey-Bass Publishers, Inc., 1975).

Alexander W. Astin, *et al.*, *The American Freshman: National Norms* (Los Angeles: Cooperative Institutional Research Program, Graduate School of Education, University of California at Los Angeles, published annually).

John W. Atkinson and Norman T. Feather, eds., *The Theory of Achievement Motivation* (New York: Wiley & Sons, 1966).

Graham B. Blaine, Jr., and Charles C. McArthur, eds., *Emotional Problems of the Student* (New York: Appleton-Century-Crofts, 1971).

Charles E. Bowerman and Glen H. Elder, "Variations in Adolescent Perception of Family Power Structure," *American Sociological Review*, Vol. 29, 1964, pp. 551–567.

William M. Boyd, *Desegregating America's Colleges: A Nationwide Survey of Black Students, 1972–73* (New York: Frederick A. Praeger, Inc., 1974).

Editors of Change Magazine Press, *Women on Campus: Unfinished Liberation* (New Rochelle, New York: 1975).

Arthur W. Chickering, *Education and Identity* (San Francisco: Jossey-Bass Publishers, Inc., 1969).

Burton R. Clark, *The Open Door College* (New York: McGraw-Hill, 1960).

John J. Conger, "A World They Never Knew: The Family and Social Change," in Graubard, S. R., ed., *Twelve to Sixteen: Early Adolescence, Daedalus*, Fall, 1971, pp. 1105–1138.

Patricia K. Cross, *Beyond the Open Door* (San Francisco: Jossey-Bass Publishers, Inc., 1971).

Fred E. Crossland, *Minority Access to College: A Ford Foundation Report* (New York: Schocken Books, 1971).

Humphrey Doermann, *Crosscurrents in College Admissions: Institutional Responses to Student Ability and Family Income* (New York: Teachers College Press, 1970).

Elaine H. El-Khawas, *New Expectations for Fair Practice* (Washington, D.C.: American Council on Education, 1976).

Kenneth A. Feldman and Theodore M. Newcomb, *The Impact of College on Students* (San Francisco: Jossey-Bass Publishers, Inc., 1969).

Kenneth A. Feldman, ed., *College and Student: Selected Readings in the Social Psychology of Higher Education* (New York: Pergamon Press, 1972).

Douglas H. Heath, *Growing Up in College: Liberal Education and Maturity* (San Francisco: Jossey-Bass Publishers, Inc., 1968).

Donald P. Hoyt, *The Relationship Between College Grades and Adult Achievement, A Review of the Literature,* Iowa Research Report No. 7, American College Testing Program (Iowa City: 1965).

Joseph Katz, *et al., No Time for Youth* (San Francisco: Jossey-Bass Publishers, Inc., 1968).

Joseph Katz and Rodney T. Hartnett, *Scholars in the Making* (Cambridge, Mass.: Ballinger Publishing Co., 1976).

Lawrence L. Leslie, "Higher Education Opportunity: A Decade of Progress," *ERIC/Higher Education Research Report No. 3* (Washington, D.C.: ERIC Clearinghouse on Higher Education, The George Washington University, 1977).

Henry M. Levin, "Educational Opportunity and Social Inequality in Western Europe," *Social Problems*, Vol. 24 (1976) pp. 148–172.

David McClelland, "Testing for Competence Rather than for 'Intelligence,'" *American Psychologist*, Vol. 28 (1973) p. 2.

Samuel Messick and Associates, *Individuality in Learning* (San Francisco: Jossey-Bass Publishers, Inc., 1976).

James E. Nelson, "Are Parents Expected to Pay Too Much?" *The College Board Review*, Vol. 92 (Summer 1974) pp. 10–15.

James O'Toole, *Work, Learning, and the American Future* (San Francisco: Jossey-Bass Publishers, Inc., 1977).

Harold S. Wechsler, *The Qualified Student, a History of Selective College Admission in America* (New York: Wiley, 1977).

Law School, Legal Practice, and Thought

American Bar Association, *How to Find the Courthouse: A Primer for the Practice of Law* (Chicago: American Bar Association, 1974); *Law Prac-*

tice in a Corporate Law Department (Chicago: American Bar Association, 1971); Lawyers in Uniform (Chicago: American Bar Association, 1974); Shall I Choose Private Practice? (Chicago: American Bar Association, 1972).

Thomas Ehrlich and Geoffrey C. Hazard, Jr., eds., *Going to Law School: Readings on a Legal Career* (Boston: Little, Brown & Co., 1975).

Lawrence M. Friedman, *A History of American Law* (New York: Simon & Schuster, 1973).

Quintin Johnstone and Dan Hopson, Jr., *Lawyers and Their Work: An Analysis of the Legal Profession in the United States and England* (Indianapolis: Bobbs-Merrill Co., 1967).

Karl N. Llewellyn, *The Bramble Bush: on Our Law and Its Study* (New York: Oceana Publications, Inc., 1951).

Julius J. Marke, ed., *Dean's List of Recommended Reading for Prelaw Students* (New York: Oceana Publications, Docket Series, 1958).

Roscoe Pound, ed., *Law In Action: An Anthology of Law in Literature* (New York: Bonanza Books, 1957).

Talbot Smith, *Opportunities for Careers in the Legal Profession* (New York: The Macmillan Co., 1961).

Rennard Strickland, *How to Get into Law School* (New York: Hawthorn Books, 1974).

James P. White, *The Legal Imagination: Studies in the Nature of Legal Thought and Expression* (Boston: Little, Brown & Co., 1973).

Robert B. Yegge, Wilbert E. Moore, and Howard K. Holme, *New Careers in Law: Meeting Present and Prospective Legal Needs* (Denver: University of Denver Law School, 1969).

Medical School and Medical Education

Marcel A. Fredericks and Paul Mundy, *The Making of a Physician* (Chicago: Loyola University Press, 1976).

Milton J. Horowitz, *Educating Tomorrow's Doctors* (New York: Meredith Publishing Company, 1964).

James I. Hudson and E. Shepley Nourse, eds., "Perspectives in Primary Care Education," *The Journal of Medical Education*, Vol. 50, no. 12, part 2 (December, 1975).

Davis G. Johnson and Edwin B. Hutchins, "Doctor or Dropout?: A Study of Medical Student Attrition," *The Journal of Medical Education*, Vol. 41, no. 12 (December, 1976), pp. 1092–1292.

Sherman M. Mellinkoff, "Are We Missing the Trees for Imagining the Forest?," *The Journal of Medical Education*, Vol. 50, no. 11 (November, 1975), pp. 1005–1009.

Index